D1601232

Private and Public

Private and Public

Individuals, households, and body
politic in Locke and Hutcheson

Daniela Gobetti

London and New York

First published 1992 by
Routledge
11 New Fetter Lane, London EC4P 4EE

Simultaneously published in the USA and Canada
by Routledge
a division of Routledge, Chapman and Hall, Inc.
29 West 35th Street, New York, NY 10001

Typeset in 10/12pt Times by
Ponting-Green Publishing Services, Berkshire
Printed in Great Britain by
Biddles Ltd, Guildford, Surrey

British Library Cataloguing-in-Publication Data
Gobetti, Daniela
    Private and Public: individuals, households and body
    politic in Locke and Hutcheson.
    I. Title
    320.5092

Library of Congress Cataloging-in-Publication Data
Gobetti, Daniela, 1952–
    Private and Public : individuals, households and body
    politic in Locke and Hutcheson / Daniela Gobetti.
        p.   cm.
    Includes bibliographical references and index.
    1. Locke, John, 1632–1746 – Contributions in political science.
    2. Hutcheson, Francis, 1694–1746 – Contributions in political science.
    3. Political participation – Philosophy.   4. Political science –
    Philosophy.   5. Political sociology.   6. Sociological jurisprudence.
    I. Title.
    JC153.L87G63   1992
    320'.01'1 – dc20   91-22774

ISBN 0–415–03174 5

a mia madre
e alla memoria di mio padre

Contents

Acknowledgements

This project has been long in the making. During these years, I have received help from many sources. I am grateful to the Fondazione Luigi Einaudi, Turin, for a fellowship from 1982 to 1984, to the Woodrow Wilson National Fellowship Foundation for a Charlotte W. Newcombe Fellowship, 1984–5, and to the European University Institute, Florence, for a Jean Monnet Fellowship, 1988–9. I especially wish to thank Professors Norberto Bobbio, Julian Franklin, Don Herzog, Steven Lukes, Allan Silver, and Salvatore Veca, who at different stages in the long life of this project have given me their patient support and insightful criticisms. I am also indebted to Michelangelo Bovero, Stephen Darwall, Jean Elshtain, Marco Geuna, Marco Guidi, Eugenio Lecaldano, Al Meyer, Luisella Pesante, Arlene Saxonhouse, and my husband Michael Bonner.

Introduction

In presenting a book on the pair private/public, I wish to accompany the reader on a journey into the world of the conceptual conventions and tacit assumptions which underlie both everyday communication and theoretical reflection. I state the obvious in saying that the terms private and public are widely used in our society. Ordinary people, politicians, scholars, men and women of the law, and so on, all talk of private and public industry, private beliefs and public opinion, the sanctity of privacy, and the dangers of secrecy in political decision-making. They all trust that the audience will share the denotations that each user assigns to the term.

Political theorists also have confidence in the power of shared meanings. They refer to private and public aspects of society, but rarely focus their inquiry on the terms themselves.[1] One reason for this is the terminological and even lexical stability of the terms throughout the history of Western thought.[2] Already employed by writers of classical Greece, the terms private and public were given their most famous definition at the beginning of the *Corpus juris*, the collection of the norms of the Roman civil code which was so influential on the subsequent development of Western political thought. The *Corpus juris* reads: "Public law is that which regards the establishment of the Roman commonwealth, private that which regards individuals' interests, some matters being of public and others of private interest."[3] Borrowed by political thinkers, and often divorced from its juridical context, this definition can be found in Aquinas, Bodin, Althusius, Kant, to name a few, until today.

In adopting the formal definition of the *Digest*,[4] political writers have changed the connotative power of the pair. Roman jurists were interested in distinguishing two jurisdictions within the Roman law, that of *jus privatum* and that of *jus publicum*, in response to the questions: what kind of legal intervention is appropriate in each case, what magistrate must intervene, and what scope will his authority have? Political thinkers substitute the universe of reference *jus* with that of the possible holders of rights within the human association; in particular, discrete individuals on one side, and the community as a whole,[5] or the state, on the other. Writers continue to think in jurisdictional terms, but the question has become: what concerns the individual and what concerns the community? Or: what can and should be entrusted to the individual, and what to the community? Where does private jurisdiction end, and public jurisdiction begin? And: what criterion should we use to make this decision?

The answers to these questions depend on the arrangement which each thinker envisages as best for the community, that is, on the conception of the nature and tasks of politics which a writer has developed. If politics are supposed to ensure the survival of individuals prone to subjectivism and to the destructive use of their personal resources, as in Hobbes, then the state must have access to, and control over, those personal resources. The private domain will be reduced to the space left available by the *silentium legis*.[6] But if politics are supposed to ensure the steady application of the already existing, although unwritten, rules through which personal resources are acquired and managed, as in Locke, then only willful misapplication of the rules will fall under public jurisdiction.[7]

To express what has just been said in another way, there are reciprocal implications between a thinker's private/public distinction and her conception of politics. This means that we can start from either of the two themes to clarify the other. We can analyze the distinction between private and public to grasp inferences about the conception of politics which the author may not have drawn, or may have left aside. And we can do the same starting from the conception of politics, in order to inquire into its implications for the distinction between private and public.

As a way to illustrate this approach, I shall introduce to my readers the thinkers whose work is the object of this inquiry. The two more important ones are John Locke and Francis Hutcheson. Both are here considered in the context of the modern school of Natural Law,[8] which flourished in Europe, in particular in Protestant Europe, in the seventeenth and eighteenth centuries. I try to show that we can better understand some aspects of the modern liberal conception of politics and of the private/public pair if we examine how Natural Law thinkers conceptualized it. In the process of establishing "what concerns the individual" and "what concerns the community," Locke and Hutcheson, in particular, recognized that all (sane) adults are individuals endowed with a private domain of a kind. This is the conclusion that we can draw if we look at the conception of domestic relations which they offer. They revise the model of the household and of the political domain dominant in Western political philosophy since classical Greece. According to this model, only heads of households have private domains which include children, women, servants, and/or slaves. And only heads of households constitute the public association.

My concern is: besides being a historically innovative feature,[9] is Locke and Hutcheson's recognition that every adult controls a private domain of consequence for their conception of politics? Do Locke and Hutcheson grant that all adults are members of the public, since all adults exercise control over their personal concerns, things, and activities? The answer is: yes and no.

One of the basic tenets of the school of Natural Law is that the political condition is supervenient to a state of nature in which power is distributed among all human beings. If we look at Locke and Hutcheson's description of the state of nature, all adults are free and equal. That is, they are all endowed with what I shall call personal and public agency. All adults can manage their own lives and resources, and enforce the law of nature on trespassers. But if we look at the process of instituting civil society, that is, the political community, only heads of households appear to be active participants, and consequently full members of the body politic.

The conception of politics that corresponds to the latter scenario holds that individuals who have the capacity for managing their private domains by consulting the law of nature, transfer functions of enforcement and coordination to the magistrate in order to avoid the inconveniences of the natural condition. This conception of politics emphasizes the delegation of crucial functions, in particular the power of life and death, to the representatives of the people. Direct participation is not required, and is even seen with suspicion. The state will monopolize both legislation and enforcement. Once in civil society, individuals engage in activities which are private in scope and nature. They only exercise their public agency intermittently, by electing their representatives, and exceptionally, by rebelling against persistent abuse on the part of their rulers.

But if we look at the state of nature, in which the activities that will be transferred to the magistrate are, at least in principle, decentralized among all adults, we can draw a different portrait. In managing their personal affairs, individuals show that their private agency has a public side, broader than the enforcement of the law of nature on trespassers in self-defense. Locke already hints at it,[10] but it is in Hutcheson's account of the natural condition that this unsuspected public side comes to the fore.

The Hutchesonian state of nature is peaceful, because individuals do more than manage their own personal affairs correctly. They are also capable of taking into consideration and furthering the welfare of the group. They can grasp the moral and juridical implications of their choices not only for those immediately linked to them, but for human-kind at large. The psychological/moral mechanisms characteristic of the human species ensure that social order can be attained, even in the absence of political coercion. Hutcheson depicts a fully developed social condition in the state of nature, as the outcome of actions regulated by the individuals performing them.

The network of social relations produced by autonomous individuals constitutes "society." "Society" is the unintended result of individuals engaging in personal transactions. But it also constitutes an abstract community (so wide that it can include all of humankind), in which all members share norms, principles of conduct, and a sense of reciprocal rights and duties. "Mankind as a system," or the "publick," as Hutcheson calls it, has no juridical personality, no precise boundary, no center. It is a regulative ideal, which gives the individual the measure of the broad implications of her choices.

It is the argument of this essay that Hutcheson's "society" provides us with a type of public domain which lacks the institutional and formal features of the state, but performs some crucial public functions, which cannot be delegated to political institutions. These functions mainly consist of the elaboration of shared norms and the integration of the group as a body politic. The fulfillment of these functions is the outcome of the direct and active participation of all adults in public life. This informal public is truly open to all, although the institutional public, in Hutcheson as in his predecessors, his contemporaries, and his successors in large numbers, is still reserved to adult males, either heads of households or independent persons.

With the analysis of Locke and Hutcheson which I propose here to my readers, I aim at contributing to the history of political thought and the current debate in political theory in three ways.

First of all, I propose a revised interpretation of seventeenth-century Natural Law. The current historiographical debate about the contribu-tion of Natural Law theory to political philosophy sees the relationship between economics and politics as the central theme. Both Marxian and liberal scholars agree that seventeenth- and eighteenth-century con-tinental and British Natural Law thinkers have one fundamental problem in mind: that of trying to justify the unequal distribution of property ensuing from the exercise of natural rights.[11] The institution of political authority would be the device through which conflict about material goods could be avoided and overcome. Thinkers are held to agree on the nature of the problem, and to differ only in their recommendations regarding the tasks of justice and the function of political participation. Retributive justice is presented as an alternative to distributive justice, and the withdrawal of citizens into a private sphere secured by general rules is contrasted with political participation and the practice of republican *virtù*.

I suggest that Natural Law thinkers are as concerned with the problem of reconstructing a hierarchical social structure out of egalitarian premises, as with the issue of material inequality. In other words, the question of personal power is distinct, in their thought, from the question of the acquisition of land and riches. But, paradoxically, the solution which they offer is such that it helps to obscure – for a long time – the relevance of personal power relations to political institutions and participation. By looking into Locke and Hutcheson's accounts of the family I can thus explain why only heads of households are politically active. For women and servants alienate part of their personal liberty to their superior in instituting or joining the family, thus impairing their capacity for political participation, and becoming, paradoxically, the agents of their own exclusion from the institutional public domain.

The second theme explores the possibility of drawing on Locke and Hutcheson in order to elaborate a phenomenology of politics. A comparison of the universal egalitarianism of the state of nature and the restricted egalitarianism of civil society enables me to capture two aspects of the public domain. The institutional public is concerned with the promulgation and enforcement of norms which must be compatible with the general principles of the law of nature. Delegation of power to the magistrate is emphasized, rather than political participation. And politics are seen to implement ends that are defined in a pre- and non-political domain. But if we look at the state of nature we can draw a different picture. In that condition, there is already political activity in the interpretation and refinement of the norms that ensure a peaceful state of nature. And this political activity is the outcome of informal participation by individuals who reflect on the moral and juridical implications of their actions for the association.

To put it in other terms, my question is: what features does direct political participation assume, and what function does it play, if we start from individualistic assumptions, and their possible subjectivist implications? A synthetic answer is: participation enables individuals who are prone to psychological and moral subjectivism to identify the shared values which inform the decisions made by political institutions, and which make concerted action possible. This view reformulates and synthesizes a leitmotif of contemporary modern and political theory: agreement on shared values is the outcome of one form or another of discursive practice. I here assimilate positions which are sometimes very different from one another: Arendt's rediscovery of political judgement as shared taste and common sense, through her interpretation of Kant's *Critique of Judgement*; Gadamer's recovery of Aristotelian *phronesis* as the faculty that guides us in the practical world; and Habermas's attempt to describe the formal requirements of an ideal speech situation.[12]

When I speak of this activity as a form of political participation, I emphasize both the adjective and the noun. We need a shared activity to overcome the subjectivist and centrifugal tendencies of modern society. And that activity is political. That is, it is different from the ethical evaluation of our deeds and aims, and from the implementation of a decision through institutional channels, although it, like a two-faced Janus, relies on both. Political participation presents a phenomenology distinct from ethics in both nature and scope. Its prescriptions may be provisional and temporary: they do not need to attain the level of incontestability which we require of moral assertions. Political participation does not have to address all the issues that are or may be morally relevant, but only those that the political association deems crucial to its own survival as an integrated society. And political participation, given the institutional delegation of power typical of representative democracy, does not entail immediate implementation and enforcement of the conclusions which have been reached by the participants. But it does require implementation sooner or later, and the split between finding a shared position and actualizing it may well be a growing source of tensions in contemporary Western societies. It goes without saying that it is impossible to attribute such a conception of political participation to seventeenth- and eighteenth-century Natural Law theorists. Nonetheless, I find in Hutcheson's work a useful precedent to illustrate some features of an activity which cuts across the liberal distinctions between morality and politics, morality and legality, justification and implementation.[13]

The individualistic premises of Locke and Hutcheson are also relevant to the distinction between private and public, the third area of inquiry of this essay. The most recent contributions to the debate about the private/public pair have come from feminist writers. They have corrected the traditional liberal view which holds that the distinction between private and public runs along the line separating the economic and the political domains. (This approach does not quite know what to do with the family.) Feminist scholars have argued that the dividing line must be drawn between the family and the rest of society.[14] Both the economic and political spheres are parts of the public domain. In so doing feminist writers have taken the pair private/public as meaning hidden/visible, rather than personal/shared. The private is what remains hidden from public view, and what remains hidden is indeed not the economy, but family life. Women, who are relegated to the family, are thus by definition excluded from the economic/political domain and deprived of public existence.

The analysis of the jurisdictional distinction between private and public shows that the dynamics of inclusion in, and exclusion from, the public arena of all adult household dependents at first, and women (and children) more recently, are more articulated than the feminist account contends. On the one hand, Locke and Hutcheson empower each adult with agency, only to enable some of them to dispossess themselves of their independence.[15] Initially, everyone's private domain is the same as everyone else's, and it coincides with the capacities and rights that make the individual an autonomous agent. But some will be able to increase their private domains by acquiring jurisdiction over the personal capacities of others; the latter will thus curtail their private endowments, and impair their capacity to act in public.

On the other hand, in principle each individual has a private domain and can be an autonomous agent. This assumption becomes consequential for the dynamics of the public domain, in two ways. First, all are subjects of rights. Public institutions can be invoked to protect those rights, and can, therefore, intrude into anyone's activities. Second, when the emphasis is shifted from the purely juridical account of the handling of personal resources, to the ethical dynamics underlying it, as is the case with Hutcheson, all adults are held to participate in the refinement of the norms that ensure the integration of the group. If we adopt the spatial metaphor so pervasive in talking about private and public, we must place this activity in the private realm of the social. But Hutcheson cannot deny its public dimension and political import.

The public domain thus can reach much further than liberal theory contends. But, from a conceptual if not a sociological point of view, it can reach even further than feminist scholarship has contended. The institutional public may have to intervene in every activity and institution, in order to protect each person's endowments. And the non-institutionalized public arena provides the space for participation. This recognition does not cancel the fact that the admission of dependents to life in public is an unintended consequence of a conception which is elaborated to address the solipsistic and subjectivist implications of individualism.

Before leaving my readers alone with the narrative, I wish to say a few words about the approach I have adopted in this study.

The story told here lies at the crossroad of political theory and the history of political thought, in that it uses historical materials as the building blocks of an embryonic theory of politics. In this case, the underlying theoretical concern is the attempt to elaborate a phenomenology of politics, and, in particular, of participation in modern society. I start from the assumption that the distinction between private and public can be of help in understanding the nature and aim of politics. And I contend that we can look at Locke and Hutcheson as two sources of a jurisdictional distinction between private and public which still shapes our way of thinking about the pair. This is the case for two reasons, one conceptual and the other historical. Conceptually, they elaborate a jurisdictional distinction based on individualistic assumptions and a subjective theory of rights. Insofar as we adopt the same assumptions, we may encounter the same problems which they encountered, and we may share some of their solutions. But there is also historical continuity between us and them, due to a characteristic feature of the Western tradition of political thought.

This feature is the tendency of practitioners of that tradition to consider notions and conceptual frameworks produced in the past as applicable to different historical conditions. The formal definition of the pair private/public offered by the *Corpus juris* is itself an example. Abstractions thus acquire a *longue durée*, which does not necessarily depend on some mystical or Platonic property of the concepts, but on their inertial assimilation by successive writers. I contend that the jurisdictional distinction between private and public based on the notion of harm, which we find in Locke and Hutcheson, is an example of a *longue durée*. What they have to say on this matter is not only exemplary of a way of thinking about the pair, but it is constitutive of our way of thinking about it.

At this more abstract and inertial level, meanings can be reconstructed by looking at the function that concepts are made to play in a theory, rather than at the interaction between the thinker and her society. As a consequence, it is the theoretical concerns that guide the choice of historical materials, and the level of contextual detail which is necessary to reconstruct the meaning and import of those materials.[16] In other words, my aim here is not to contribute to ascertaining the "historical identity" of a thinker, a vocabulary, or a theory.[17] My aim is to reconstruct systematically how concepts and arguments have been, and can be, used in the elaboration of a theory.[18]

"Historical identification" and "systematic reconstruction" are two distinct intellectual enterprises, but they need not be starkly separated, as they have been, in particular, in twentieth-century Anglophone culture. And they should not be starkly separated because each of the two is to a degree indebted to the other. "Historical identification" starts from the tacit assumption that we share our deep logical structure with people who wrote centuries ago;[19] otherwise we should be unable to understand what they meant. This implies that there is a level at which meanings are quite independent of the specific historical conditions in which they are elaborated or used. On the other hand, "systematic reconstruction" must take into account variations in the range and mode of employment of concepts due to differences in the historical context.[20] But if we wish to summarize the thrust of each endeavor, we can say that "historical identification" makes us more aware of what differentiates us from our predecessors. It also tends to use their contributions as exemplary of possible argumentative strategies, but discontinuous from ours. "Systematic reconstruction" emphasizes what links us to our predecessors, and it looks at their contributions as living parts of our conceptual apparatus.

A work such as this which aims at clarifying tacit assumptions cannot avoid being based on tacit assumptions. As readers will soon realize, the most important such assumption regards the concept of power. I am well aware that there may be very different interpretations of what "power" is, and of what it means "to exercise power." But in this essay I have chosen to rely on the well-known Weberian definition of power as *Macht*: "the probability that one actor within a social relationship will be in a position to carry out his own will despite resistance, regardless of the basis on which this probability rests."[21] This choice is partially motivated by the fact that we can subsume under that definition the concept of power used by the thinkers analyzed in this study.[22] I have therefore chosen not to call into question the plausibility of considering power (and the tightly connected concept of "will") in rather essentialist terms, as those writers do. By accepting their point of view, I can capture the implications of the jurisdictional distinction between private and public.

I also take for granted the distinction between persuasion (or education) and manipulation as employed by Hutcheson. Hutcheson understands as education practices which we should consider forms of manipulation. Or, if you like, he believes in a stark contrast between the two, whereas we are more cynical. His distinction is grounded on the idea that practices that enhance our (positive) natural endowments are educational. He therefore inscribes in human nature (or so it appears to us) the characteristics that education must reinforce. The procedure is circular, but exploring its implications is beside the point of this inquiry.

Finally, a stylistic remark. I use gender pronouns interchangeably, for it seems to me the least troublesome way of referring to a neutral subject. But in a work such as this, in which the inclusion (or exclusion) of women is one of the crucial issues, I have had to use the formula he/she, his/her. I have tried to do that only when it has seemed aesthetically acceptable and heuristically relevant.

1 Domestic society/political society

Toward the rejection of the Aristotelian model

BOOK ONE OF ARISTOTLE'S *POLITICS*

The contemporary political arena is, at least in principle, open to all adults.[1] Widespread agreement on this principle has been achieved only recently, and its practical implementation is by no means universal, as we may see in the ongoing struggles of women and of non-white groups. The philosophical seeds of universal equality were planted by seventeenth-century Natural Law theorists. In the name of reason, they waged a war against tradition and received wisdom, a war which took the philosophy of Aristotle and his late epigones as its polemical target. Hobbes stated clearly in his *Leviathan* that a thorough elimination of Aristotelian errors would lead to a new political science.

While Aristotle underwent profound criticism, two other classical traditions were central to natural jurisprudence: Stoic philosophy and Roman civil law. Throughout the Middle Ages, Roman legal concepts were employed to analyze the social and political realities of medieval Europe. The fortune of Roman legal terminology went through ebbs and flows, but it gained particular force in the seventeenth century, in a process which led to the elaboration of the *jus publicum europaeum*, on one side, and the vocabulary of Natural Law thinkers, on the other. The latter adopted concepts of Roman private law to conceptualize the relationships between citizen and state, church and state, nation and nation. They also adopted the formal definition of private and public offered by the *Corpus juris*, and they used it to discuss the limits of the legitimate spheres of competence – or jurisdictions[2] – of the citizen/subject and the state.

The adoption of a juridical vocabulary for constructing a political philosophy is of consequence for what can and what cannot be expressed through the medium of that specific vocabulary. As Pocock has remarked, the political philosophy which takes Roman civil law as its starting point frames questions in a different manner from that of Aristotelian republicanism.[3] The latter focuses on the participation in office by equal males prompted by their nature to engage in political activity; on the virtue requisite for being a good citizen, capable of preferring the common good over private interest; and on the maintenance of freedom in the community as the main objective of political life.[4] Natural Law theory, on the other hand, draws attention to pre-political relations among free and equal human beings, who resort to politics in order to pacify social relations which are endangered by conflicts about equally legitimate claims over scarce resources.

Pocock is indeed correct in seeing the vocabulary of the Aristotelian–Machiavellian republican tradition as antithetical to the vocabulary of Natural Law. But in analyzing the private/public distinction, one soon discovers that the antithesis does not hold absolutely. By way of Stoic, Roman, and medieval readings, elements of the Aristotelian paradigm filtered through the conceptual framework of Natural Law theory. As we shall see, Aristotle was reinterpreted, and often misinterpreted,[5] by later thinkers. But we cannot understand the seventeenth-century conceptualization of the distinction between private and public, which culminated in the work of Locke, unless we acknowledge the Aristotelian frame of reference which was, at first, uncritically accepted, and eventually dismantled and rejected.

Aristotle's main legacy to subsequent thinking about private and public takes the form of a rhetorical strategy, a way of arguing about domestic and political society as the two fundamental institutions of the community, considered, respectively, as the private and the public domain. Aristotle, like other Greek thinkers, was not particularly interested in the jurisdictional aspect of the distinction between private and public. But his way of framing questions about household and body politic could be adopted for discussing jurisdictional issues. Aristotle employs a three-step strategy: the identification of household and body politic as, respectively, the private and public domains; a comparison of the domestic and political associations on the basis of the types of power exercised in each; and a distinction between domestic and political power derived from his conception of politics. In so doing, he establishes a relation of reciprocal implication between two themes: the distinction between private and public power, and the conception of the nature and tasks of politics. The Aristotelian comparative strategy, and its implications for a theory of politics, were accepted and reproduced even by seventeenth-century Natural Law theorists, until Locke offered an alternative approach.

Aristotle introduces the discussion of the relationship between private and public sphere in Book Two of the *Politics*, while criticizing Plato's ideal state as presented in the *Republic*. Aristotle rejects Plato's proposals to eliminate private property and families among the members of the guardian class, and analyzes less extreme versions of the community of goods, to which he is not, however, completely opposed.[6] From Aristotle's discussion of Plato's ideas it can be inferred that family and property are the two main elements composing the private sphere. These are, in Aristotle's language, the "things" of which a man can say: "they are mine," thus excluding others from enjoying them. On the other hand, citizens share in common the political community itself, that is, the system of relations and exchanges among persons of different kinds which enables the community to attain self-sufficiency.[7]

The theme of ruling and being ruled in turn is central to Aristotle's discussion of the household and the body politic in Book One, which is devoted to identifying the specific nature of political rule in contrast with other types of rule, and especially the domestic one.

According to Aristotle, what transforms a group of scattered human beings into an association is sharing a common purpose, and the means by which that purpose can be attained. But no group can act in coordination without a ruling principle, a source of authority, which organizes the performance of various functions, and regulates inter-action among the members. The exercise of power, without which no ordered social life is possible, is the thread running through all types of associations, and is a fundamental analytical element around which the comparison of domestic and political society revolves. In an association, power must belong to one or more individuals, since

> in all cases where there is a compound – constituted of more than one part but forming one entity whether the parts be continuous (as in the body of one man) or discrete (as in the relation of master and slave) – a ruling element and a ruled can always be traced.[8]

Although power permeates all aspects of life, not all hierarchical orderings are identical, and one of the tasks of political philosophy is to discover the best one for the body politic.

In comparing household and body politic, Aristotle has a clear polemical target in mind: those (read Plato) who see in the *polis* merely a great household, and who therefore assimilate the statesman to "the monarch of a kingdom, or the manager of a household, or the master of a number of slaves."[9] It is not merely size, and the number of people over whom one rules, which distinguish various associations, and particularly the domestic from the political community, but rather a difference in "kind." From the point of view of the type of authority exercised in each, the political association is set apart from all others by the fact that its component members are (relatively) equal free men, as they are not slaves, and share the leisure provided by the household, over which they exercise control. This similarity of condition explains why "the members of a political association aim by their very nature at being equal and differing in nothing."[10] Equality makes it problematic to ascertain what criteria should be used in assigning power, for nature does not provide any guide for ascertaining who may exercise authority, and who must be subject to it.[11] Aristotle's solution is, as is well known, that political rule will consist in "ruling and being ruled in turn,"[12] allowing all active citizens full participation in political activity.

In the household, on the contrary, the head exercises different types of rule, but his power is unquestioned, because grounded in nature. The free adult male rules, not because of acquired skills, or because of choice on the part of his dependents, but rather because of innate superior capacities. According to Aristotle, "masters are not so termed in virtue of any science they have acquired, but in virtue of their own endowment."[13] Even in the case of the rule over the wife, which is "like that of a statesman over fellow citizens,"[14] the natural superiority of the male makes his entitlement to power self-evident, and rotation between him and the woman inconceivable.

Aristotle's comparison of domestic with political society can be used to ground a distinction between private and public domain on three accounts.

First, there is the contrast between a domestic world, characterized by a natural and unquestioned hierarchy, and a public world in which equal free men express their political nature. The separation of private and public spheres is grounded on the rationale that only human beings capable of sharing both ruling and being ruled are entitled to a public life.[15] The natural subordination of household dependents to the adult free man justifies granting him control over them as parts of his private sphere. As partially impaired human beings, women, children, and slaves are entrusted to the man, who takes care of their welfare while taking care of his own.[16] Their lives and their possessions, if they have any, are managed by the head of household, and even in the case of adult free persons, such as women are, their capacity for autonomous agency is drastically curtailed. The condition of natural inferiority of household dependents, even when they are free, as in the case of women, thus bars them without appeal from enjoying full citizenship.

The second criterion of distinction between private and public consists in the different handling of personal and common good. The head of household is entitled to treat his dependents' good as his own. But the condition of relative equality enjoyed by free men in the public sphere entails a more complex and problematic relationship between individual and common good. There does indeed exist a good of the community which is greater than the sum of the good of its members, and for the sake of which each citizen will have to sacrifice his own selfish inclinations. But individual good, and last but not least, individual properties, will remain distinct from what is shared, so that only on certain terms will the public be justified in crossing the boundaries that fence off private endowments. Ignorance of these boundaries, and a tendency to treat citizens and their property as if they were part of the ruler's property, are symptoms that despotism has set in. A body politic managed by a ruler who treats it as if it were his own household is no longer a political association, capable of attaining the good life. It has become a big family, and the power relations within it will resemble those obtaining between the free man and his dependents, in the worst case, his slaves.

The third criterion of distinction is a piece of Aristotelian metaphysics, and it is the one that the subsequent tradition will soon reinterpret. Aristotle contends that each being or human association aims at some good, the highest of which it is capable. Among humans, only adult free men are endowed with the capacities to attain the highest practical good, which consists, as remarked, of being alternately a ruler and a subject. The practice of rotation in power allows the members of the community to express all the virtues of which they are capable, in particular, justice. But the household does not provide the arena in which such a high level of virtue can be practiced. The free man is destined to rule, for no other member of the group can compete with him in virtue. Politics, as a mode of being and acting, are forever banned from the domestic association.

It is this third and, for Aristotle, crucial factor that later thinkers, especially Christian ones, will abandon. The natural inferiority of the members of the household will be maintained, but the term "inferiority" will acquire a new meaning. In a culture shaped by the Christian tenets about the universal equality of all humans before God, and about the universal capacity to attain the good, that is, eternal salvation, Aristotle's metaphysical/ethical differentiations become problematic. The inferiority of women, children, and servants is recast in the much more mundane language of material dependence. Inferiors are less able, less intelligent, less strong, less autonomous. They cannot survive without being directed by an adult free male. But the innate superiority of the male is reflected in, and slowly confused with, greater access to material resources. Access to the public arena remains a prerogative of heads of households, and it is still maintained that only the political association can reach self-sufficiency.[17] But this is reinterpreted as control over the resources that allow the community to live in peace, to prosper, and to remain independent from neighboring communities.[18]

This profound change in metaphysical assumptions does not prevent writers from adopting Aristotle's general argument, and in particular Aristotle's comparative strategy. His basic question: is political rule different from domestic rule? – with its corollaries: how do family and body politic differ, and what are the implications for the distinction between the private and public domains? – becomes a recurrent theme in subsequent thinkers. But before turning to the Natural Law theorists who are the focus of this inquiry, a few remarks about the Aristotelian procedure are in order. For ultimately, it is a modification of these basic assumptions which will prompt thinkers to abandon the Aristotelian approach.

We have reconstructed Aristotle's criteria of distinction between private and public by interpreting his inquiry into the nature of political rule. To understand what activities are proper to politics, and how human beings relate to one another when engaged in them, Aristotle turns for comparison and clarification to the household. The comparison takes the form of a game of mirrors, in which household and body politic are set one before the other, in order to identify common features and elements of differentiation. The game can of course start with either of the two, but Aristotle starts with the family, for its structure is unquestioned and seemingly unproblematic. The household thus provides the background against which the features typical of the body politic are supposed to emerge more clearly.

This argumentative strategy remains plausible as long as thinkers share with Aristotle the belief that the political association is an aggregation of families. Families are full-fledged societies, linked to the body politic through the persons of their heads. This means that thinkers consider both households and individual free men as the basic components of the political association, depending, in turn, on what the term "political association" is taken to include. The political association is thus the whole community, comprising free and unfree members, full citizens and dependents. But it is also the part of the community where political activity takes place, since the body politic only includes independent heads of households.[19]

Household and body politic thus have a double structural relationship. As models of full-fledged societies, they are compared with each other as if they were independent and separate associations. But they are also the two fundamental institutions of the same community. This double relationship ultimately explains why the account of similarities and differences between domestic and political society is consequential for the distinction between private and public. For the descriptive account of the dynamics of each group will translate into prescriptions about their optimal relationship once they are seen as the lesser and major parts of the same association. What governs the prescriptive dimension is thus a description of domestic and political society which is in turn informed by each writer's conception of the nature and task of politics. This hermeneutic cycle remains heuristically significant for Western writers until the late seventeenth century, when the Aristotelian model is finally rejected.

THE REVIVAL OF NATURAL LAW THEORY IN THE SEVENTEENTH CENTURY

Crises of legitimation engender questions about the entitlement of those in power to rule, and about the obligation which subjects have to obey them. This was so even before the vocabulary of legitimation, entitlement, and obligation became current coin for discussions of the relationship between ruler and ruled. That vocabulary, which now appears indispensable, was first elaborated in the period of formation of the Western European nation-states, between the fifteenth and the eighteenth centuries. A crucial phase in the elaboration of the modern vocabulary of politics occurred in the seventeenth century. It started on the Continent, and culminated in the England of the Civil War and the Glorious Revolution.

The main protagonists of this endeavor were Natural Law theorists, who took opposing sides, in favor of, or against, absolute monarchy, but who developed a common conceptual framework. Their discussion of the issues of legitimacy and obligation is directly relevant to the analysis of private and public in jurisdictional terms. When do we owe allegiance to the ruler? Concerning which aspects of life should his jurisdiction take precedence over ours? How do we know? That is, what criteria should we use to establish the respective areas of competence?

The centrality of these issues prompted Natural Law theorists to inquire into the proper spheres of competence of subjects and ruler within the body politic. The need to clarify the limits of legitimate authority led them to adopt a conceptual framework which articulated problems in jurisdictional terms. And the adoption of that specific framework further led people to think of political questions first and foremost from the point of view of their jurisdictional implications. The revival of Natural Law theory thus not only prompted a renewed interest in Stoic themes, a rationalistic interpretation of the nature of norms,[20] and the attribution of a central role to the will in politics; it also entailed the framing of political issues in a vocabulary rooted in the juridical language of the *Corpus juris*.

Several notions of Roman civil law appear in the terminology which these writers employ to express their concern for the balance between individual interest and common good. They discuss the *dominium* which a private individual enjoys over his possessions, the *potestas* which he exercises over his dependents, and the *contractus* which binds him to his wife and servants. They compare *privata potestas* with *jurisdictio*, the latter being taken to denote the supreme power of the political ruler.[21] They argue as to whether the people or the sovereign has *majestas realis*, that is, as to who is sovereign in the community.

By the time seventeenth-century Natural Law theorists had accomplished their redefinition of the nature, tasks, and limits of political power, the transformation of this juridical language into a specific and autonomous political one was a *fait accompli*. The elaboration of an autonomous language of politics determined a change not only in conceptual framework, but in vocabulary as well. Thus when Locke writes the *Two Treatises*, property has replaced *dominium*, sovereignty, *jurisdictio* and *majestas realis*, and rights, *libertates* and *privilegia*.

This use of the Roman juridical vocabulary implies not only that modern political philosophy has grown out of a juridical framework, but also that elements of Stoic philosophy, which are abundantly present in the *Weltanschauung* of the Roman jurists, occupy a central role in the work of Natural Law thinkers. The Stoic inheritance, corrected by Christian interpretations, provides basic metaphysical assumptions about the role of laws in shaping all aspects of reality. The term law denotes both regularities of conduct in the non-human world, and normative principles in human beings. And these normative principles are available to us through reason. The world can be rational, provided that human beings set their minds to understanding that rationality, and their wills to actualize it. But some Aristotelian assumptions are still present, at least insofar as the analysis of household and body politic, private and public, is concerned. An interweaving of juridical, Stoic, and Aristotelian elements, the latter filtered through medieval, and especially Thomistic, revisions, is apparent in Francisco Suàrez, who, at the beginning of the seventeenth century, plays a crucial role in rekindling interest in the Natural Law tradition.

Suàrez adopts the Aristotelian strategy of comparing the domestic with the political association so as to emphasize the specificity of political rule. He lists three reasons why family and body politic differ. The first is the superiority which the head of household enjoys over his dependents; the second is the greater coercive power to be recognized to the political ruler if he is to perform his task; and the third is the fact that the head of household minds only his own good, whereas the political ruler must take care of the good of the community.[22]

Although Suàrez's discussion is formally and strategically Aristotelian, the sociological realities comprised under the headings "domestic" and "political" are the ones described by the medieval commentators, first and foremost Aquinas, who fuse Aristotelian philosophy and Roman jurisprudence. The contrast of household and political community, which Aristotle articulated in terms of the ontological differentiation of associations capable of attaining different levels of goodness, is reinterpreted in juridical terms. The perfect community is the only one capable of exercising full and autonomous jurisdiction – that is, sovereign power – over its members. It can enforce its own decisions, and can therefore produce laws, that is, rules which are binding for those subject to them; it can carry sanctions against transgressors.[23]

The use of force plays such a central role in Suàrez's thought because his main problem is the legitimacy of imposing commands on free human beings. In discussing this issue, Suàrez agrees with Aristotle that the household, as the first, "natural," and indispensable unit of social life, is useful for clarifying issues about the body politic. But here the comparison focuses upon the legitimating principles of various forms of power. The household is a perfect case-study because a wide range of legitimating principles can be found in it: nature alone, or nature and convention, or convention alone. Children are providentially created inferior by nature; women give their free assent to a condition of natural subordination; and free men become their master's servants or slaves through a voluntary act of subjection. The latter case provides the blueprint for what happens when adult free men give life to a political community. As someone may become another's slave and entrust his life to him completely, so a people may assign sovereignty to a ruler. For Suàrez, the problem consists in explaining and justifying how independent adult males, who still maintain the condition of freedom into which human beings are born by nature, can become subjects, for they can only be forced to fulfill those obligations which they have voluntarily accepted. It is thus supposed that human beings have authorized the ruler to regulate their relations by imposing laws, and to coerce them when they do not comply with their duties.[24]

The insistence on legislation and the use of force, including the power of life and death, as distinct traits of political rule, partially modifies the terms in which Suàrez articulates the comparison of household and body politic. Domestic power differs from political power because, being exercised over personal dependents, it may not extend so far as may political power; the head of household may neither sentence his subordinates to death, nor legislate. Only a political community composed of peers who have voluntarily transferred their powers to a ruler can and must produce laws which will ensure the common good.

In contrasting household and body politic, Suàrez proves to have abandoned the Aristotelian argument about the attainment of ontologically different levels of the good by different "natures" – the slave's, child's, woman's, and man's. Suàrez indeed subscribes to a hierarchical view of non-human and human nature, but one that no longer identifies ethical and ontological orderings. Despite these changes in metaphysical assumptions, the contrast of independent with dependent human beings, of self-sufficient with "partial" associations, has the same consequences as in Aristotle. Women, children, and servants are excluded from the political domain; and their inferior condition prevents the household from ever being a body politic.[25] The implications for the private/public distinction are also traditional: dependents are incorporated into the person of the head of household, and are part of his private property, whereas heads of households, who maintain separate domains, join other chiefs of families in the public sphere. The head of household has only to further his own good, whereas the sovereign must take care of the good of the community. In pursuing the latter, he may appropriate part of his subjects' private possessions, although prudence and the laws of God and nature set limits to his discretion.

As this brief summary of Suàrez's arguments shows, the emphasis on the juridical component of social and political relations changes the focus of the comparison between domestic and political society. Both associations are seen as aggregations of persons who regulate their relationships through juridical means, mainly oriented toward accepting, assigning, or instituting the authority of a superior. Aside from the authority of parents over the child, which is directly established by nature, the husband's power over the wife, the master's power over the servant or slave, and the sovereign's power over the subject, all owe their existence to a combination of natural and conventional factors. There exists a common denominator in all transactions regarding the attribution of power: the procedure through which that power is accepted by those who will be subject to it. As a consequence, relationships become, so to speak, more ready of comparison, and show remarkable procedural similarities; and more analogical inferences can be drawn between household and body politic.

Natural Law theorists draw mainly on the civil law concept of contract, as the means by which individuals give official sanction to mutual engagements, in particular those onerous to one of the parties, as is the case when one subjects him-/herself to another. This emphasis on contract entails a prima facie acceptance of the other aspects of the legal procedure which are indispensable for rendering the transaction valid. The parties must be free and competent to perform the trans-action, the conditions must be reciprocal,[26] and there must be the possibility of seeking redress, at least in private matters. Dependent members of the household are thus taken to employ the same procedure as do the heads of households in instituting the body politic. Can we continue to maintain a stark distinction between dependents as natural inferiors, and adult males as equals, as Suàrez still does? And if individuals have the same capacities, since they perform the same operation, what distinguishes the domestic from the political associ-ation? In asking these types of questions, Natural Law theorists show that they still adopt the Aristotelian comparative strategy. But they offer answers which begin to call into question the plausibility of that strategy.

SUBJECTIVE RIGHTS

Questions about the procedure for assigning the power of life and death are crucial to Natural Law theorists who contend, against mainstream Protestant doctrine, that this power is not assigned to rulers directly by God, but rather that it is given by God to all human beings, who then assign it to rulers. But the field of Natural Law splits over the following question: if all have it initially, do they then transfer it once and for all, or do they maintain the possibility of taking it back, so to speak, under certain conditions? If the power of life and death is originally within our jurisdiction, to renounce it once and for all means that we curtail that jurisdiction dramatically and place ourselves without reservation in the hands of a fellow human being. If each of us gives it up only to a degree, or under certain conditions, what does this imply for the ruler's supreme jurisdiction? And since the power of life and death is obviously the most important, but not the only power which one may exercise, what else is comprised in personal jurisdiction, both before and after the use of force has been transferred to the sovereign?

It is in Hugo Grotius, who is considered the first important representative of the modern school of Natural Law, that we can find interesting responses to these questions.[27] For Grotius, the ruler's coercive power is originally in each human being because God has given everyone all the means necessary for survival. Quoting Cicero's *De Finibus*, Grotius points to self-preservation guided by reason as the fundamental principle of human life. Reason makes us understand how to harmonize self-preservation with the other basic principle governing the species, natural sociability. According to Grotius, "right reason and the nature of society which claims the second, and indeed more important place in this inquiry, prohibit not all force, but only that which is repugnant to society, by depriving another of his right."[28] In a situation in which no other remedy is at hand, force may be repelled by force, and we may engage in a personal war with someone who tries to deprive us of what is legitimately ours.

The condition in which each individual is responsible for his own survival is the state of nature.[29] In it, human beings can only rely on their reason to regulate their interaction with others. Reason not only tells us that the use of force is not incompatible with social life; it also provides us with the principles necessary for dealing with all aspects of life, even in cases less dramatic and extreme than those of personal "war." The set of all those principles constitutes the law of nature, which can be summarized in the formula: respect one another's rights.[30]

It is relevant to the present argument that Grotius emphasizes the aspect of rights in Natural Law. He begins *Of the Law of War and Peace* with an analysis of *jus*, which is explored in all its possible meanings. *Jus* is both what the law establishes as being rightly due to someone, and what someone may legitimately claim as being due to him/her. In other words, *jus* can be considered as the center of either an objective or a subjective theory of rights. Grotius significantly opts for the latter.

Jus has three meanings, according to Grotius. The first is the objective one: right is what is just, or, as Grotius says, as he is discussing war, what is not unjust. The second sense of right points to the subjective side of *jus*:

> Right is a moral quality annexed to the person, justly entitling him to possess some particular privilege, or to perform some particular act. ... This moral faculty (*in personam*, and *in rem*) when perfect is called a faculty; when imperfect, an aptitude.

Jus is therefore the capacity, or the very faculty itself, of having and claiming rights: it is a meta-right, so to speak, which enables human beings to be the subjects and objects of rights. And thirdly, right is synonymous with just, or proper: it is what the law obliges us to do above and beyond what retributive justice strictly taken obliges us to.[31]

It is Grotius's analysis of *jus* as a faculty that clarifies what is entailed by a subjective theory of rights.

> Civilians call a faculty that Right, which every man has to his own; but we shall hereafter, taking it in its strict and proper sense, call it a right. This right comprehends the power, that we have over ourselves, which is called liberty, and the power, that we have over others, as that of a father over his children, and of a master over his slaves. It likewise comprehends property.... There is a third signification, which implies the power of demanding what is due, to which the obligation upon the party indebted, to discharge what is owing, corresponds.[32]

The faculty of claiming what is one's own is exercised, as it were, in three fields: over ourselves, as the power to dispose freely of our own persons; over those who are legitimately subjected to us; and over our property, that is, external possessions. If all over which *jus* as a faculty is exercised composes the category "our own," and what is our own is what is proper to us, then the category of property comprises our liberty, our power over others, and our possessions. Grotius appears to establish a proprietary relationship not only between a person and things, but also between a person and another, and between the person and one of her specific features, that is, her liberty to dispose of herself unhindered.

If a proprietary relationship between a person and things is the standard and unproblematic one,[33] and the tradition has prepared us to conceive of slaves as an article of material property, it is more questionable to describe in those terms the interaction of parent with child, and the person with herself. It may indeed seem unwarranted to think of the relationship between the person and herself as a form of property. In saying "I have a right to my liberty," I do not necessarily use "my" as I would use it in saying "That is my house." "My" is simply used reflexively, and indicates the subject which exercises that specific faculty, that is, freedom.[34]

Grotius does, however, have a proprietary model in mind. In fact, the consequences of the use of that liberty are very similar to those deriving from having property in things. There is an exclusive relationship between me and my liberty: there are things I can do with it which are forbidden to others. And one of the things I am entitled to do is to renounce part or, for Grotius, all of that liberty, if I believe I may gain from that act. I can give myself in self-enslavement, as has already been mentioned, and turn myself into the property of another.

The proprietary model is also valid in the case of power over others which can be acquired as material possessions are.[35] "Among those things, which belong to no one, there are two that may become the subjects of occupancy; and those are jurisdiction, or sovereignty, and property."[36] Lesser forms of power than sovereignty can also be acquired as if they were property-items.

> The third way [of making a promise] is, where such a determination is confirmed by evident signs of an intention to convey a peculiar right to another, which constitutes the perfect obligation of a promise, and is attended with consequences similar to an alienation of property. There may be two kinds of alienation, the one of our property, the other of a certain portion of our liberty.[37]

Grotius is aware that property can correctly be predicated only of material possessions, but he analogically treats a person's liberty, and her legitimate power over others, as if they were property. Similarities therefore exist between the procedures and rules which people employ to handle material possessions, and those which they use to handle transactions regarding personal endowments.

It is by exercising their natural faculties that human beings can ensure their own survival: "God has given life to man, not to destroy, but to preserve it; assigning to him for this purpose a right to the free enjoyment of personal liberty, reputation, and the control over his own actions."[38] The care for one's own life leads individuals to expand the original stock of endowments which they received at birth. A significant addition occurs through the appropriation of resources, material and animal, which God gave to humankind in general. Already in the state of nature, consent (of our fellows), occupancy, and labour attach a resource to a specific person, and render it illegitimate to deprive one of one's "property" without one's consent.

When such an attempt has been made, the attacked party is entitled to defend him-/herself by the use of force, to ask for redress and compensation, and to punish the transgressor. The right to defend one's rights, or, in other words, to enforce the law of nature, is recognized by Grotius as belonging to all: "The power of inflicting the punishment, subservient to this end [to discourage people from committing crimes], is allowed by the law of nature to any one of competent judgement, and not implicated in similar or equal offences."[39]

When personal endowments are the object of a transaction, individuals must treat them as they treat material resources that have already been appropriated. As personal endowments "belong,"[40] by definition, to the person, we cannot get access to them without the person's consent, and if we do so we expose ourselves to the other's legitimate reaction. Such is the case with all services that require the direct participation of the person performing them: labour, sexual intercourse, etc. Transactions regarding specific resources, such as labor for money, only involve a "traffic of exchange," "accompanied with an obligation on both sides."[41] But when we alienate a portion of our liberty, we transfer our resource, as it were, to the other person, thus instituting or accepting a superior. In doing so, we grant him the right to appropriate that resource, and to dispose of it as he likes, within the limits of the law of nature, and not simply to demand the performance of a service. In discussing whether we can be compelled to the supererogatory duty of charity, Grotius argues:

> The transactions of equals with each other, must be regulated upon principles very different from those that regulate the mutual relations of sovereigns and subjects. For an equal cannot compel an equal to the performance of any thing, but what he is strictly bound by law to perform. But a superior may compel an inferior to the performance of Other duties besides those of Perfect Obligations; for that is a right peculiarly and essentially belonging to the nature of superiority.[42]

If the transference of liberty is essential for instituting political authority, there are however other transactions in which we perform an action of the same kind: marriage, servitude, and self-enslavement. The institution of a position of power thus appears to require that we dispossess ourselves of something that originally belonged to us, and that we assign its possession to another person. There is an alienation on one side, and an appropriation on the other. The consequences of employing a proprietary model become clear. We can only dispose of what belongs to us.[43] If we want to grant others the right to use some of our resources, we can only do that by transferring our title of ownership to them.[44] But we have first to possess those resources, in order to be able to transfer them. Our liberty is therefore listed as one of our proprietary endowments, because we should otherwise be unable to assign control over it to others.

This detailed analysis of the dynamics of the transference of liberty allows Grotius to answer the question: how is the power of life and death transferred from its original bearers, individuals, to the political ruler? Renunciation of all or part of one's natural liberty is in fact the means through which the right to defend oneself and punish transgressors is assigned to the sovereign. It is by curtailing their original endowments that human beings empower the magistrate to ensure peace and order in the community. Once they have joined the body politic, citizens can only use force when their lives are immediately in danger; they must resort to the magistrate to obtain redress in all other cases.

The alienation of liberty is indispensable for instituting both political and lesser forms of power. As has been shown, the acquisition of power is framed in the same vocabulary and principles that account for the acquisition and transference of material possessions. Material and personal resources differ, for the former are originally unappropriated, whereas the latter never compose a common stock, but are intrinsically someone's. If appropriation in the strict sense is ruled out for personal endowments,[45] transference is nonetheless possible, and is essential every time two (or more) human beings intend to institute a permanent relationship between themselves. A common terminological and conceptual thread thus connects all types of transactions in which human beings engage;[46] this will appear all the more clearly when we consider that very similar procedures have been devised for instituting and regulating all kinds of relationships and associations.

This reading of Grotius's work is of consequence for the analysis of personal and political jurisdiction in two ways. First, the proprietary model, which he applies to both material and personal resources, helps us to understand what is comprised in personal jurisdiction, in a conception centered on the individual as a bearer of subjective rights. Second, the reconstruction of the procedure through which one's property is partially alienated points to the question: what control does the individual retain over his own jurisdiction once the political ruler has been instituted? And since defining the proper jurisdiction of the individual and the body politic implies defining the boundaries of the private and public domains, what conception of private and public can we extrapolate from Grotius's theory?

PERSONAL AND POLITICAL JURISDICTION

As we have seen in the definition offered by Grotius, the "right, which every man has to his own" comprises the power one has over oneself and others, property, and the capacity to claim what is due, that is, one's rights. The "things" predicated as proper to a bearer of subjective rights do not appear to be homogeneous and commensurable, for they comprehend power, things, and faculties. What they have in common is that they are all, at least to a degree, at the disposal of their owner, including the capacity of claiming what is one's own. And in fact, in enslaving oneself, one alienates, together with one's liberty, one's capacity to be an independent subject of rights.

There exists, therefore, a set of characteristics proper to the bearer of subjective rights that appear indispensable for constituting a personality capable of autonomous agency.

> Since the Common Right to Things has been established, the Common Right to Actions follows next in order, and this right is either absolute, or established by the supposition of a general agreement amongst mankind. Now all men have absolutely a right to do such or such acts as are necessary to provide whatever is essential to the existence or convenience of life.
>
> Right in this place means what is strictly so called, signifying the moral power of action, which any one as a member of society possesses.[47]

The features composing personal agency are two-faced. As constitutive of personality, they enable the individual to be the author of his/her own actions; those who are deprived of them are not responsible for what they do, as is the case with children, idiots, and mad people. On the other hand, faculties and capacities can be, like things, objects of transactions, and they can be voluntarily decreased by transferring them to others.

Each individual's personal jurisdiction thus comprises all those "things" of which one can dispose. Since some of those "things" are faculties which are constitutive of the person as an agent, the inevitable conclusion is that individuals have jurisdiction over the capacities that make them competent. This conception may sound odd to us, who starkly separate what defines us as persons from the domain of what can be the object of transactions.[48] In seventeenth-century thought, however, it is a commonplace: alienability of characteristics that are essential to human personality is indispensable if positions of power are to be instituted.

In establishing a sovereign, persons therefore renounce at least a portion of their personal jurisdiction, thereby giving life to public jurisdiction. The latter will collect all that individuals have given up: primarily, their power to defend their rights and enforce the law of nature, by punishing transgressors. This is the most basic function of the state, "for the end of society is to form a common and united aid to preserve to every one his own."[49] Grotius further denies that the state can lose its political capacity by acting unjustly, "as long as its laws and tribunals and other necessary parts of its constitution remain, to administer justice and give redress to foreigners, no less than to private subjects in their actions against each other."[50] All that regards the use of force, both in domestic and in foreign affairs, belongs to public jurisdiction.

Since force was used by individuals in the state of nature to defend what was their own, the state now has the task of doing that on their behalf, by ensuring redress and punishing transgressors. The jurisdiction or area of competence of the state thus includes, as is the case for individuals, the capacity to act in view of certain aims,[51] and the actions whereby those aims can be attained; and it extends over the actions performed by members of the community that may endanger other citizens and what belongs to them.

If we reconstruct a definition of public jurisdiction by considering which natural capacities individuals transfer to the sovereign, we are led to conceptualize a very narrow and specific conception of politics. Politics are concerned with maintaining order and peace in the community, by enforcing a system of regulations, the law of nature, which is mainly focused on identifying and assigning to everyone his/her own. In this perspective, politics are required only to confirm and sanction what human beings do by managing their personal endowments, provided that they abide by the norms comprised in the law of nature. In other terms, politics only regard those aspects of personal agency that lead to deviant and transgressive behavior. Does this imply that Grotius entrusts individuals with full and uncontrolled competence on all other things, activities, and relations which result from individuals' exercise personal agency?

As one might expect, the answer to this question is negative. Grotius combines two elements to justify the institution of a public authority which, though constituted through the transference of the power of life and death by individuals, acquires a nearly unlimited power over them. The first element, which we have already mentioned, is that the institution of a superior entails a transference of agency which goes beyond the specific terms of the transaction.[52] The second is that, for Grotius, a body politic cannot exist if the only aim of collective – i.e. public – activity is to avoid internal war.

Drawing on the analogy of domestic and political association, Grotius says:

> But whether any one presides over an household, or a state, the first and most necessary care is the support of his dependents and subjects. For the household forms but one body with the master, and the people with the sovereign.[53]

Although the essential task of politics is the protection of subjects from the injuries which they may inflict upon each other, it appears that the performance of that task is not enough if human beings are to live in society. The care and support of the members of the community go well beyond ensuring the enjoyment of what is legitimately in their possession.

The analogy of domestic and political association is here not merely rhetorical, as household dependents and subjects find themselves in the same condition before their respective superiors. Although Grotius does not describe in detail the procedure through which "fathers and masters" acquire power over their dependents, they are the superiors of their children, wives, and servants as the political ruler is of his subjects. And superiors can, as Grotius has emphasized, impose obligations which are not merely the ones prescribed by the principles of justice strictly defined. There is an obligation to obey the ruler, the content of which remains unspecified and dependent upon the ruler's will. The instrument for legitimating such a broad power is the voluntary transference of one's natural liberty, which entails the loss of part of one's personal agency in favor of the sovereign. Ultimately, this means that the autonomy and separateness of each individual are impaired. The condition of heads of households who have become the subjects of someone is thus similar to that of children, women, and servants. These are incorporated in the head's person, and have only a vicarious political existence; independent adult males are incorporated in the body politic, and retain only a partial control over their persons and private possessions.[54]

Grotius's theory has thus led us to somewhat paradoxical conclusions, for he relies on a very individualistic and egoistic conception of the nature of human agency to construct a plausible justification of how that agency can be substantively curtailed and impaired. The condition of subjects in political society is similar to that of household dependents, who retain a limited personal agency, if any at all, and are dispossessed of any public agency they might have had as human beings in the state of nature. Grotius's version of the analogical approach to the domestic and political associations emphasizes more and more the similarities between the two. The ruler/ruled relationship has become more like that of husband and wife, master and servant. And yet, household members are supposed to conclude transactions with their personal superiors which are procedurally very similar to those in which free men engage when they subject themselves to the sovereign. The analogy thus works both ways, as it were, and the social universe of the household and that of the body politic are conceived by Grotius as increasingly homogeneous.

Grotius's theory leaves some important problems open. First, he explores the features of personal agency only to the extent necessary to legitimate the institution of absolute power. Although he appears to hypothesize equally competent human beings in the state of nature, he never explicitly affirms that household dependents were initially on an equal footing with their personal superior; and he does not explain how and why, if all were really equal, only heads of households became endowed with political agency.

The second problematic issue is the analysis of political agency itself. Grotius's analogy of the power enjoyed by the head of household with that enjoyed by the sovereign implies that adult free men curtail their public agency in entering civil society, as much as dependents curtail their personal (and, consequently, public) agency in joining a family. To leave the state of nature, individuals perform a political action by transferring the power of life and death; and since this transference is interpreted by Grotius as the alienation of one's liberty, individuals renounce most of their capacity to act autonomously. Just as the head of household is the only one entitled to make decisions for the family, so the sovereign is the only one entitled to make decisions for the political community. Only the sovereign thus enjoys public agency in civil society. The need to ensure peace and order by protecting what legitimately belongs to everyone prompts individuals to assign that task to the sovereign, at the cost of dispossessing themselves of the competence to participate in public life.

This analysis of Grotius's theory has shown the implications of a proprietary model of personal jurisdiction. Not only things and services, but one's own capacities are parts of that jurisdiction. In emphasizing this point, Grotius makes human agency into an item which can be an object of transactions. He also prompts us to reflect upon the role played by agency in our inquiry into private and public. Personal and political relations are created by individuals, who are endowed with the skills necessary for bringing those relations into existence. Those skills are themselves resources that compose the personal jurisdiction of each adult, and can be increased or decreased through a voluntary contract. Not only can individuals be richer or poorer, they can also be "more" or "less" agents. And if one is left with no autonomous agency at all, as is a slave, can one still have public agency? Can a slave exercise the power of life and death in the state of nature? Can a slave participate in instituting civil society? In other words, what type of personal agency does one need to have in order to express public agency? The distinction between private and public in Natural Law theory thus regards not only what people control in the private or public domains, but also what type of agency individuals express in those domains. It is Samuel Pufendorf who thoroughly explores the implications of the juris- dictional distinction between private and public for a conception of personal and political agency.

NATURAL EQUALITY, PERSONAL DEPENDENCE, AND POLITICAL INEQUALITY

The most interesting aspect of Pufendorf's theory for the present inquiry is his detailed and original analysis of the state of nature.

> The *Natural State* of Man, consider'd *with relation to other Men*, is that which affects us upon the bare account of an Universal kindred, resulting from the similitude of our Nature, antecedent to any Human Act or Covenant, by which One Man is render'd peculiarly obnoxious to the power of Another.[55]

Pufendorf is aware of the universalistic bias of this starting point, and of its implications for a theory of human agency. Human beings are moral persons, capable of entering into relationships with others regulated by "operative moral qualities," which can be active or passive. The active ones are articulated in turn in "power, right, and obligation." In the faculty of "power" Pufendorf sees the focus of agency. By exercising it, we structure our relationships with ourselves, the world, and others. Power enables us to act autonomously, to fulfill our obligations and claim our rights, and it is also the outcome of the actions we perform. As a faculty, "a *Power* over *our own* Persons and Actions is called Liberty."[56] As a result of those actions, power can take the form of "propriety" or "domain," empire or authority, and servitude – that is, access to things that belong to others.[57]

A human being considered independently of all social interaction is therefore a person endowed by God with the capacities for acting in the world. The rights of nature are logically derived from this original and hypothetical condition, in which each individual would tend to preserve him-/herself, in a situation of complete independence. It should be emphasized at this point that, unlike Grotius, Pufendorf does not consider rights as *dominia*, which each human being has over the world independently of anybody else. Rights and duties do not exist in nature, prior to human interaction. For they are not *entia physica* – physical entities – but *entia moralia*: qualifications superimposed by indi- viduals upon things, their person, and their transactions.[58] When a person legitimately uses her natural power in such a way that another recognizes that he has an obligation to allow her to behave as she does, the person has acquired a right.

> For the clearer Illustration of this Point, it is necessary to observe, That not every Natural Licence, or Power of doing a thing is properly a *Right*, but such only as includes some Moral Effect, with regard to others, who are Partners with me in the same Nature.... But then at length, it turns into a proper Right, when it creates this Moral Effect in other Persons, that they shall not hinder him in the free use of these Conveniences, and shall themselves forbear to use them without his Consent.[59]

This approach implies that Pufendorf does not adopt a proprietary view of the relationship between oneself and one's faculties, as the one we saw in Grotius. The individual is not an owner of his capacities, which he can transfer and alienate to others. Nonetheless, a capable adult can engage in transactions which have the same consequences as those envisaged by Grotius's proprietary approach.

> A *perfect Promise* is, when a Man not only determines his Will to the Performance of such or such a thing for another hereafter, but likewise shews that he gives the other a full *Right* of challenging or requiring it from him. When we engage to give away a particular thing, or to perform a particular Service, the former is a Kind of *Alienation* of our Goods, or at least somewhat in order to it; the latter is an *Alienation* of some part of our Natural Liberty.[60]

Although the transferor does not have a proprietary right in his liberty – a right which he transfers to another through a contract – the language and the implications of the transaction are those of the proprietary model. The beneficiary acquires (Pufendorf's term) a right to govern the dependent, who has alienated part of a faculty which inhered in him before the contract. Despite the original liberty and equality recognized to all in the state of nature,[61] human beings increase or decrease their original stock, thus modifying their original equality. They acquire possessions, by "specifying" material resources which are by nature common, and acquiring control over people. But the rejection of the proprietary model enables Pufendorf to see more clearly the difference between property in things and rule over people. In discussing the master/servant relationship, Pufendorf argues:

> But altho' *Dominion*, which is properly the Right of governing Another's Person, when establish'd with the free Consent of the

Subject, cannot, regularly, be transferr'd without his good liking.... Yet so long as the Subjects enjoy any Remains of Liberty, we cannot in seriousness say, that the Men themselves are thus alienated or made over, but only the Right of governing them, as being join'd with Some Use or Advantage. Every Sovereign may indeed, as Mr Hobbes remarks, say of his Subject *hic, meus est, this Man is my Property*; yet 'tis in a quite different sense that we call a *Thing* our *own*. For, by the former Expression, I mean no more, than that I and none else have the Right of governing such a Person; yet so as to be myself under some kind of obligation to him, and not impower'd to exercise that Right upon him, in an unlimited absolute manner. But, on the other side, the Property I claim over a Thing, implies a Right of using, spoiling, and consuming it, to procure my Advantage, or to satisfy my Pleasure; so that what way soever I dispose of it, to say it was *my own* shall be a sufficient Excuse.[62]

Pufendorf's universalistic assumptions become explicit in his discussion of the rights which husband and wife acquire over one another through the marriage contract.

We suppose before-hand, that all Human Persons, whether of one Sex or the other, are naturally equal in Right; and that no one can claim the Sovereignty over another, unless it be obtain'd by the free Act of one of the Parties.... Therefore whatever *Right* a Man holds over a Woman, in as much as she is by Nature his *Equal*, he must acquire, either by her Consent, or by the Sword, in a just War.[63]

In describing the wife/husband relationship Pufendorf constructs two states of nature. The first is completely hypothetical and perfectly egalitarian. In it, human beings would engage in temporary relationships, without giving life to any stable institution. Man and woman would conclude *ad hoc* agreements, on the initiative of either party and without including reciprocal submission. The child born of their intercourse would be in the mother's power, for in such a condition, motherhood, not fatherhood, is certain.[64]

This perfectly egalitarian, egoistic, and Hobbesian state of nature, in which all adults are free and equal, is a fiction of the imagination, since it has never existed on earth. There is, says Pufendorf, a historical state of nature, dating back to Biblical times, in which most human beings do not live in isolation, but live in small societies, first among them, the family.

In as much as upon the divine Authority of the Scriptures, we believe all human Race to have proceeded from one Original Pair. Now it's plain, that *Eve* was subject to *Adam*, *Gen* iii. 16, and those who were born of these Primitive Parents, and so on, did immediately fall under Paternal Authority, and under Family Government.[65]

This condition is no longer perfectly egalitarian: wives are subjected to their husbands, children to their parents/fathers, and some individuals will soon become servants or slaves. Degrees of superiority and inferiority are inherent in the social condition, and ascriptive differences in gender, capacities, and situations of need are sufficient grounds for explaining asymmetrical power relations.[66]

The state of nature as a condition of isolation and insecurity does not concern all human beings, but only those who live outside a domestic association. At the very beginning all belonged to one family, and it is only with the proliferation of the species that individuals began to live scattered about, with no permanent ties with their fellows. In this situation, enmity and, ultimately, the degeneration of the state of nature into a state of war became possible, until individuals decided to constitute civil society, establish an impartial judge, and put an end to an insecure albeit independent life.

However, the hypothetical state of nature plays an important role in Pufendorf's theory. First, all individuals who do not have a superior in the historical state of nature are in the condition described by the hypothetical one. For these individuals, the hypothesis is a fact. Second, even the condition of those who live in a family, and therefore have a superior, can only be justified by referring to the features and capacities of abstract and equal human beings. Their reasons for subjecting themselves to another may arise from ascriptive characteristics which doom them, so to speak, to a subordinate condition. But only the consent which they give as if they were perfectly free to avoid subjection can legitimate the superior's power.[67]

The original – even if only hypothetical – condition of equality of all human beings means for Pufendorf that every individual is endowed with a personal sphere of competence, of which he/she can dispose freely. Being free, every person has the right to dispose of his/her power as he/she prefers, within the limits of the law of nature. Pufendorf sees liberty, power, and right as synonyms, in that each of them emphasizes a specific aspect of the fact that human beings are moral persons, capable of performing actions which have a moral effect.[68] As for Grotius, that original sphere of competence can be curtailed. Some individuals will thus broaden their personal domain at the expense of others. And although Pufendorf stresses the difference between property in things and power over people, the procedure for transferring personal endowments is similar to that used in transferring material resources, and the vocabulary is that of the proprietary model.[69]

The possibility of transferring part of our natural liberty explains why in the historical state of nature there are individuals who enjoy power over others, notably heads of households who rule over children, women, servants, and slaves. Heads of households will carry their broadened personal domain with themselves into civil society.

> *Fathers of Families*, who being the chief Rulers before the Institution of Publick Governments, brought into such Governments the Power which they before held over their Wives, their Children, and their Servants. So that this Inequality being more Ancient than the Erection of Civil Societies, can by no means owe its Original to them; nor do they give this Power to the Fathers of Families, but leave it in their Hands as they found it.[70]

Heads of households and adult males not attached to any family[71] establish civil society when the growing complexity of social relations in the historical state of nature makes that condition unstable and dangerous. At the center of the procedure leading to the creation of the body politic there is the transference of the right to dispose of one's self, capacities, and possessions. The most important power transferred is that of using force in self-defense. The fundamental drive of human nature is in fact the desire for self-preservation, which entitles people to do all they can to ensure their own survival. Individuals can appropriate material resources, exchange freedom for assistance and help, and use what belongs to others in cases of extreme need. They can also, as in Grotius, defend themselves from aggressors, by employing force and using all means to make sure that attacks will not be repeated in the future. However, says Pufendorf,

> whoever enters into a Community, divests himself of his natural Freedom, and puts himself under Government, which, among other things, comprehends the Power of Life and Death over him; together with Authority to enjoyn him some things, to which he has an utter Aversion, and to prohibit others, for which he may have as strong an Inclination: so that 'tis possible he may often, in Obedience to this Authority, be oblig'd to sacrifice his private Good to that of the publick.[72]

Civil society as we know it is the doing of independent adult males. But the assumption that all human beings are by nature equal leads Pufendorf to abandon once and for all the notion that dependent members of the family are by definition incapable of political agency. All individuals possess the instinct of self-preservation and the capacities for doing what is necessary to satisfy it, including the faculty to assess when to use the power of life and death in defense of one's own person and endowments.[73] Pufendorf depicts two possible scenarios in which adults transfer to a superior the power to use force and punish transgressors, thus instituting a political community. The first is the transformation of a family into a political community; the second, the institution of civil society in the strict sense of the term.

In analyzing the nature and extent of the husband's power over the wife, the father's over the child, and the master's over the servant, Pufendorf rejects the notion that the power of life and death is inherent in domestic authority. Resorting to the traditional comparative strategy, he denies that the husband's power is a full power of government, by explaining that "the End of Marriage is not like that of Commonwealths, the Defence and Security of Men; but is directed wholly to the Propagation of [the] Human Race." But a few lines later, he accepts the idea that a family is like a small state, so that "the Wife when she is admitted into it, ought, one would think, to yield Submission to the Lord and Director of the Society." And this can happen because "a *Family*, if encreas'd with a numerous Train of Servants, hath two Ends and Designs, once common, the other proper. The common End consists in mutual Defence and Security, arising from the united Strength of so many Persons." The other end is, of course, the reproduction of the species. So that, after much debating, Pufendorf concludes:

> Not that is repugnant to the Law of Nature, for a Wife to be subjected to her Husband in the way of strict *Political* Government. For the fear of supreme Authority, and the Endearments of Conjugal Affection are really, no more destructive of each other, than the Sovereignty of the Prince extinguisheth the Love of the Subject.[74]

As the analogical approach emphasizes, the consequence of assuming that all are equal, and therefore capable of concluding any type of transaction, is to make wholly contingent the differences between the domestic and the political association. According to Pufendorf's argument, in the historical state of nature, individuals decide on the basis of their specific needs what type of power to assign to a superior. It is the extent of the power attributed to the person chosen as the ruler of the association that distinguishes the household from the body politic. If the superior must ensure the security of the group from aggressors, dependents may decide to assign him the right to use the power of life and death on behalf and in the name of all. In this case, he exercises political authority, and the association can be considered to be political. But when the superior only rules over his wife, children, and servants to ensure the propagation and survival of the species, his power will be much more limited, and the association will remain domestic. Whether an individual who joins a household transfers his natural right to use force, and thus recognizes his superior as a political ruler, depends on the type of transaction in which the parties engage. We must look to procedural and therefore formal aspects, to establish if we have to do with a body politic or a domestic association.

There are significant differences between the transformation of a family into a little commonwealth, and the institution of civil society – the second, more interesting, and historically relevant scenario depicted by Pufendorf. The institution of civil society consists of the aggregation of several families in a body politic, which is realized, as seen above, by heads of households alone.[75] The steps of the operation are much more complex, and subjected to a greater number of conditions, than is the attribution of political power to a personal superior by a dependent. The acquisition of full authority by a head of household is in fact a typical case of a dual transaction in which one of the parties alienates his/her natural power to use force, and therefore his/her liberty. The relationship between a husband who enjoys absolute power over his wife and that wife is the same as that between an absolute monarch and his people, Pufendorf remarks. The convention between them is a *pactum subiectionis*, through which the powers of the man as husband (or father, or master) are broadened so as to include the power of life and death.

But in instituting civil society, the *pactum subiectionis* is not enough, since the association itself has to be created. Whereas husband and wife are already united by the marriage covenant, and by a relationship of superiority and inferiority which makes one body of the two, scattered heads of households or unattached adult males are disconnected entities. Their first step is to become one body, which will be able to act as one moral person uniting the forces and wills of all members. The *pactum societatis* guarantees to all participants that the terms of the convention[76] to which they subscribe are reciprocal.

It will be necessary, first of all, that they covenant each with each in particular, to join into one lasting Society, and to concert the Measures of their Welfare and Safety, by the publick Vote....This Covenant may be made either Absolutely or Conditionally. The first is done, when a Man engageth himself to stick to this Society, whatever Form of Gov. shall afterwards be approved of by the major Part. The latter, when the Person engaging adds this Clause, provided such a Form shall be introduced, as is agreeable to his private Judgement.[77]

After choosing the form of government, the body politic subscribes to a *pactum subiectionis*, through which the ruler/s is/are chosen. The regular procedure – and the one Pufendorf prefers – is when the body politic alienates its freedom to act to an absolute ruler. For Pufendorf, sovereignty is absolute and irrevocable (except by the sovereign himself), resistance is not permissible, and subjects surrender their natural "forces" into the hands of the sovereign. The action performed by a body politic is thus the same as that performed by an individual subjecting him-/herself to a superior.[78]

Although the procedure which leads from the state of nature to civil society is much more complex than that which individuals follow when they endow their personal superior with the power of life and death, the final result is the same. Pufendorf himself remarks:

> Yet it is not so utter an Impossibility, that Civil Empire might arise from Paternal Government; such we mean as extended it self to some Breadth, taking many petty Villages under its Direction. 'Tis true, the Command of Fathers, belongs properly to the Care of educating Children, as that of Masters, doth to the Management and Improvement of Estates; nor can either be alter'd by the bare *Number* of Children, or of Servants. Yet there is not so wide a Distance between Paternal and Civil Government, but that Men might pass from one to the other, without the Production of any new Sovereignty by the immediate Power of God.[79]

The individualistic and universalistic premises of Pufendorf's theory explain the similarities between domestic and political society. Associations can only be constituted through the voluntary transference of the natural power of their members. The power to act, which every natural or artificial person must possess in order to attain its ends, is first of all in human beings, who give it to the institutions they found. More precisely, they assign it to the person/s who will act on behalf of, and in the name of, the institution in question. We must therefore hypothesize that every sane adult is competent to perform the transaction that will lead to the creation of an association. The function of the hypothetical state of nature is that it allows us to see which characteristics human nature must possess if power is to be instituted.

Although all individuals are competent to conclude political transactions, that is, those regarding the power of life and death, only adult independent males and heads of households can form a political association. Those who are excluded have *de facto* or must be presumed to have curtailed their agency, through having become someone's dependents. By clarifying the dynamic by which individuals end up by constructing personal domains of different "sizes", so to speak,[80] and by showing the implications of that dynamic for political agency, Pufendorf also provides the material necessary for clarifying the relationship between personal and public agency, and private and public domain.

PRIVATE AND PUBLIC

The jurisdictional bent of Natural Law theory provides the common denominator between the conception of agency held by Grotius and Pufendorf and the definition of private and public contained in the *Corpus juris*. This definition is used in Roman jurisprudence to distinguish between two broad jurisdictional areas, that regarding individuals and that regarding the Roman commonwealth. The distinction is made from the point of view of the legislator, who issues norms to regulate transactions, and who assigns competence over those transactions to different magistrates. The adoption of this definition by political thinkers entails a shift in the universe of reference of the terms, as has happened with all juridical concepts taken from the Roman tradition and turned to more strictly political use. Grotius still employs the distinction in separating private from public *jus*, but *jus* is by now a very different notion from the Roman one, with wider and broader implications for the distribution of power in society.

> Right [*jus*], strictly taken, is again twofold, the one, private, established for the advantage of each individual, the other, superior, as involving the claims, which the state has upon individuals, and their property, for the public good. Thus the regal authority is above that of a father and a master, and the sovereign has a greater right over the property of his subjects, where the public good is concerned, than the owners themselves have.[81]

This excerpt illustrates the political meaning which the distinction between private and public is now acquiring. *Jus* here has both objective and subjective connotations. There is in political society something called *jus*, which can regard either individual endowments, that is, property, or the public, that is, common, good. But for the subjects of each domain – individuals on one side, and the sovereign on the other – that *jus* is subjectively predicated, and each subject can claim different *rights*. For Grotius, the most important function of the distinction is to order domains in jurisdictional terms, for the *jus* of the ruler takes precedence over that of his subjects, to the point that he can legitimately claim their property as part of his jurisdiction. The distinction between private and public law thus turns out to be a distinction between private and public jurisdiction, that is, a distinction between areas of competence over which natural and artificial persons have control thanks to their capacity for agency.

Pufendorf's more detailed rendering of how individuals increase or decrease their original stock helps us to understand the exact composition of each individual's domain – whether that individual is an independent human being in the hypothetical state of nature, a wife in the historical one, or a head of household about to join other adults in civil society.

If a person's private sphere is composed of all the capacities that may become the objects of transactions, and of all that one acquires by exercising them, then the public sphere is composed of all that individuals have transferred to the sovereign. The state collects the powers that its members have given up, and acquires an independent personality. It becomes a moral person – albeit an artificial one – capable of action as each individual is, and endowed with its proper sphere of competence. Pufendorf draws an explicit analogy between the power which each person enjoys over his/her personal domain and that which the state enjoys over the public domain.

> As we cannot conceive, in single Persons, a higher and more absolute Liberty, than that they shall determine and dispose of their Goods, and Actions, not by the Will of another, but by their own Judgement and Pleasure, yet still with a full Obedience to the Law of Nature; and as this Liberty Naturally belongs to all Persons, who are not subject to the Command of Others: so, where Many Men cleave together in an established *State*, there too, as in a *Common Subject*, must necessarily reside the same Liberty, or the Power of choosing by their own Judgement, all Means and Methods tending to the Preservation of the whole Society. And this Liberty is attended with an Absolute Command, or a Right of prescribing those Means to the particular Members, and of compelling them to a due Obedience and Conformity.[82]

This institution of an absolute sovereign implies that the distinction between private and public domain has become merely rhetorical. In instituting an absolute sovereign, citizens surrender to him the faculty of judging what constitutes the common "good," that is, of deciding what should be of public concern.[83] In so doing, subjects renounce the possibility of questioning the sovereign's policies regarding the transference of parts of the individual's private endowments to the public. As a consequence, establishing the boundary between private and public becomes a wholly contingent and subjective operation: contingent, because no rule independent of both sovereign and subject is maintained to fix that boundary; subjective, since the ruler cannot be obliged to adopt shared standards in deciding what is of private, and what of public, competence.[84]

Pufendorf is aware of all these implications, for he devises another possible outcome of the *pactum subiectionis*, by which an agreement is attained to establish fixed limits to the ruler's faculty of defining what is the public good.

> The Condition of the Subjects, under such a Constitution, rather depends on their own Choice, than on the Prince's Pleasure. Yet they could not but find it necessary, to abridge themselves of their Natural Liberty in such a Degree, as the Form of Government required which they are now about to introduce.[85]

As in all contracts regarding the transference of natural power, individuals have some discretion over the degree of authority which they assign to their superiors. The wife need not subject herself completely to her husband; the subject does not have to institute an absolute sovereign. Although the institution of an authority necessarily implies that some degree of discretionary power will be legitimately exercised by the superior, that power need not be absolute. But Pufendorf, like Grotius, assigns each individual a broad power over him-/herself, so that individuals can legitimate unlimited rather than limited authority. We confront the paradox that the subjective theory of rights put forward by Natural Law writers, recognizing very specific endowments and far-reaching powers for human beings, is used to dispossess individuals rather than empower them.

I have already stressed that this conclusion is further supported by Grotius and Pufendorf's emphasis on the analogies between domestic and political society. As dependent members of the household curtail their independence by joining the family, heads of households curtail theirs by joining civil society. The sovereign will exercise control over their private domain, at his discretion. Typical is the case of the restrictions imposed by the state on paternal authority: "After the erecting of Commonwealths, of these Rights which before belong'd to Fathers of Families, some were contracted, others quite taken away.

Yet so much Authority was almost in all places allow'd, as appear'd sufficient for Educating the Children."[86]

The analogy between family and body politic also stresses the reciprocal dependence of private and public domain, private and public aspects of agency. We can impair our public persona by transferring agency to a personal superior, as women and servants. But the alienation of our political competence inevitably affects the private domain, because the ruler is entitled to decide which personal resources must be appropriated to further the common good.

> And since all the Members of the State, in submitting their Wills to the Will of a single Director, did, at the same time, thereby oblige themselves to Non-resistance, or to Obey him in all his Desires, and Endeavours of applying their Strength and Wealth to the Good of the Publick; it appears, that He who holds the Sovereign Rule, is possess'd of sufficient Force to Compel any Persons to a Discharge of the several Injunctions, which he lays upon them. So, likewise, the same Covenant affords a full and easy *Title*, by which the aforesaid Sovereignty appears to be Establish'd, not upon Violence, but in a Lawful manner, upon the voluntary Consent and Subjection of the respective Members.[87]

Both Grotius and Pufendorf introduce the notion of "common good" to justify the unquestionable authority attributed to the ruler. The sovereign's right to intrude into his subjects' personal domains is justified by his duty to ensure the welfare of the community, not merely to prevent individuals from encroaching upon each other's rights. But even if only the latter were the aim of political intervention, the sovereign depicted by Grotius and Pufendorf would be entitled to intrude into his subjects' private domains, for both substantive and procedural reasons.

From a substantive point of view, the sovereign is invoked to regulate and give stability to a network of personal relationships which very much regard individual rights, claims, and possessions. Once it has been accepted that the more basic concern of politics is the conflict which arises at the level of personal exchange, it is private transactions and, inevitably, the personal sphere of competence that become the objects of regulation. And procedurally, adult males transfer their autonomous agency to the ruler, thus giving him a power which goes beyond the specific terms of the transaction, as Grotius emphasizes.

If we accept that politics must prevent personal transactions from becoming antagonistic, but if we also wish to avoid Grotius and Pufendorf's solution, two main questions appear unavoidable. The first has to do with conflict itself, its frequency and gravity when human beings are not controlled by an absolute ruler. The second question concerns whether the alienation of personal agency is necessary to the ruler in order to perform his task. If we hypothesize that citizens need not be completely dispossessed of their competence, then a new notion of public agency has to be elaborated. In particular, allowing individuals to retain personal competence will inevitably affect how we think of public agency – that of the state, and that of individuals who give life to it.

Both the question of the role and scope of conflict in the state of nature, and that of the inviolability of the personal domain, are central to Locke's work. While accepting the basic tenets of the tradition of Natural Law which we have been exploring here, especially in the version of Pufendorf, Locke applied fundamental corrections to it. But between Pufendorf's intriguing two-level theory of the state of nature and of agency, a theory which managed to tame the Hobbesian premises, without completely losing their radical flavor, and Locke's more moderate conception, another writer will have to be considered. This writer is Robert Filmer, who was important in his own right as a pamphleteer during the English Civil War. Filmer acquired a post-humous theoretical importance because several Natural Law theorists, and especially Locke, engaged in serious debate with him. Filmer was a patriarchalist and a fierce critic of Natural Law theory. In adopting a view which is as radical as that of Hobbes, but based on opposite assumptions, Filmer stressed the implications of playing with the analogical strategy and the similarities between household and body politic. And in subjecting Filmer's theory to thorough scrutiny and criticism, Locke provided an alternative view of domestic and political relations and the distinction between private and public.

2 Patriarchalism

The radical view of Sir Robert Filmer

ASSIMILATION

The comparison of power relations in the household and the body politic led Grotius and Pufendorf to emphasize the similarities between the two associations. Both substantively – in the tasks they should perform, and the ends they are expected to attain – and formally – in the procedures through which positions of power are assigned – domestic society and political society are described as fundamentally analogous. Analogy does not mean identity: the family remains distinct from the commonwealth, for its head may not and usually does not exercise the power of life and death.[1] As Pufendorf explicitly contends, at the moment when transactions between husband and wife, and master and servant, extend to negotiating the use of force, the family becomes *transformed* into a little kingdom. In the (historical) state of nature this happens easily, and the transition from domestic to political power may well occur through a tacit convention. Dependent members spontaneously turn to the head as the arbiter of their disputes, and their defender against external aggression. But conceptually, the difference stands, and it cannot be brushed off as marginal. If a specific act were not necessary to justify the attribution of political power to the head of household, then the power of the sovereign could also be acquired without the active consent and participation of future subjects. It is therefore important to establish clear criteria for distinguishing a large association in which the power of life and death is still *de jure* in the hands of each adult, and a small one in which that power has been assigned to a specific person or group. Growth in size is not sufficient for changing the nature of the society; a specific act is required to effect that change.[2]

Pufendorf especially insists on the use of force as the factor which sets the political association aside from all others. But in alienating their natural liberty and power, to either a domestic or a political ruler, individuals will find themselves similarly dispossessed. Adults who have preserved their natural independence and are therefore politically active renounce their political agency in instituting the sovereign. Their condition with respect to the ruler is not dissimilar from that of their dependents within the household. The Aristotelian strategy of comparing the two associations has thus prompted opposite conclusions to those of Aristotle: domestic power and political power show remarkable analogies. And the analogical motif is not merely a rhetorical device, but indicates that the two most important institutions structuring social relations are increasingly perceived as homogeneous.

As remarked, this view is consequential for the distinction between private and public, because it follows from the nearly complete alienation of one's personal competence that subjects cannot call into question what the ruler does, even if there is an objective or intersubjectively valid ground for establishing what pertains to the individual, on one side, and the community, on the other. The sovereign will be the only judge, and as such will be entitled to consider the private spheres of subjects as part of his own jurisdiction. Not only does the public take precedence over the private,[3] but the criteria for deciding when that is necessary are chosen unilaterally by the ruler. The distinction between private and public is therefore reduced to a technical one, in the sense that the ruler must discriminate between the personal possessions of one of his subjects, and what is already part of the public domain.[4]

Grotius and Pufendorf's permissive interpretation of the use which individuals may make of their rights weakens the normative force of the distinction between private and public. But the subjective theory of rights elaborated by Natural Law thinkers provides a sophisticated tool for distinguishing between the private spheres of individuals. As Pufendorf shows, the notion that each individual has the competence and the responsibility for doing what he/she does with his/her personal endowments allows us to identify with precision the boundaries of each one's private domain. Some individuals maintain and broaden their original stock at the expense of others, thus enlarging their private spheres, to the point where they alone retain public agency. They will have a direct relationship with the sovereign, whereas dependents will be entrusted first of all to their personal superior. When writers discuss the ruler's right to appropriate private possessions for the common good, they are referring to the endowments of the head of household, for dependents have no active public standing, having lost their personal autonomy. Although the head of household's private sphere is at the disposal of the community, that private sphere is real enough: it includes all individuals who are no longer masters of themselves. And in relation to the latter, the adult male can exercise his personal competence as he thinks fit, short of exercising the power of life and death.

If the household proves to be the realm in which the head exercises private discretion, that discretion is, however, already partially restricted. First, because the state can deprive the individual of what is his own; second, because it will ensure that the power of life and death is not abused; and, last but not least, because even dependents retain a residual personality, and are therefore direct interlocutors of the sovereign, although with a passive voice. Pufendorf insists on this point in contending that the original equality of human beings can never be alienated completely.[5] And since that equality was conceived in terms of equal liberty, power to act, and rights, individuals remain, albeit minimally and only in principle, persons capable of autonomous action, and endowed with a personal sphere of competence. As we shall see, this factor will become more and more important in Locke and Hutcheson, and will profoundly modify the conception of the public, as both a collective subject, a domain of life, and a mode of action.

These remarks will serve to emphasize the contrast between the view of Natural Law theory and that of patriarchalism, especially in the version offered by Robert Filmer.[6] If for Natural Law theory the relation between domestic and political society can be defined as "analogy," for Filmer that relation can be defined as "assimilation." "Assimilation" is an extreme form of analogy, which denies that the two associations differ in any significant respect.[7] The choice of a noun indicating verbal action – "assimilation" – indicates that this procedure seeks to make conceptually identical two structures which are initially understood as distinct.

If, as they are for Filmer, the domestic and political associations are the same, society can be seen as either a "big household" or a "small kingdom." Which is the "model," and which the "copy"? Does Filmer extend the characteristics of the household to the commonwealth, or vice versa? In the abstract, both operations are possible, and we have seen that supporters of the analogical view play a double-mirror game. For Filmer, however, the household, as the first and more basic structure, is the model for society as a whole, which will be seen to reproduce on a bigger scale the dynamics typical of the family. The ends of the political community will therefore be survival and physical welfare, politics will be reduced to household management, and rulers will govern thanks to their superior capacities or because of a gift from

God, not because they have been chosen by their peers. If household and body politic cannot be distinguished, can we still separate a private from a public jurisdiction within the community? Filmer struggles with this problem, without offering a satisfactory answer, but his critics will have no doubt that the distinction between private and public here becomes logically problematic, and practically questionable.

In comparing the power relations typical of domestic and political society, Natural Law theorists focus their attention on the transference of personal endowments between adults. Although children, as future subjects, are of great concern to writers, their condition of dependence and subordination is seen as transitory. The power which parents – but usually fathers – enjoy over them may be more or less extensive, and derive directly from nature, or, as in Hobbes, be based on a contract *a posteriori* which sanctions a power *de facto*. But children are supposed to grow out of that condition, and become independent individuals.

For Filmer the father/child relationship is on the contrary the paradigmatic one for understanding the world of ruler and ruled. He argues that no relevant difference can be detected between paternal and political power. Their origins, natures, scopes, and ends are identical. The king's power is identical to that which God granted to Adam over the earth and its inhabitants. All humans are Adam's descendants; and, upon Adam's death, his authority automatically passed to his oldest son. A kingdom is thus a huge household, where the monarch rules at his own discretion over subjects who wholly depend on his will for their survival. As the giver of life and their keeper, the father/monarch has full jurisdiction over his children/subjects and may therefore exercise the power of life and death at his own discretion.[8]

Filmer grounds his assertion that family and kingdom, and paternal and political power, are identical on the assumption that all human beings are not free at birth, and that only their superior's decree can make them so.

> Every man that is born, is so far from being free-born, that by his very birth he becomes a subject to him that begets him: under which subjection he is always to live, unless by immediate appointment from God, or by the grant or death of his Father, he become possessed of that power to which he was subject.[9]

By emphasizing universal inequality, Filmer completely assimilates the status of heads of households to that of their dependents. The condition of adult males with respect to the monarch is the same as that of women, children, and servants with respect to the head of household. Although he rejects the fundamental tenets of Natural Law theorists,

Filmer does not fall back onto the traditional argument opposing the natural hierarchy of the household to the condition of equality of the full members of the body politic. On the contrary, he employs the comparative strategy to show that what is true of dependent members of the household holds true for all subjects in the kingdom. His conception of politics provides the ultimate ground for his assimilating procedure. Fathers and kings exercise the same type of power because they share the identical duty of preserving the association over which they rule.

> If we compare the natural duties of a Father with those of a King, we find them to be all one, without any difference at all but only in the latitude and extent of them. As the Father over one family, so the King, as Father over many families, extends his care to preserve, feed, clothe, instruct and defend the whole commonwealth. His wars, his peace, his courts of justice, and all his acts of sovereignty, tend only to preserve and distribute to every subordinate and inferior Father, and to their children, their rights and privileges, so that all the duties of a King are summed up in an universal fatherly care of his people.[10]

In Filmer's view, family and kingdom are merely two names attached to the same institution, since they perform the same task: the preservation of human life. Although human beings appear to engage in very different activities, their goal is the same, as are the means necessary to attain it.

Even if the household is Filmer's model, his description shows that the assimilating procedure prompts an exchange of characteristics between the two associations. This becomes apparent when Filmer maintains that the exercise of kingly power is identical with paternal care, but the care of a father who is as mighty as a monarch. Filmer sees fathers as omnipotent, because he transfers to them the capacity and force of the absolute ruler. The natural power of fathers is thus unduly increased by reading features back into it which pertain to the political power of kings. What matters to Filmer is that, if by nature fathers enjoy such an absolute and irresistible power, and if the authority of fathers and kings is the same, then kings too will be endowed by nature with the same might. Fathers are thus assigned the might of kings, while on the other hand, kings have the rights of heads of households, and are not accountable to anyone except God for their deeds. If a king rules like a head of household, tyranny is as good a form of government as any other, and is only another name for monarchy. Filmer thus ends up by "domesticizing" political relations, and "politicizing" domestic ones.[11]

If the father/child relationship is the archetype of all power relations, we should expect generation to be the foundation of the superior's power. However this is not the case, because Filmer, whose theory provides as good an example as any of overdetermination, also contends that Adam's authority was grounded in his being the first and only legitimate proprietor of the earth and all it contained. Filmer thus adopts a radical version of the proprietary frame of reference which Natural Law theorists also share, by maintaining that property in things and *dominium* over people are logically coextensive. To possess an object and to rule over a person are species of the same genus, and the ruler governs thanks to his being a proprietor. In adopting the juridically based vocabulary shared by Natural Law theorists, Filmer shows how that conceptual framework can be bent to support the most various positions. But the seeds of Filmer's radical view are already present in Natural Law theorists themselves. Grotius, for one, accepts the idea that the sovereign can hold sovereignty with a full property title, especially when he has obtained it by conquest.[12] It is the extension of that principle to all social relations that, better than anything else, shows the unpalatable aspects of a proprietary approach to the foundations of power.

ANARCHY

The ultimate ground of paternal/kingly power thus appears to be the proprietorship over the earth and its creatures which God assigned to Adam in creating him. Filmer assigns immense significance to the choice which God made at the moment of creating the world, among the infinite number of possible alternatives available to his omnipotence. He chose to create one adult self-sufficient male. This fact has determined the features of all of society and human history. God granted Adam dominion over Eve, his children, and his future servants, and made the entire earth his exclusive property.[13] All human beings, starting with Eve, are thus not merely Adam's dependents, but rather his possessions, in the manner of material things, and he can dispose of them just as any proprietor disposes of his belongings.

The grounding of Adam's power in proprietary relations shows the extent to which Filmer "privatizes" the realm of politics. Filmer contends not merely that members of the household depend on the adult male for survival, but that they are living parts of the head's property. In other words, they share the condition of Aristotle's slaves. As Aristotle maintains that certain individuals can be enslaved because they are capable of becoming someone else's property, so Filmer holds that dependents must be considered as possessions of the father/king, because they are incapable of directing their own lives. Individuals remain throughout their lives in a condition of minority resembling that of children.[14]

Filmer's mistrust of the capacity of his fellow human beings for reliable and autonomous agency appears in his reinterpretation of Aquinas's passage on the necessity of government before the Fall.

> Government as to coactive power was after sin, because coaction supposeth some disorder, which was not in the state of innocency: but as for directive power, the condition of humane nature requires it, since civil society cannot be imagined without power of government: for although as long as men continued in the state of innocency they might not need the direction of Adam in those things which were necessarily and morally to be done; yet things indifferent, that depended merely on their free will, might be directed by the power of Adam's command.[15]

According to Filmer, human beings cannot be left on their own, and must be told what to do even when their actions are inconsequential from a moral point of view, as "things indifferent." Filmer here uses this notion in a peculiar way, not as a criterion to identify the realm where political rule can be exercised as a matter of discretion, because natural and divine law are silent, but rather as a means of emphasizing that political rule must regulate all aspects of social life. From a political point of view, there are no "things indifferent," and there is, therefore, no space left for individual discretion. Individuals cannot enjoy any degree of autonomy, and no decision can be entrusted to their will.[16] If subjects are denied independence, they are also relieved of responsibility. This is assigned wholly to the father/king, who enjoys a power commensurate with the magnitude of his duty. Since dependents are incapable of directing their own lives, they must be considered passive instruments in the superior's hands, as are the things which he possesses.

This assimilation of paternal and political power entails that chaos and anarchy ensue whenever that power is not exercised. Everyone will then be free to follow his/her will, and since dependents are incapable of self-direction, the social order will be completely disrupted. But we can see the most important consequence of adopting an assimilating procedure in Filmer's reading of the portrait of the state of nature offered by Natural Law theory. If the state of nature is a condition of freedom and independence, then this must apply to all human beings. If in the state of nature political power is not vested in any person, the logical conclusion must be that there is no power at all, since in Filmer's view the elimination of political power entails the elimination of the power of the head of household.[17] The statement that in this condition there is "no superior on earth" must be taken literally as meaning that each person can then do whatever he/she wishes. This is precisely the same as anarchy, "for anarchy is nothing else but a broken monarchy, where every man is his own monarch or governor."[18]

Filmer's interpretation of the state of nature corresponds to the hypothetical version of it offered by Pufendorf, who contended that such a state never existed. Filmer states that even the Hobbesian state of nature is not a condition of complete anarchy, and goes on to maintain that it is not a state of nature at all.[19] The only accurate description of a condition of natural liberty is therefore the one that grants to all – including women, children, and servants – complete independence and equality, and especially, equal political agency. And if political power is instituted, all must participate in instituting it. Filmer cannot accept the consequences of this reasoning.

> It is further observable, that ordinarily children and servants are far a greater number than parents and masters; and for the major part of these to be able to vote and appoint what government or governors their fathers and masters shall be subject unto, is most unnatural, and in effect to give the children the government over their parents.[20]

Filmer thus sees an insoluble contradiction in the account of the state of nature offered by Natural Law theorists. If these maintain that some forms of power survive in the state of nature, then this state of nature is no longer a condition of equality and freedom. If they maintain that no power whatsoever is exercised, they must accept the radical conclusions entailed by their premises. For Filmer, the response to this dilemma is easy. There is no atomistic and anarchic state of nature, because paternal/political power is never "lost." Since paternal authority owes its origins to a grant of God transmitted through generation, every father is automatically endowed with it. If "political" authority is not exercised, heads of households will maintain order by controlling their dependents.[21] And since the power of fathers is the same as the power of the political ruler, the condition where heads of households are independent of one another is not a semi-social state of nature – as Pufendorf had contended – but in every respect a political condition. In it chiefs of families will rule over communities which differ from monarchical states only in size.

Filmer thus draws the conclusion that political authority cannot be instituted by independent heads of households, since political power is already in existence. If we accept the assumption of Natural Law theory that in the state of nature political power does not yet exist, even the authority of fathers has to be explained and accounted for, since they enjoy, according to Filmer, the same authority as kings. And if political power is instituted, the paradoxical answer must be that, if all are free and equal, even paternal power is instituted by those who will be subject to it – a statement devoid of meaning.[22] It is much more plausible to contend that human beings are not free and equal, that they are born into a condition of subjection to their father/monarch, and must comply with his orders, however tyrannical, without any right of redress.

CONFLICTING JURISDICTIONS

Filmer's view of social relations is structured around a radical interpretation of the proprietary model used by Natural Law thinkers. If dependents/subjects are their superior's possessions, and if possessions are at their owners' disposal, then human beings may be treated as if they were material resources. Of course Filmer does not argue that the father/monarch is entitled to dispose of his people ruthlessly. On the contrary, superiors have the duty to support and defend those entrusted to them, and they will answer to God for their deeds.[23] But conceptually, inferiors are assimilated to material resources, in the sense that the relationship between superior and inferior is the same as the relationship between the owner and his property.

Dependents must be ruled absolutely by the sovereign because they are incapable of regulating their own actions by themselves. As Filmer's description of the state of nature shows, he is convinced that granting autonomous agency to the average human being would doom society to chaos. His pessimism is exacerbated by his assimilation of all forms of power to the political one, so that where that is missing, no ordered life is conceivable. Filmer shares with the Natural Law theorists whom he opposes the notion that the state of war is the one in which individuals, left on their own, rush to mutual destruction instead of to cooperation.[24] To control them, absolute political power is indispensable, and Filmerian individuals are denied the personal competence which in Natural Law thought is granted to them, and which they then alienate in instituting sovereign authority.

What are the implications of Filmer's conception of paternal/political power for the distinction between private and public?

Filmer assimilates domestic and political society both at the descriptive and at the normative levels. The tasks and structural features of the two are described as being the same, and the principle of legitimation is identical in both cases, as fathers inherit, together with Adam's property in the earth and its creatures, the divine justification of his (Adam's) power. In Filmer's case, the traditional comparative strategy has yielded the peculiar result that no difference exists between the domestic and political associations. But what happens when we move from the level of the comparison of two separate institutions, to the relationship between those institutions within the same society? If paternal power and political power have the same origin, foundation, nature, and extent, then a problem of conflicting jurisdictions immediately arises once the two authorities have been set side by side within the same community. If God's donation to Adam is renewed through generation, all fathers possess it in their capacities as fathers. They will exercise the same authority as do monarchs, and, since this authority is supreme, the commonwealth will comprise as many supreme authorities as fathers. Far from being a cohesive and ordered social structure, the kingdom reproduces the anarchic features of the state of nature, where equal and free individuals do not recognize any superior on earth, and where each of them exercises the power of life and death. Filmer recognizes the problem of conflicting juris- dictions, but only when hypothesizing that the power of fathers would conflict with that of the people in a popular form of government.

All power on earth is either derived or usurped from the fatherly power, there being no other original to be found of any power whatsoever; for if there should be granted two sorts of power without any subordination of one to the other, they would be in perpetual strife which should be supreme, for two supremes cannot agree; if the fatherly power be supreme, then the power of the people must be subordinate, and depend on it; if the power of the people be supreme, then the fatherly power must submit to it, and cannot be exercised without the license of the people, which must quite destroy the frame and course of nature.[25]

Filmer's contention that monarch and father share the same power and have the same duties leaves us in a predicament. We either accept the normative implications of the assimilating procedure, and devise a social structure in which the distinction between a private and a public sphere is merely rhetorical, and where fathers, dispossessed of their natural authority, will only exercise authority over household depend- ents as delegates of the sovereign; or we maintain a separation between private and public domain, and recognize to all fathers autonomous jurisdiction on the basis of fatherhood, thus creating a conflict of jurisdictions. In the logic of assimilation, the monarch dispossesses fathers of their power, and incorporates their domains into his. Households are no longer the private possessions of adult males who can dispose of them at their discretion, but are merely branches or agencies of a centralized public power.[26] If we wish to reject these extreme conclusions, we have to sacrifice the coherence of the argument, as Filmer in fact does, when maintaining that there exists a public good distinct from the private good of heads of households. His position is *de facto* that upheld by all absolutist writers, including Natural Law theorists.

> He [the sovereign] must remember that the profit of every man in particular, and of all together in general, is not always one and the same, that the public is to be preferred before the private and that the force of laws must not be so great as natural equity itself.[27]

If a public good distinct from and superior to the good of each citizen is to exist, their private spheres must also be preserved, and heads of households must be assigned a certain independent jurisdiction over them. Although Filmer declares that domestic society and political society are the same, he maintains that the body politic is not one huge household, but rather is composed of households which preserve distinct juridical and physical existence – both among one another, and in relation to the political sphere. A kingdom is thus a social structure containing smaller groups (families), which are physically distinct, but which are governed by individuals (fathers) who have yielded to the sovereign the power accruing to them from their role in generation. In a kingdom, the only one who exercises paternal authority is the monarch, because

> though by the laws of some nations children when they attain to years of discretion have power and liberty in many actions; yet this liberty is granted them by positive and humane laws only, which are made by the supreme fatherly power of princes, who regulate, limit, or assume the authority of inferior Fathers for the public benefit of the commonwealth: so that naturally the power of parents over their children never ceaseth by any separation, but only by the permission of the transcendent fatherly power of the supreme prince, children may be dispensed with, or privileged in some cases, from obedience to subordinate parents.[28]

The assimilation of paternal and political power shows that, if the latter has to be supreme in a commonwealth, the former cannot be exercised by all fathers living in it, but only by the monarch. Fathers cannot preserve the power corresponding to their role as fathers, because this would make of royal authority a mere *flatus vocis*.

The problem of conflicting jurisdictions which arises from a consistent application of Filmer's premises highlights the paradoxical consequences of assimilating domestic and political society. The assimilation creates a hybrid – the paternal/monarchical power – produced by the fusion of the two basic institutions and forms of authority present in society. Filmer's conclusions are not, however, so different – leaving logical consistency aside – from those of the Natural Law theorists who adopt an analogical approach. The description of household and political society as increasingly similar institutions (institutions with very similar tasks and ends, governed by a ruler who alone maintains autonomous competence) makes it problematic to ground the normative distinction between private and public. Thomas Hobbes openly hypothesizes that political power, besides being instituted by consenting adults, may be "acquired" by a superior. Acquisition implies that dependents sanction an authority which is already exercised by giving their consensus to it, as happens in the case of paternal authority over children. And in all these cases, the authority of the ruler is unquestioned, and interference into the subjects' "private domain" is left to his discretion and prudential considerations.

But Filmer's version is particularly relevant to this inquiry because he does not admit that if king and father enjoy the same type of power, based on the same grounds, conflict of jurisdictions inevitably arises. After Filmer, any attempt to solve this quandary requires that domestic and political authority be each justified on its own grounds. If political power is supreme, and has the use of force at its core, then what is paternal power? What is its nature and extent? And if political rule is not the same as domestic rule, the latter must be redefined so that all features typical of the former disappear from the household. New foundations and new justifications are as necessary for domestic relations as for political ones.

Filmer argues in favor of patriarchal monarchy on three different grounds: because God has ordained it, by making Adam the sole proprietor of the earth and its creatures; because generation is the mechanism through which that power has been handed down to Adam's heirs; and because only absolute power can maintain peace and order among human beings who are as incapable of autonomous agency as are children. Filmer's challenge thus has to be met on these three grounds. The first requires a rethinking of the proprietary model of Natural Law theory, and the limits of its applications. The second must clarify the relationship between the divine and natural factors shaping human existence and the capacity for contrivance and artifice typical of the species.[29] The third must prove that conflict does not permeate human society to the extent that only an absolute sovereign can prevent the onset of a state of war.

It is to these three issues that Filmer's critics devote their attention. But only John Locke succeeds in specifying the nature of domestic and political power, the nature and ends of politics, and the distinction between private and public.

CRITICS OF PATRIARCHALISM: GEE AND TYRRELL

Patriarchal motives and images recur constantly in seventeenth-century political thinkers, who rely on the model of the domestic power structure to reinforce the asymmetry of the ruler/ruled relationship. One need not be a patriarchalist in the manner of Sir Robert Filmer to contend that sovereigns and fathers end up by playing a very similar, if not always identical, role in their respective domains. A *de facto* theorist such as Anthony Ascham suggests that it may even be desirable that

> the laws of a State or City ought to be modelled out of those which belong to families, and he who rules in either hath obligations of care and tenderness over us, as we are reciprocally bound *debito grati-tudinis* to render the like to him.[30]

Filmer's peculiarity lies in his insistence that Adam's paternal role as begetter included the power of life and death, and that his dominion over the earth and its creatures was transmitted to his legitimate successor through generation, so that consequently only fathers can be kings, more precisely, only one father at a time can be Adam's rightful heir. The identification of paternal with political power entails that the painstaking attempts of Natural Law thinkers to distinguish between private and public forms of rule, dominion over things, and authority over people are wiped out with a single stroke. It is the issue of conflicting jurisdictions that shows the serious problems of Filmer's assimilating procedure. Criticism of this point can already be found in Edward Gee's *The Divine Right and Originall of the Civill Magistrate from God*.

> The power of the Father is in every Father over his children: and if from it you raise a Civil Political power, then, either it must be said to be in, or to be the right of every Father; and if so, as soon as one Civil Power, begins a new Common-wealth, and he, and his children

are exempt from his Fathers (if living), and all other Civil superiority; and the Fathers power, and the Common-wealth he is over shall be dissolved by his having Nephews, or by his childrens fatherhood; and this will make every family, though but of two persons, to be a civil state, and that no Common-wealth can consist of more than the children of one Father, and for ever prevent or deny the compounding a Common-wealth of many families, and the distinction of the Common-wealth from the Family.[31]

It is noteworthy that Gee's critique of Filmer is only partially based on the principles of Natural Law theory. Gee is a fairly traditional Protestant writer, who tries to adapt the Pauline tenet that "all power comes from God," to a consensual procedure whereby authority is instituted and legitimated. For Gee, all positions of power are ordained by God, but they can only become operative if human beings freely and voluntarily choose the specific persons who will fill them. Human choice determines the coming into being of a power relation, but is not constitutive of its specific features, which are divinely prescribed.[32]

Human contribution is indispensable because (legitimate) power is not a metaphysical quality inherent in things and relations, but is rather a moral quality, which only God or human beings can bring about. This distinction is necessary because "moral" inferiors are most of the time physically superior to their rulers.[33] To enable human beings to bring about the institutions necessary to social life, God acts through Providence, not by assigning power directly, but by providing the means through which individuals can enact his will. The directing principles are contained in the law of nature, and the procedure for empowering a specific person is the contractual one.

It brings home the law, which in it self runs in terms universal, or indefinite, to its singular matter, by applying it to particular persons, things and times; and by that means that commandment or direction which is delivered generally to all of like case and condition, it gives occasion or call to this or that man in particular to put in particular.[34]

Gee's position represents a compromise between radical patriarchalism and radical Natural Law theory, as he couples an ascriptive view of power roles, with an elective procedure for bringing them about. By adopting a traditional view of the social structure, Gee bypasses the problem of conflict and anarchy which Filmer believes would inevitably arise if all human beings were left free to manage their own lives. Not surprisingly, Gee accepts the Thomistic notion that a hierarchy of social institutions was already present in the state of innocence.

However, Gee's strategy of combining a God-ordained and therefore natural hierarchy of power roles, with a voluntaristic and therefore artificial procedure of legitimation,[35] does not answer Filmer's challenge. The compromise between innatism and voluntarism strikes a balance between radical patriarchalism and radical Natural Law theory, but avoids the problems which Filmer highlighted. This shortcoming becomes apparent in Gee's style of argumentation, which appeals to tradition and shared consensus while handling the thorny issue of the conflict of jurisdictions. In attacking Filmer's view that paternal/political power is handed down to the oldest son, Gee oscillates between denying that paternal power is political, and admitting that, in ancient times, public power may have resided in the father, and may then have been assigned to the first-born by agreement of the other children. Did the father enjoy political power *qua* father or on some other ground? Did that power pass down to the oldest son? Gee does not clarify this crucial point, and his teleologism may lead one to suspect that, in agreeing to obey the oldest son, the children actualized a political power somehow present in him *in potentia*. They would therefore do what fathers of families are supposed to do, according to Filmer, if Adam's power becomes lost. As Gee does not provide a clear distinction between paternal and political authority, he also fails to provide a viable criterion for distinguishing between private and public domain. He relies on the shared and long-standing consensus that "since the erection of a public state as a distinct society from a household, and compounded of a multitude of families, the paternal power has been taken as distinct from, and inferior to the power of the magistrate."[36] But reliance upon tradition and a consensus which is no longer so obviously shared does not suffice to meet the challenge Filmer presents.

A much more serious attack on Filmer's work is offered by James Tyrrell's *Patriarcha, non Monarcha*, and *Bibliotheca Politica*.[37] Although the titles would suggest otherwise, it is the latter of the two that deals more extensively with patriarchalism. *Bibliotheca Politica* takes the form of a dialogue between Mr Meanswell, a Civilian, and Mr Freeman, a Gentleman. The first represents a patriarchalist's view, the latter, Tyrrell's. Tyrrell emphasizes the problem of conflicting jurisdictions ensuing from Filmer, and tries to address it by bringing a fairly radical interpretation of Natural Law to bear upon the problem of the nature and extent of paternal and political power. Aspects of Pufendorf's conception are here present. But Tyrrell abandons the dual vision of the state of nature which Pufendorf had adopted in order to rescue Hobbes while reducing the import of his radicalism. For Tyrrell there is only one state of nature that can be used to assess the legitimacy of existing power relations. That state of nature, however radical it may be, will not be as radical as Pufendorf's hypothetical one. If we accept the latter, it means that we espouse a Hobbesian view of human relations, which would prevent us from meeting Filmer's challenge that a truly Hobbesian state of nature would be pure anarchy. Tyrrell tries to take on all the issues which Filmer's patriarchalism made prominent: that individuals not governed by political authority would live in a condition of anarchy akin to a state of war; that all forms of power are reducible to the paternal/political one; and that contractual relations are a logical and practical impossibility. Tyrrell tests all three of these assertions in the household, and extends his conclusions to the body politic. In doing so he provides one of the last significant examples of the analogical mode of treating domestic and political society, with all its implications for the distinction between private and public.

Tyrrell emphasizes that the conflict of jurisdictions ensuing from Filmer's conception depends on his identification of paternal and political power. If fathers of families enjoy the power of life and death in the state of nature, they must renounce it in entering civil society, "unless you will fall into the Absurdity of supposing two absolute independent Heads, or Masters, in one and the same House, which, what a Confusion it would bring, I leave to your self to judge."[38] If it may be true that heads of households are the political leaders of their small communities, the question becomes whether, in doing so, they exercise the power inherent in their condition of fathers and proprietors. The task is therefore to inquire into the similarities and differences between the domestic and political associations, thereby reversing Filmer's assimilating procedure.

Domestic society and political society differ because they are meant to attain different ends, so that the power exercised by their respective rulers will be commensurate with the tasks which each community has to fulfill.[39] Tyrrell refers to social life before the Fall – a theme dear to Filmer – as a proof that family rule does not include the power of life and death, unless one wishes to argue that political authority was necessary even when human beings spontaneously complied with their duties.[40] Tyrrell then deduces that the characteristics of domestic authority remained the same, even after sin had altered human nature and made it prone to misconduct. Tyrrell's contention that paternal power need not be political in historical times thus means that there is a connection between the type of power necessary to rule a group and the human capacity for compliance with norms. The family is portrayed as an institution whose members – for various reasons – appear to be capable of peaceful cohabitation, and therefore do not need to be repressed by an authority endowed with the power of life and death. Behind the rhetoric of means and ends, it is possible to detect an indirect answer to Filmer's concern about the inevitable conflict tainting social relations, both within and without the family.

Is Tyrrell unrealistically contending that family relations, even after the Fall, are immune to lethal conflict? The answer is of course in the negative, and Tyrrell's formulation is tenable only if we keep in mind its normative import. He offers his account as a description, but his statements are also meant to carry normative implications.[41] He makes this point clear in distinguishing between paternal authority *de jure* and *de facto*.

> It is true, a father in the state of nature, and considered as the head of a separate family, has no superior but God ... yet it does not follow that such absolute submission is therefore due from the children, as does oblige them either to an active or a passive obedience in all cases to the father's will, so that they neither may, nor ought to defend themselves in any circumstance whatsoever. There is a great deal of difference (in the state of nature) between calling a man to an account as a superior, and defending a man's self as an equal. For a man in this state has a right to this latter against all men who assault him, by the principle of self-preservation: but no man has a right to the former, but only in respect of those over whom he has an authority, either granted him by God, or conferred upon him by the consent of other men.[42]

Tyrrell's contention that familial relations do/should not generally require the exercise of political power is consequential for answering the questions: what happens when conflict arises, and who is entitled to use force, either to punish transgressors, or to defend the innocent? Tyrrell's answer is radical and coherent: everyone. In fact he assigns to every adult the right to employ the power of life and death in self-defense, or to help a weaker party attacked by a superior who abuses his power.[43]

If every adult is entitled to use the power of life and death – which is the paramount power – then every adult is endowed with all other rights constituting personal agency. As Pufendorf has already made clear, once it has been granted that everyone is entitled to use force, personal competence in the wider sense is recognized to all. Attribution to all of the right of self-defense is in fact the translation into operative terms of the tenet that all are equal by nature. Are not human beings in the state of nature all equal, having the same rights over the same things? "And if they are thus equal, they must likewise, when they attain to Years of discretion, be endued with a Power of judging for themselves, concerning that things are necessary to their Happiness and Preservation."[44]

The presumption of universal equality is consequential for the institution of both personal and political power. Unlike Gee, Tyrrell contends that human will does not merely actualize power roles, but is constitutive of them. The clearest sign that we are facing the transition from ascriptive to elective power roles is the negotiability of the terms of, for example, the marriage contract. Tyrrell strikes a balance between the Pufendorfian hypothetical state of nature, in which no asymmetrical power relation would be instituted, and Gee's ascriptive social hierarchy. On the one hand, the woman is subject to the man "by the word of God"; on the other, the terms of the contract are negotiable. Since Tyrrell subscribes to a permissive interpretation of Natural Law, this means first of all that the prospective dependent may assign to the superior more power than is ascriptively inscribed in their respective positions.[45] But it also means that the husband's superiority starts to be treated as the generalization of observable experience; where experience tells a different story, norms and practices must adjust to it.

> I have already proved that the authority over the wife, commences from that contract we call marriage and though by the word of God the woman is made subject to the man, yet the reason of that subjection naturally depends upon the man's being commonly stronger both in body and mind than the woman; and where that ceases, the subjection will likewise of course cease, even amongst us.[46]

As is usual in Natural Law thinkers, Tyrrell bridges the gap between the presumption of natural equality and the power roles indispensable to attaining social order, with the attribution of personal competence to all adults. If human beings are all equal, but society requires asymmetrical power relations, we must suppose them to be able to dispose of their endowments so that authority can be instituted and legitimated.

Filmer, however, explicitly contended – if anyone still had doubts about it – that to recognize personal competence to everyone meant, by the same token, to grant political agency. If the state of nature is characterized by universal equality and the absence of a centralized political authority, then everyone must be considered a political agent. Tyrrell has no choice but to agree that, prior to the institution of civil society, everyone is entitled to pass judgement over and punish even superiors, if these transgress the law of nature.

Tyrrell's state of nature thus appears to be a relatively peaceful condition in which order is maintained, at least within families, thanks to the human capacity for compliance with unwritten norms. Compliance entails the assumption of obligations which generally include the institution of asymmetrical power relations. Each dependent member of the household is thus described as being in the paradoxical situation that he/she curtails his/her personal domain in favor of the head; at the same time as he/she retains full control when life itself is at stake. In other words, Tyrrell combines Pufendorf's hypothetical and historical states of nature, for he considers that, when self-defense is concerned, universal equality is empirically and not only theoretically consequential.[47] However, the submission to personal superiors supersedes the right to use force in self-defense as the defining factor of political agency. Only heads of households are engaged in instituting the commonwealth, for they incorporate the other members of the family. An egalitarian state of nature need not be read as an anarchic and destructive condition, nor as a prelude to active participation by all in political affairs.[48]

Tyrrell's critique of Filmer's conception highlights two very important points for a distinction between private and public based on the conceptual framework adopted by Natural Law theorists. First of all, the definition of jurisdictional boundaries is connected to the foundation of the power exercised in each sphere of competence. Second, unlike in the Aristotelian model, the boundary between private and public domain is a movable instead of a fixed one.

In criticizing Filmer, Natural Law theorists show that they establish a direct link between the scope of a jurisdiction and its foundation. For Filmer, the power of the king and that of the father share the same foundation: God's gift of the earth and its creatures to Adam *qua* the first father. For Tyrrell this means that the jurisdiction of the king and that of the father are coextensive. This approach shows the extent to which Natural Law theory operates within the juridical frame and concerns inherited from Roman jurisprudence. Judges have competence over different actions and domains, according to the type of authority delegated to them by the person enjoying *merum imperium*. In the case of Natural Law theory, power is instituted by human beings. A power is legitimate when it rests on its proper foundation. That foundation is provided by the contractual procedure through which we give our consent to the exercise of power. It is therefore this contractual procedure – which is often reduced to giving our free consent to a power already in being[49] – that indicates the nature and limits of the authority which is being founded; authorities having identical foundations will also extend over the same jurisdiction. This point is further proved by the condition of universal equality in the state of nature. Since God assigns to all human beings the same power to preserve their lives, their jurisdictions will also be identical. It is only by creating an authority with a jurisdiction bigger than, and superior to, that of each member that mutual destruction can be avoided. This approach also explains why the creation of social order tends to be conceived in terms of a hierarchy of powers, for this is what happens in a judicial system, in which the higher court overrides the decisions of the lower one.

Since jurisdictions can be distinguished on the basis of their respective foundations, the question becomes: how do foundations differ? We have seen that significant analogies characterize domestic and political society. Their respective members are initially endowed with the same competence, and in both cases the procedure for instituting a legitimate authority is the same, namely contract. It is therefore through the analysis of each procedure that specific features can be detected. If at first Natural Law theorists still contrast procedures which merely confirm a natural position of superiority with procedures in which superiority is artificially constructed, the tendency is nonetheless toward narrowing the import of that distinction. Both household and political power roles are constituted by the active and free will of the members. Differences are increasingly described as contingent and empirically determined, as Tyrrell's rendering of the marriage contract shows. A fairly wide range of options is open to contractors, who will choose on the basis of their current needs and aims. A woman may agree to obey her husband only in matters regarding their society – the family – and may bargain with him to retain partial control over their children;[50] but she may also decide to enslave herself to him, thereby making him the political leader of the household.

If the woman, servants, and adult children accept that the head monopolizes the power of life and death, they have transformed the household into a political community. Tyrrell does not explore this possibility thoroughly, for it would lead him to the inevitable conclusion that dependents are full political agents, able and entitled to play a politically active role. However, his permissive interpretation of the right to dispose of oneself in the state of nature[51] indicates that all human beings can engage in transactions regarding the power of life and death, which is also at the core of the procedure for instituting political authority. This aspect is important, not only because it shows the implications of assuming natural equality, but also because it brings to the fore the fact that no fixed boundary can be assumed to exist between the private and public domains.

The Aristotelian description of household and (ideal) body politic as two associations aiming at attaining two incommensurably different levels of the good can justify a stark normative separation between private and public domain. It is ontologically impossible for the household to perform the functions of an (ideal) political community. Given the primacy that Greek thought assigns to the public, this does not mean that the private is protected and insulated from public interference. It rather means that the public is insulated from the spilling of private dynamics into the political domain. But having clarified this point, it remains true that the separation between private and public domain is rigid, fixed once and for all, and unquestionable.[52] Some persons, activities, and relationships will be permanently located in their appropriate domain.

Natural Law theorists, on the contrary, explore the hypothesis that relationships among those living in the same household can be intrinsically political. In the state of nature, all human beings may have to exercise the power of life and death, or renounce it in favor of a superior, and all human relations may generate conflicts which will require the institution of political authority. No association is immune from the onset of violent and dangerous forms of interaction among its members, even if the general rule is that peace and harmony characterize it. Husband/wife, parent/(adult)child, and master/servant relationships may all degenerate into a state of war. In Tyrrell's language, members of the family may need protection from other members, but especially their superiors, as much as independent adult males in the state of nature end up by needing protection from one another. Tyrrell tries to hypostasize the difference between domestic and political society by contending that different ends characterize each of the two: procreation and upbringing of children, for the former; security and defense, for the latter. But he has to admit that the family "may have a twofold end: the one peculiar to it self, the other common with that of civil government. The common end is considered that defence and security, resulting from the conjunction of many into one body."[53]

If the need to regulate the use of force characterizes the procedure which leads to the institution of political power, then the handling of force will be the core of public jurisdiction. And if we conceive human beings as being originally all equal, and contend that politics have to prevent them from inflicting harm upon each other, all relationships will sooner or later fall under public jurisdiction. As a consequence, politics no longer occupy a specific area of social life, but become a characteristic which activities and relations may acquire, and an attribute of all the persons and institutions deputed to employ force.

Human transactions are private *until* they need not be regulated by the coercive power of the political ruler.

Filmer's radical view that politics pervade all forms of interaction presents a serious challenge to his adversaries. But, paradoxically, he merely endorses at the normative level a perspective which Natural Law theory itself has brought to the fore. The challenge for Filmer's adversaries therefore becomes: is it possible to hypothesize a less ubiquitous role for politics? Can we describe family and civil society so that we can uphold a normative distinction between private and public domain? But can we maintain egalitarian assumptions as the starting point of all social relations, without admitting that politics may have to intrude in all of them? The Natural Law thinker who comes closest to reformulating a stark distinction between non-political and political aspects of society, private and public, is John Locke. He partially succeeds and partially fails, thus permitting us to acquire a richer view of the inevitable implications of structuring the distinction between private and public around the notion of personal and political jurisdiction.

3 Private/public

John Locke

FILMER AND THE PROBLEM OF CONFLICTING JURISDICTIONS

The problem of conflicting jurisdictions was the most serious flaw which Filmer's critics detected in his work. But in order to present a successful alternative to the assimilation of household and body politic, three broader themes had to be addressed. It was Locke who devoted himself most thoroughly to this task.[1] The first area of concern was that Filmer and Natural Law theorists shared a proprietary model of personal and material resources, which could be used to dispossess human beings completely. If this outcome is undesirable, the proprietary model must be revised. The second was the relationship between divine will and human reason. For Locke, God is necessary if we wish to defend the existence of a non-conventional social order. But does it have to be the god of the patriarchalists? What is the role left for human reason? What is the proper interweaving of nature and convention? And the third theme regarded the question of whether egalitarian assumptions must entail antagonistic relations in the state of nature.

Underlying Locke's effort there is the attempt to walk the tightrope between Hobbesian egalitarian anarchism, and patriarchalist authoritarianism. This is the framework within which Locke's attack on Filmer must be set.[2] On the one hand, Locke rejects the view of the family as a political association. On the other, he depicts a state of nature which is less radically egalitarian than the Hobbesian one, or the hypothetical natural condition of Pufendorf, because Locke, like Tyrrell, accepts Filmer's charge that a radically egalitarian original condition is anarchic and asocial. For Locke, the point is to prove that there exists a natural order compatible with universal freedom and equality. Human beings have the capacity to regulate their interaction autonomously, including voluntarily accepting asymmetrical relations. This ensures that anarchy is not inevitable, and that the use of force is not indispensable to ensure peaceful social interaction. It is thanks to this hypothesis that family relations can be classified as non-political, in the narrow sense that negotiation over the power of life and death need not be included in the procedure through which the family-household is instituted.

Demonstrating that relations in the household can be peaceful, even if the power of life and death is not assigned to the adult male governing it, solves two problems at once. It proves that there exists at least one institution, the family, in which adults need not be controlled by an all-powerful ruler; and it addresses the question of conflicting jurisdictions. If the power which the heads of households need to ensure order is not political, it will be compatible with the power of the magistrate, and heads of households will be entitled to maintain it even within the political association.

In attacking Filmer's assimilation of family and kingdom, Locke adopts the comparative strategy for analyzing the two institutions. His own conception is cast in the rhetoric of the similarities and differences between the authority of the father of a family and the ruler of a body politic. But Locke's use of the comparative approach leads him to dissolve this *topos*. Two factors combine to produce this result. The first is that Locke's individualistic premises undermine the view of the domestic association as a group endowed by nature with an unquestionable and coherent structure, centered around the natural power of its adult male head. And the second is the insistence on the specificity of each type of interpersonal relation, both within and without the household. Father/child, husband/wife, master/servant, and generic adult/adult relationships obey specific dynamics, depending on the purpose for which each relation has been established. In his effort to counteract Filmer's assimilation, Locke emphasizes that social relations are not reducible to one overarching model, for each responds to particular needs and aims, which will affect the allocation of power between the individuals concerned. And those needs and aims are, in their turn, different from the ones that prompt human beings to start a political association. Each transaction will therefore require a specific process.

But these elements would not suffice to weaken the similarities between household and body politic, and with them, the comparative strategy. As Grotius, Pufendorf, and Tyrrell show, it is conceivable that members of the family will engage in transactions which are meant both to satisfy specific needs, and to transfer to the head the right to use the power of life and death. A family can easily become a little commonwealth, for each dependent may decide to assign to his personal superior more power than is necessary to structure their relationship.[3] A permissive interpretation of the subjective theory of rights does in fact endow each adult with the faculty to alienate his/her own person completely even in personal transactions. But Locke offers a restrictive reading of the subjective theory of rights. He rules out once and for all that transactions that concern only two individuals may regard the power of life and death; and since all transactions required to set up a family-household are dual ones, the society established by husband and wife, or master and servant, cannot have anything in common with political society, which is instituted by a plurality of human beings.[4] This conceptual move decisively sets family and body politic apart, and thinkers after Locke will employ the comparative strategy less and less.[5]

Locke's revision of the domestic power structure is of consequence for the analysis of the private/public distinction. Locke still appears to subscribe to the traditional view that heads of households controlling a domestic association share a public sphere which comes about when they found the political association.[6] But his individualism, coupled with his restrictive interpretation of the subjective theory of rights, points in a new direction. The basic units of human associations are individuals endowed with autonomous agency, as the depiction of the state of nature makes clear. Most of these individuals will curtail their sphere of competence by subjecting themselves to a superior. But both in the state of nature and in political society, they remain subjects of rights, persons capable of acting autonomously, and thus holders of a private sphere, even if limited in size and scope. What type of public domain corresponds to the private domain of these only partially autonomous individuals?

Modern readers, when presented with the notion that all adults can use the power of life and death in the state of nature, tend to infer that political agency will consist of handling that power directly, including its alienation, or delegation, if a magistrate is to be instituted. This inference is logically correct, and ultimately no one can be said to possess political agency if he/she cannot exercise control over the essential feature of political authority. But the route taken by the thinkers we are analyzing here to construct public agency is less direct and more complex. Their first step was to consider all adults as capable of concluding the transactions necessary to regulate their personal relations. It is to this minimal aspect of agency, as it were, that one must look to identify the criterion for distinguishing what concerns each individual, and is therefore private, from what concerns the community, and is therefore public. As will be shown in our analysis of the works of Locke and Hutcheson, this change in the conception of the boundary between private and public, and in the characteristics of the social universe of which privateness and publicness can be predicated, will deeply affect the conception of the public sphere, and with it, the nature and tasks of politics.

Locke presents his own conception of the family in criticizing Filmer's views. He devotes the whole *First Treatise*, and several parts of the *Second*, to a thorough analysis of the patriarchalist's views. Locke starts from Filmer's contention that political power is in the father as begetter. If generation is the only foundation of authority, paradoxical conclusions are inevitable, which Locke emphasizes by exploring all the possible implications of the contention that begetting assigns power to the begetter. Dominion from generation, according to Locke, can only be recognized of God, because he is the maker of all life. But even if we grant that parents are the real makers of new human beings, the mother has a stronger title to power over her children; and if all those involved in begetting are considered, several people will share the same power. Father and mother, fathers and grandfathers, fathers and monarchs – which of these will be supreme? And what criterion can we adopt to establish a hierarchy among them?[7]

Filmer's theory is so implausible that even he can be shown to have applied it inconsistently. Although he tries to reduce all forms of authority to one, Filmer has to resort to grounds different from sheer generation to justify the subjection of Eve, or that of servants, for there are power relations the foundation of which is not, and can never be, biological reproduction. Locke detects four grounds of authority in Filmer: creation, donation, subjection (of Eve), and fatherhood.[8] Locke does not deny that power relations may have any of these four foundations, because he, like Filmer, holds that God's choice in creating humankind is indeed consequential for the distribution of power. But, first of all, those grounds are not all synonyms of generation; and, second, how are they to be interpreted? Filmer uses them to argue that God's will, whether expressed through creation, donation, or decree, manifestly establishes a natural hierarchy among human beings. On the one hand, Filmer's contention that fatherhood is the source of all power is untenable; on the other, the question lying behind it – namely what relationship is there between God's will, human nature, and power? – is the crucial one.

For Locke, the question must be split into two parts: does God through nature assign political power to specific human beings? And: can natural differences justify lesser forms of authority? In criticizing Filmer, Locke is concerned with the first of these two, but he operates within a conceptual framework in which all types of authority are set on a continuum, so that his discussion of political power inadvertently slips into an analysis of power in general. He therefore finds himself caught in an argumentative strategy which is not so different from the one adopted by Filmer. If we call political power into question, are we calling into question all forms of authority? A solution to this problem is one of the important results of Locke's analysis, but in elaborating that solution Locke often oscillates between talking of political power and talking of power in general, thus creating ambiguity for his readers.

The issue is further complicated by Locke's acceptance, at least in principle, of some of Filmer's categories. In the *Essays on the Law of Nature*, Locke contends that there are three ways in which authority can arise.[9] The first is begetting (or creation), the second donation, and the third contract.[10] The moral obligation to obey a superior is in this early work grounded in the independent authority of the law-maker, which may have various foundations.

> And so the force of this obligation seems to be grounded in the authority of a law-maker, so that power compels those who cannot be moved by warnings. However, not all obligation seems to consist in, and ultimately to be limited by, that power which can coerce offenders and punish the wicked, but rather to consist in the authority and dominion which someone has over another, either by natural right and the right of creation ... or by the right of donation ... or by the right of contract, as when someone has voluntarily surrendered himself to another and submitted himself to another's will.[11]

It is the rejection of Filmer's position that prompts Locke's specification of the role played by nature, donation, and contract in grounding obligation.

In endowing human beings with the set of characteristics that compose their nature, God has manifested his will. What does "nature" tell us about the proper distribution of power? By nature we are born dependent on our parents, and therefore to an extent under their authority. And it is indeed true that some among us enjoy superior physical and intellectual endowments. What relationship is there between nature and power, between diversity of innate endowments and the right to exercise dominion? For example, between the natural inferiority of children, and the right of parents to rule over them? It is undeniable that children receive their lives from God through their parents, and that the condition of dependence of the newly born actually gives adults control over their lives for a long time. Children are in debt to their parents for what they have received since birth, and they must reciprocate by honoring and respecting them.[12] Nonetheless, does nature grant to parents, in Filmer's words, "royal authority," and "absolute monarchical power," that is, absolute power of life and death? Or is not this "power" only a means of fulfilling the duty to preserve lives that have been entrusted to us by God? Although it is true that the one who gives life has power over the created creature, God, as the creator, is the only one who can be said to exercise power over humankind by right of fatherhood: "For he is *King* because he is indeed Maker of us all, which no Parents can pretend to be of their Children."[13]

A "correct" reading of nature teaches us that the authority parents have over children is not political, and is not, juridically speaking, a form of power at all, for it does not generate any claim of adults against their offspring. Does nature give us clearer indications concerning other authority relations, such as the one which subjects one party to the other in marriage? Does nature assign political power to Adam, a more limited authority, or none at all? If nature is taken to be God's will as expressed in the Scriptures, Locke is confident that no absolute grant was made to Adam over Eve in punishing him for his sin. Like Pufendorf before him, Locke contends that God used subjection as a sanction for Eve's yielding to temptation, but not that he created women intrinsically inferior to men. He insists on the accidental rather than necessary character of women's destiny, so much so that

> there is here no more Law to oblige a Woman to such a Subjection, if the Circumstances either of her Condition or Contract with her Husband should exempt her from it, than there is, that she should bring forth her Children in Sorrow and Pain, if there could be found a remedy for it.[14]

If nature is to be prescriptive in regard to marriage, we must be sure that the practice we are considering is the natural one. Only "where the Practice is Universal, 'tis reasonable to think the Cause is Natural."[15] Historical experience does not, however, provide any uncontroversial indication of the "natural" form of marriage, for different arrangements have been practiced throughout time. Although in most cases women have been subjected to their husbands, there are records and examples of the opposite, and of societies in which wives have more than one husband.[16] Independently of the judgement one might pass on these arrangements, these at least prove that custom cannot be brought to bear upon the contention that women's subjection is determined by nature. However, Locke hesitates to rule out prevailing habits as carrying normative weight. In the case of women, he says, "there is, I grant, a Foundation in Nature" for their subordination, for "generally

the Laws of Mankind and customs of Nations have ordered it so."[17]
But, again, what type of power can husbands exercise on the ground of
natural superiority? The power of life and death, or a less extreme form
of authority?

Locke's reluctance to admit generation and nature as acceptable
foundations for the exercise of (political) power is also motivated by
his interpretation of divine donation. Locke admits that donation can
ground legitimate authority, for God can decide to grant part of his
power to a human being, toward whom we should then be obligated.[18]
Filmer had relied upon donation as a foundation of Adam's unlimited
authority over the earth and all its inhabitants, and Locke's concession
that donation is a legitimate source of authority appears to bring him to
a position very close to that of the patriarchalist. But Locke treats this
type of entitlement to authority as a powerful argument against Filmer's
theory. Far from having given Adam "private dominion" (that is,
propriety) over the planet and all living creatures, God has used
donation to rule out once and for all the possibility that a single
individual may ever claim it for him-/herself, by giving the earth and
inferior creatures to humankind in common. Locke offers an interpretation of Genesis opposite to Filmer's, and one in which Eve is made
to play a relevant role. Against Filmer's contention that God has chosen
to create one adult male, Locke maintains that God has donated the
earth to both Adam and Eve, as representatives of humankind.

> Whatever God gave by the words of this Grant, 1 *Gen.* 28, it was not
> to *Adam* in particular, exclusive of all other Men: whatever *Dominion*
> he had thereby, it was not a *Private Dominion,* but a Dominion in
> common with the rest of Mankind. That this Donation was not made
> in particular to *Adam,* appears evidently from the words of the Text,
> it being made to more than one, for it was spoken in the Plural
> Number, God blessed *them* [Adam and Eve], and said unto *them,*
> Have Dominion.[19]

Locke's interpretation of Genesis thus hypothesizes an original condition of plurality, in which all members of the species equally share in
the enjoyment of the earth and its resources. The hypothesis of an
egalitarian original condition – which regards both men and women –
allows Locke to contrast Filmer's reading of Genesis with an equally
plausible reading. But if human beings are all on the same foot, it
becomes harder to argue in favour of a natural hierarchy, both in
political and in non-political terms. If inequality is to be rejected at the
roots, and expunged, that is, from God's will itself,[20] it cannot be

reintroduced through the back door by accepting naturalistic legitimations of subjection and authority.

However, no social order is possible without the exercise of authority. If neither creation, nor nature, nor donation establish an unquestionable hierarchy, and if all human beings are born equal, then power can only be brought about by human beings themselves. They institute it by concluding a contract with their prospective superior, or, at least, they signal their consent to his exercise of power over them. As we have already seen in other Natural Law theorists, consent is employed in a way rather puzzling to twentieth-century readers, because these writers appear to treat as consensual procedures what we should not accept as being so. Locke is no exception. He does not clearly distinguish between the act of making a contract and the act of consenting, and sees the two as at least partially overlapping. Consent itself is never defined, neither in the *Essays* nor in the *Treatises*.[21] The most thorough analysis is in the *Essays,* where consent is said to be either positive or natural. Positive consent

> arises from a contract, either from a tacit contract, i.e. prompted by the common interests and convenience of men, such as the free passage of envoys, free trade, and other things of that kind; or from an expressly stated contract, such as the fixed boundary-lines between neighbouring peoples, the prohibition of the purchase and import of particular goods, and many other such things.[22]

Natural consent is even vaguer, and dissolves into the blind or semiconscious acceptance of prevailing practices, customs, opinions, and moral values. If tacit consent is taken to be the acceptance of any asymmetrical power relation as it is given in society, it becomes apparent that the source of obligation is no longer contract, but something else, either prevailing social practices, or natural endowments, both of which have been ruled out by their variety, and consequent exclusion of their normative import.[23]

The problem of the subjection of women to their husbands seems definitely to show Locke oscillating between considering contract-making as constitutive of the rights and duties contained in a relationship, or else as merely the legal procedure by which consent is given to socially or naturally given asymmetries. On the one hand, women can modify the terms of contract with their husbands, to the point of refusing a subordinate position. On the other hand, women are taken to have no alternative to yielding to the man's superior natural endowments or social standing.

The same ambiguity appears in the master/servant relationship. In discussing whether property in land (to Filmer, one of the sources of dominion) gives "Authority over the Persons of Men," Locke contends that "the Authority of the Rich Proprietor, and the Subjection of the Needy Beggar began not from the Possession of the Lord, but the Consent of the poor Man, who preferr'd being his Subject to starving."[24] The beggar is thus described as being in a position which, independently of the will of the two persons involved, leads him to accept an unfavorable bargain. Although the specific rights and duties of each party can be negotiated, the institution of servitude structurally requires an asymmetrical power relation.

Locke's ambivalent description of power dynamics in social relations is part of an argumentative strategy which skirts, rather than confronts, Filmer's contention that, if all human beings are born free and equal, no power relation can exist among them. Locke does not call into question that paternal, marital, and despotic power exists. He only argues that the sources of power that Filmer takes into consideration do not grant to the holder the right to exercise the power of life and death, but only lesser forms of dominion. By taking social power relations for granted Locke indirectly dismisses Filmer's anarchist reading of Natural Law theory. But he never answers Filmer's charge that to assume universal equality entails the very impossibility of a social order, because no power relation whatsoever is compatible with natural equality. In dismantling the patriarchalist's doctrine Locke merely reduces the import and extent of non-political power relations, without considering the possibility of their disappearance.

Locke thus strikes a balance between the two extreme social theories available at the time: the Hobbesian–Pufendorfian radically egalitarian and anarchic state of nature; and the Filmerian radically inegalitarian and pervasively political condition. Locke's manner of walking the tightrope between the two explains why both egalitarian and inegalitarian elements overlap in his account of domestic relations. When the use of power in a personal relationship may raise the possibility that force will be employed, the parties will be considered equally entitled to it. When assuming equal capacities leads to the possibility of conflict and disruptive interaction, one of the parties will be granted the surplus of authority necessary to maintain the relationship in being. For Locke, natural equality and non-political forms of dominion are logically compatible assumptions, for he insists that authority falling short of the exercise of the power of life and death does not impair natural freedom.[25]

The workings of these complex dynamics are best grasped in the state of nature, for the absence of political institutions allows us to see clearly how human beings manage interaction when left to themselves. Conflict is not endemic in the human condition, although the political association will ultimately be instituted to address the issue of the misuse of force. It is important that we be able to show that human beings can regulate their relationships by applying rules which are not dictated by a political ruler, for this approach will permit us to set limits to the ruler's power. For Locke, the uncoerced application of the laws of nature means both that *generally* social relations do not require the use of the power of life and death, and that everyone may resort to it if necessary. But the first of these assumptions plays a much larger role in Locke than it does in previous Natural Law thinkers. It is thanks to the description of a non-antagonistic state of nature that Filmer's catastrophic view of a non-political condition can be rejected, and the demand for an all-powerful political authority made obsolete.

DOMESTIC RELATIONS IN THE STATE OF NATURE

Widely accepted interpretations[26] of Natural Law theory argue that conflict over scarce resources is the cause of the exit from the state of nature and the institution of political society. Scholars who accept this argument subscribe to Hume's contention that the rules of justice are produced as a response to conflict over external resources, as the latter are the only ones which human beings can enjoy separately from their original possessor.[27] Hume thus contends in the *Treatise*:

> There are three different species of goods, which we are possess'd of; the internal satisfaction of our minds, the external advantages of our body, and the enjoyment of such possessions as we have acquir'd by our industry and good fortune. We are perfectly secure in the enjoyment of the first. The second may be ravish'd from us, but can be of no advantage to him who deprives us of them. The last only are both expos'd to the violence of others, and may be transferr'd without suffering any loss or alteration; while at the same time, there is not a sufficient quantity of them to supply every one's desires and necessities. As the improvement, therefore, of these goods is the chief advantage of society, so the *instability* of their possession, along with their *scarcity,* is the chief impediment.[28]

In this passage, Hume not only offers his own view of the origin of justice, and consequently of political society, but indirectly provides a reinterpretation of seventeenth-century Natural Law theory. Of all social relations in the state of nature, those centered around access to possessions are the only ones relevant for politics.

If we adopt a sociological perspective and ask: who are the persons who have conflicts over external resources? the answer has to be: independent adults. Who is independent in the state of nature? Not married women, for they have granted their husbands the power to rule in order to further the good of the family. Neither are servants, for they too have incorporated into their master's household. Independent adults are thus heads of households, who argue with others like them over transferable resources. But why cannot conflicts over other resources, inseparable from their possessors, but crucial for social reproduction, such as labor and sexual services, be counted as causes of conflict which only the ruler will be able to regulate?[29] If the "Humean" interpretation of the paradigm of Natural Law theory is correct, then the only plausible answer to these questions is that the other possible sources of conflict have been eliminated once and for all before civil society has been instituted. They have not been eliminated from the scene in the sense that they are not the object of transaction. On the contrary, sexual services, for example, and labor can be acquired even in the state of nature through a contract between two parties. But these resources are not considered relevant for politics, apparently because they do not trigger potentially lethal conflict. There are two means for avoiding the outbreak of conflict: compliance by each individual with his/her obligations; and transference of one's natural power to a personal superior who will impose his own will on his dependents. When, in transferring a personal resource, a human being becomes someone else's dependent, the beneficiary acquires control not only over the resource in question, but over the person of the possessor as well. The independence and autonomy of the latter are juridically incorporated in the person of the beneficiary. The intriguing and paradoxical result is that both the dependent and his concerns vanish from sight, and are not a cause of conflict. If his resources have now become part of someone else's endowments, conflict over them would be intrapersonal. It would occur, that is, between the person and his own possessions. This would indeed be a very peculiar case, although in principle anything may happen.

Readers of works in the Natural Law tradition can easily check the plausibility of this interpretation by considering how rare it is for these writers to inquire at any length into the potential for conflict in the relationships structuring the family-household. Only in passing do writers mention that husband/wife, parent/child, and master/servant relationships may generate lethal struggle. They admit it indirectly, as Hobbes and Pufendorf do in contending that man and woman may go to war with each other; or as Tyrrell does, in granting, in opposition to

Filmer, that children are entitled to defend themselves from their father's violence. But more often they sidestep the issue, by presenting these relationships as inherently peaceful and naturally regulated. This is far from being a marginal theme, for the description of a peaceful state of nature hinges precisely on the description of family relations. The very same relations that are, by definition, excluded from being politically relevant. Locke is the thinker who most insists, against Filmer, that conflict can be ruled out from the household, so that the need for political regulation will not arise.

Nonetheless, Locke's assertion that domestic relations are intrinsically less antagonistic than extra-domestic ones must not be taken to mean that individuals can be allowed to behave spontaneously. Familial relations are peaceful only if human beings coerce their own conduct by following the laws of nature which God has assigned to humankind. If people obey the norms provided by their creator, their personal interaction will be harmonious. Locke thus offers as a description of domestic relations a normatively charged interpretation of the human capacity for self-control, and compliance with natural duties.

This interweaving of descriptive and normative elements, which is common in seventeenth-century epistemology, appears in the language Locke uses in giving an account of the origin of social life:

> God having made Man such a Creature, that, in his own Judgment, it was not good for him to be alone, put him under strong Obligations of Necessity, Convenience, and Inclination to drive him into *Society,* as well as fitted him with Understanding and Language to continue and enjoy it.[30]

Locke juxtaposes obligations and drives as two homogeneous explanations for the innate sociability of the species. The law of nature connotes two aspects of reality which are for us distinct: the law as regularity of behavior, and the law as norm or command, which we may or may not obey. Locke can thus talk of the drives leading human beings into society as features of human nature shaped both by a blind, irresistible force, and by our voluntary compliance with God's commands.[31]

Instincts and obligations are present, needless to say, at every stage of social life, including marriage. The biological desire for copulation prompted human beings to give life to the first society, the main features of which can and ought to be derived from the "intention of nature." The latter includes "not merely Procreation, but the continuation of the Species," which in turn will require marriage to last "so long as is necessary to the nourishment and support of the young

Ones, who are to be sustained by those that got them, till they are able to shift and provide for themselves."[32] A strong instinctive attachment ties parents to their offspring, and makes human beings take care of the newly born even at the cost of their own lives. But this instinct is reinforced by a law of nature which commands parents to look after their children: "And after them [Adam and Eve] all *Parents* were, by the Law of Nature, *under an obligation to preserve, nourish, and educate the Children*, they had begotten."[33]

Obligations specify how instincts can be correctly satisfied.[34] The instinct of self-preservation offers the clearest example of the problematic relationship between innate drives and their proper satisfaction.

> God having made Man, and planted in him, as in all other Animals, a strong desire of Self-preservation, and furnished the World with things fit for Food and Rayment and other Necessaries of Life ... directed him by his Senses and Reason, as he did the inferior Animals by their Sense, and Instinct ... to the use of those things, which were serviceable for his Subsistence, and given him as means of his *Preservation*.[35]

The desire to survive must not be taken to mean, first, that human beings may desire not to continue to live, as if it were a matter of preference. As God's creatures, we have no choice: "Every one ... is *bound to preserve himself*, and not to quit his Station willfully."[36] And although every individual has a *"Right of Self-preservation,"*[37] physical survival cannot be ensured at any cost. Enslavement to another human being, for example, is illegitimate and void. If we do not have the right to take our own life, we may not transfer that power to another human being:

> For a Man, not having the Power of his own Life, *cannot,* by Compact, or his own Consent, *enslave himself* to any one, nor put himself under the Absolute, Arbitrary Power of another, to take away his Life, when he pleases.[38]

If we are in such a powerless condition that our survival depends on another's will, a compact leading to self-enslavement would merely reinforce the power the stronger already has over the weaker.

The desire of self-preservation thus cannot be satisfied unless we discover the appropriate way to implement it according to the law of nature. To grasp what is appropriate is a matter not of instinct, but of reason, which is the manner of existence typical of the species. Reason reveals to us the existence of a law of nature through which human actions and relationships can be regulated. "And Reason, which is that

Law, teaches all Mankind, who will but consult it, that being all equal and independent, no one ought to harm another in his Life, Health, Liberty, or Possessions."[39]

Reason connects and harmonizes the deterministic and normative aspects of the principles structuring human experience. In the case of parents and children, reason specifies the duties incumbent on adults toward their offspring. The former must *"preserve, nourish, and educate the Children*, they had begotten, not as their Workmanship, but the Workmanship of their own Maker, the Almighty, to whom they were to be accountable for them."[40] The fulfillment of this duty entails the exercise of a certain authority over children, whose dependence makes it necessary that they be ruled until they reach the age of discretion. Power is thus reintroduced, nearly surreptitiously, as a necessary means to enable parents to comply with the law of nature. Children's physical and intellectual dependence is an objective, or factual datum, which legitimates their parents' rule. Although this is a peculiar type of power, for it does not entitle adults to lay claim upon their children's lives and possessions, it is still a governing activity. Reading correctly the law of nature therefore provides us not only with the appropriate interpretation of how to use our drives constructively, but also with a strong justification for the exercise of power.

Locke holds that children's dependence also indicates the limits to the parents' authority. For the individual who

> is in an Estate, wherein he has not *Understanding* of his own to direct his *Will*, he is not to have any Will of his own to follow: He that *understands* for him, must will for him too; he must prescribe to his Will, and regulate his Actions; but when he comes to the Estate that made his *Father a Freeman*, the *Son is a Freeman* too.[41]

As a form of guardianship, rule over children does not extend to the full control over their lives and possessions, and must cease when the need for it ceases. The (normative) limits built into the parent/child relationship also eliminate the issue of conflict altogether. Since interaction is not supposed to affect the person and possessions of the child, there is no reason why conflict should arise. So much so, that Locke does not hypothesize any device to ensure that parents will exercise their power within those limits, except natural affection. Locke does not provide any institution or controlling authority to defend children from their parents' abuse, both in the state of nature and in civil society. The magistrate does not exercise control over parents, and the child is a non-entity for the state:

> *A Child is born a Subject of no Country or Government.* He is under his Fathers Tuition and Authority, till he come to Age of Discretion ... the Power that a Father hath naturally over his Children, is the same, where-ever they be born; and the Tyes of Natural Obligations, are not bounded by the positive Limits of Kingdoms and Common-wealths.[42]

It is therefore only the human capacity for self-restraint, supported, according to Locke, by our innate affection, which shelters children from aggression and abuse.

In order to appreciate Locke's depiction of a peaceful state of nature, we must focus our attention on relations between adults, for nature does not provide for them prescriptions as clear as those regarding parenthood. In the case of marriage, the "intention of nature" is the preservation of the species. But there can be several correct applications of this natural injunction.[43] The variety of familial arrangements in different cultures testifies to the wide range of choices left to human beings. Locke refers to "those parts of *America* where when the Husband and Wife part, which happens frequently, the Children are all left to the Mother"; and to the family as an association where either the "Master or Mistress of it ... [have] some sort of Rule" proper to it.[44] Even if we specify that the family ought to widen its ends to include "Support, and Assistance, and a Communion of Interest too, as are necessary not only to unite their [husband and wife's] Care, and Affection, but also necessary to their common Off-spring,"[45] a broad range of choices is left to the parties, who are entitled to negotiate the terms of their marriage contract.

A "lower" and an "upper" limit define the space left for human beings to devise acceptable arrangements. The lower limit is the satisfaction of the "intention of nature," and the upper limit is the power which a human being can legitimately transfer to another. We are not entitled to alienate completely our persons and lives, for the latter belong to God, and we cannot give away what is not our own.[46] Like suicide, self-enslavement is not permissible, both of a servant to a master, or of a wife to a husband, contrary to what both Pufendorf and Tyrrell contended.

The two parties can negotiate all that lies between those limits, in respect of both real and personal rights.[47] Men and women can reach various agreements about the control of property, and the distribution of authority between them.[48] After children have grown, marriage can be ended at the request of either of the two parties,[49] and, as Locke emphasizes in the *First Treatise*, the woman can legitimately try to avoid subordination to the man. But even in the more common form of marriage, in which the woman transfers to the man part of the autonomy which she enjoys by nature as a human being, she still retains control over her personal property, either bestowed on her by compact, or acquired through her own labor.[50]

Locke has up to this point described a situation in which two adults, equally capable of interpreting the law of nature, regulate their inter-action by finding a common ground between their respective needs and interests. As in the case of children, the relationship, albeit long-lasting and complex, appears not to generate the type of conflict that makes the use of force necessary. This picture is, however, partial, and Locke can confidently exclude conflict from the portrait of marriage relations only by reintroducing an asymmetrical power relation.

> But the Husband and Wife, though they have but one common Concern, yet having different understandings, will unavoidably sometimes have different wills too; it therefore being necessary, that the last Determination, *i.e.* the Rule, should be placed somewhere, it naturally falls to the Man's share, as the abler and the stronger.[51]

In this passage, Locke merely hints at the possibility of conflict, but this possibility is a reason strong enough to assign power to one party, not surprisingly, the man. A new description of woman's fate in life supersedes the egalitarian assumptions which are necessary for hypo-thesizing a contractual procedure between two adults. Like the child, the woman will find herself in an "objective" condition of dependence which will induce her to choose one particular interpretation of the law of nature regarding familial arrangements. Repeated pregnancies make the woman unable to provide for herself and her offspring, so that she will have to rely on the man's protection and support.[52] This condition of need thus makes her subscribe to a marriage contract in which the man will rule. She freely consents to an asymmetrical power relation which is founded on a condition of dependence over which she has, for the time being, no control, and which is not in her power to alter.

Locke's account of familial life thus shows that the capacity which human beings have to manage their relationships without resorting to the power of life and death draws upon various sources: instincts, conscious reflection, rational reading of the law of nature, and contract-making. The combination of these elements enables Locke to imagine forms of social interaction which usually do not require "political" regulation. Locke therefore does not follow his predecessors, and omits any reference to the use of force by family dependents in the state of nature.[53] Whereas Tyrrell acknowledged that women, servants, and even children might have to defend themselves from the head of household, Locke portrays a domestic association in which interaction does not lead to lethal conflict. The power structure of domestic society is however the same as that hypothesized by the other Natural Law theorists. The husband is granted

> Conjugal Power, not Political, the Power that every Husband hath to order the things of private Concernment in his Family, as Proprietor of the Goods and Land there, and to have his Will take place before that of his wife in all things of their common Concernment.[54]

Only by reintroducing inequality in the household does Locke, as did Pufendorf and Tyrrell, ensure that conflict can be avoided, and that politics can be ruled out of domestic relations. Would the family still be a self-regulating institution if its members, and particularly the husband and the wife, were as equal after the marriage contract as they were before?[55]

Locke's favorite way of summarizing his conception of the domestic association manifests all the ambiguities of his approach.

> The ends of Matrimony requiring no such Power [of life and death] in the Husband, the Condition of *Conjugal Society* put it not in him, it being not at all necessary to that State. *Conjugal Society* could subsist and obtain its ends without it ... nothing being necessary to any Society, that is not necessary to the ends for which it is made.[56]

Behind the quasi-Aristotelian teleological terminology there lies the combination of descriptive and normative elements which the present analysis has tried to unravel. Locke describes individuals as being capable of assuming moral obligations, which are both "natural" (as in the case of parenthood), and "conventional" (as in the case of marriage), and as being capable of abiding by them without being forced by an authority external to the relationship. They are compelled by their reason to respect the norms which God has given to the species.[57] When they assume conventional obligations, they may and usually do accept an asymmetrical power relation. This is true not only of husband and wife, but of master and servant: "A Free-man makes himself a Servant to another, by selling him for a certain time, the Service he undertakes to do, in exchange for Wages he is to receive." The servant may become part of the master's household, and be subject to his authority, although one falling short of the power of life and death.[58]

Even more than in the case of marriage, naturalistic elements appear to have been excluded as a foundation of the master's position. The prospective servant is a human being who, unlike the prospective master, has misused, or underused, his natural endowments, and who therefore finds himself in an objective condition of need. Responsibility for his state of dependence thus falls on his own shoulders, and cannot be attributed either to nature, or to his future master. As Locke remarks in the *First Treatise*, the advantaged situation of the proprietor does not force the needy beggar to become his servant, although, as in the woman's case, the alternative to accepting subordination is starvation, and, ultimately, death. What matters to Locke is that the proprietor is not directly responsible for the other's disadvantaged condition, and does not physically coerce him into servitude.[59] Both the woman and the future servant are, anyway, juridically as free as their superior, and they are as able as the latter to negotiate their transactions. It is therefore only their consent that legitimates the power which the husband/master will exercise.

Locke thus portrays domestic society as an association regulated partially by semi-spontaneous mechanisms of adjustment to other human beings' needs and rights, and partially by the conscious acceptance of duties and obligations freely accepted through a contract. Locke presents the exclusion of political power as a fact, deriving from the intrinsically non-antagonistic nature of familial relations. The "fact" is however a compound of descriptive and normative elements. First, the assumption that there is no ground in nature for the exercise of political power; second, a normatively loaded description of human beings as capable of avoiding conflict in domestic life; and third, the statistically plausible contention that familial relations are less antagonistic than relationships between strangers. The husband/master is not entitled to use force against his dependents, and does not in any case need to, partially because dependents freely recognize and accept his superiority.

DOMESTIC SOCIETY AND POLITICAL SOCIETY

The exclusion of political power from the authority relations of the household is definitive only if one accepts Locke's descriptive/normative conception of domestic society. Political society can only come about "where every one of the Members hath quitted this natural Power, [and] resign'd it up into the hands of the Community in all cases that exclude him not from appealing for Protection to the Law established by it."[60] However, after going to great lengths to show that the head of household ought not and need not be a political ruler, Locke, like other Natural Law theorists, cannot avoid admitting that the family can become a little kingdom. The quotation is long, but too important to summarize it.

> Though the *Father's Power* of commanding extends no farther than the Minority of his Children, and to a degree only fit for the Discipline and Government of that Age: And though that *Honour* and Respect ... which they indispensably owe to their Parents ... gives the Father no Power of Governing, *i.e.* making Laws and enacting Penalties on his Children ... yet 'tis obvious to conceive how easie it was in the first Ages of the World ... for the *Father of the Family* to become the Prince of it; he had been a Ruler from the beginning of the Infancy of his Children: and since without some Government it would be hard for them to live together, it was likeliest it should, by the express or tacit Consent of the Children, when they were grown up, be in the Father, where it seemed without any change barely to continue; when indeed nothing more was required to it, than the permitting the *Father* to exercise alone in his Family that executive Power of the Law of Nature, which every Free-man naturally hath, and by that permission resigning up to him a Monarchical Power, whilst they remained in it.[61]

Locke thus relies on the process of socialization as the means through which a person can monopolize the power of life and death, and become the political leader of the group. As in all other associations and personal relationships, human beings tend to accept as legitimate factual positions of superiority. Women and servants are induced by their condition of need to yield to husbands and masters' authority, and to make their superiority legitimate by giving their consent. Children are induced by the habit to obey their parents (effectively, fathers), and to let them extend their dominion from parental to political.

In telling this story, Locke offers a portrait of a plausible (to him) historical scenario, in which adult children accept their father as their political ruler. What is striking about it is that supposedly non-antagonistic familial relations must have given way to antagonistic ones, if the monopolization of the rule of force has become necessary. Locke does not offer enough details for allowing us to answer the several questions raised by this turn in his thought. Why does conflict arise? Does it only arise between the father and his adult children, but not between the master and his servants, and the husband and his wife? Why is that so? Because children become their father's equals once they have come of age? Because only between them does potentially lethal conflict occur? Are women and servants excluded from the process because, like in Pufendorf, the partial alienation of their natural independence through a personal contract has deprived them of the agency necessary to institute political authority, and has already assigned to the head of household sufficient power to keep them under control?

If the passage cited above generates more questions than it is possible to answer by dissecting Locke's work, it highlights, however, two important points. The first is that the exclusion of conflict from domestic relations is a normative rather than a factual statement. Locke's concessions to "historical" development show that conflict can pervade every human group, including the family. Consequently, whether a group is a political association or not only depends on the type of negotiation in which its members engaged. Did individuals negotiate over the power of life and death? Did they possess the competence to do that? Were they entitled to negotiate the use of force? The procedure through which a group transforms into a political association becomes crucial to understand what differentiates political society from other aggregations, especially the domestic one. The comparative strategy can once again be of help to understand the criteria whereby the two institutions are set apart. But new elements will have to be taken into account to justify Locke's forceful assertion that

> the *first Society* was between Man and Wife, which gave beginning to that between Parents and Children; to which, in time, that between Master and Servant came to be added: And though all these might, and commonly did meet together, and make up but one Family, wherein the Master or Mistress of it had some sort of Rule proper to a Family; each of these, or all together came short of *Political Society*, as we shall see, if we consider the different Ends, Tyes, and Bounds of each of these.[62]

When instituting a political association, individuals aim at the "preservation of the property of all the Members of that Society, as far as is possible."[63] The attainment of this end requires that human beings give up their natural power to enforce the law of nature, so that "all private judgement of every particular Member being excluded, the Community comes to be Umpire, by settled standing Rules, indifferent, and the same to all Parties."[64] In the state of nature, on the other hand, each person is entitled to enforce the law of nature; direct enforcement destroys the very foundation of civil society.

In joining civil society, individuals entrust to it a much greater part of their lives than they do by engaging in any other transaction. First, they grant the public and its representatives the right to monopolize the use of force. Second, there is no temporal limit to the existence of the political association, at least in relation to the life-span of the individual. Civil society lasts over a great number of generations. Every person who comes of age can indeed choose whether to remain in the commonwealth into which he was born,[65] but, once he has fully incorporated, exit is made onerous. If one quits the body politic, he must leave his possessions behind. It is much more burdensome to terminate one's subscription to the social contract than to a personal one.

Since entering into civil society is such a consequential act, the contractual procedure through which individuals give life to it requires the compliance with very strict conditions, if the contract is to be legitimate.[66]

The suspension of each one's right to exercise the power of life and death is the first public act,[67] and is the act that constitutes the "publick." Two requirements are necessary to make it valid: universality and reciprocity. Universality ensures that all human beings actively engaged in that act give their consent; and reciprocity guarantees that no one gives up more than any other. Whereas in private contracts, the parties can subscribe to non-reciprocal contractual terms (as do husband and wife, and master and servant), in public contracts all those who subscribe to the contract must give up and receive in return the same. No one in the community loses or acquires more authority than anyone else. In other words, no one acquires the right to exercise the power of life and death while all others lose it (as happens with the absolute monarch). What was true in the state of nature – that *all* may enforce the law of nature – remains true, *mutatis mutandis*, in civil society: *all* are subject to the public authority of the magistrate, because no one is entitled to be judge in his own case.

The rule of reciprocity points to the second crucial feature of the social contract, that is, the structural characteristics of the social universe which can give life to a political community. Besides the features of universal freedom and equality (from mutual jurisdiction), which individuals must enjoy before the contract is performed, the other structural requirement is that more than two persons participate in it. Unlike personal contracts, which are more often concluded between two parties, the social contract requires the presence of a multitude. Plurality is the prerequisite for instituting civil society, where plurality is distinguished from both singularity and duality.[68] Plurality is crucial because individuals instituting a political association negotiate the exercise of the power of life and death. If two individuals negotiate that particular matter, two outcomes are possible. The two make a reciprocal exchange, thus remaining in the original condition, that is, the state of nature; or they make an uneven exchange, meaning that one of the two renounces his/her right to exercise that power, and he/she grants it to the other, thus remaining in, or entering, a state of war. In the former case, the contract is meaningless. In the latter, the contract is illegitimate and void, for human beings do not have jurisdiction over their own bodies, and their very survival.[69] The life of a person belongs to God, as creator, and God alone can dispose of it. Consequently, any exchange between two individuals must fall short of the transference of the power of life and death, or, to put it more precisely, there can be no exchange concerning the control of all of one's own "life, liberties, and possessions," that is, of one's person in its entirety.[70]

This implies that a contract between two persons regarding the use of force can never give life to a political relationship, or a political association. Only where *several* human beings come together can a political association be brought into existence. Even in the case of the quasi-spontaneous transformation of the family into a paternal monarchy, Locke always mentions the father and his *children*,[71] thus tacitly ruling out a situation of duality. A family composed of a father and his child will never become a political society; but, in case the father monopolizes the power of life and death, it turns into a despotic society, in the Aristotelian sense of the term, in which the despot treats his dependents as his private property. For Locke, this means that the parties are still in the state of nature, more precisely, in an open state of war.

Finally, a dual situation gives life to a despotic, and not a political, association, because the presence of a third party arbitrating between the two is *a priori* excluded. In setting up civil society, human beings transfer their right to exercise the power of life and death (and therefore to be judge in their own case) to a magistrate, who will be the impartial arbitrator between two litigants. Two individuals in the state of nature can only "appeal to Heaven," if they believe that they have been wronged by the other party. Without a judge recognized by both of them, their interaction will sooner or later degenerate into physical confrontation: "But force, or a declared design of force upon the Person of another, where there is no common Superior on Earth to appeal to for relief, *is the State of War*."[72] A typical dual situation is that of the married couple. Conjugal society does not require the exercise of the power of life and death, because individuals are deemed to be capable of regulating their relationship, and of avoiding conflicts that would require the use of force. But the possibility always exists that individuals will ignore or trespass the limits proper to the situation.

In the case of marriage, the man, as the abler and the stronger, and as the one who is generally assigned power by contract, will be more likely to take advantage of his position and exercise an illegitimate power. In the state of nature the wife must be supposed to have the right to defend her own life against aggression, and to "appeal to Heaven" to protect her rights.

The institution of civil society however seems to give rise to problems similar to those faced by two human beings in the state of nature. In entrusting political power to the magistrate, human beings divide the body politic into rulers and ruled. Who judges between the two parties, in case they disagree? According to Locke, it is the ruled themselves who retain the right to pass judgement over their governors' actions. As in the case of two individuals, however, a problem of self-reflectiveness is inherent in this solution. The ruled constitute one artificial body – the "publick" – and they are entitled to evaluate the magistrate's performance toward themselves, that is, toward the interested party. When the contrast between the people and the magistrate reaches the breaking point, Locke contends that the only remedy is the "appeal to Heaven," that is, to God.[73] When the "publick" acts as a monolithic entity, an artificial person, against magistrates who have betrayed the trust received by the public itself, God's judgement reestablishes the triadic situation which is indispensable to impartial and fair judgement.

The "appeal to Heaven" is anyway a rare event, for the magistrate must have repeatedly attempted to trespass the limits of his authority, if the people must resort to the use of force to defend their sovereignty. When no such crucial matters are at stake, the "publick" performs a controlling function in another way, and one which is made possible by the condition of plurality referred to above. Although, by becoming a society, the multitude has given life to one "body," this body is composed of discrete individuals, who maintain their separate existence within the collective. As individuals, they appeal to the magistrate when disagreement arises among them. In this case the "publick" controls the performance of the ruler toward one or a few member/s of the community, making sure that the magistrate does not encroach upon each individual's rights.[74]

We can thus imagine a triadic situation: discrete individuals, the magistrate entrusted with the legislative and executive power, and the "publick." The first go about performing transactions, carrying out exchange, and concluding contracts, as they do in the state of nature; the second intervenes as arbitrator and/or regulator of those dealings; and the third checks the magistrate to make sure that he does not trespass his proper limits. When only two natural actors are on stage, this reciprocal checking becomes impossible, because two parties must perform three different but overlapping roles. Both of them are in fact the interested parties, and, in case of disagreement, the one who trespasses can only be checked by the other, because the society they had instituted – which would play the role of the "publick" – has been destroyed by their disagreement.

In describing the procedure through which human beings give life to civil society, we have already hinted at the differences between a body politic and a domestic association. A domestic association is first of all the society between man and wife, and since only two individuals are involved, their transaction can be legitimate only if the transference of power from one to the other does not include the use of force. The assumption that two human beings are not entitled to negotiate the power of life and death constitutes a prima facie unsurpassable limit to the institution of a family in which political authority is assigned to one of the parties. But the family-household is far from being a society of two. As Locke himself remarks, the group which, in primitive times, gave origin to the political association comprised children, even adult children, and servants. It is a group composed of several members, and it can in fact be transformed into a body politic. Why cannot women and servants, if not children, get together and negotiate with their prospective superior? Why can Locke rely on the contrast between dual and plural contract-making as a strong element that differentiates the domestic from the political association? The answer is to be found in Locke's insistence on the particular "ends, ties, and bounds" of the various transactions comprised in the household. In other words, the specificity of each power relation is the element that explains Locke's distinction between household and body politic.

Locke considers the family-household as an institution in which different social relations happen to be found together. Each of those relationships is structured by dynamics and procedures which cannot be assimilated one to the other. It may well be that the question: who has power over whom, how much, and why? is crucial for all of them. But the specific ends and needs of the persons involved, and the different resources to which individuals want to get access, make it impossible to cluster all the transactions under one and the same heading. In the case of parents and children, no negotiation is involved in establishing their relationship, and parents cannot advance any claim against their children, in exchange for their taking care of them. Husband and wife, and master and servant, indeed assign power to one of the parties and establish the terms of their relationships. And they use the same device, contract, to reach that goal. But they do not negotiate over the same resources, and for the same purpose. Husband and wife need access to each other's body, and are tied by affection and mutual care. Master and servant exchange wages for labor, and, at times, negotiate incorporation of the servant into the master's family; an incorporation that, however, always falls short of granting the master control over the whole life of his servant. The specificity of each transaction makes it wholly implausible that the woman and servants negotiate together with their future superior. The family-household, although made of more than two human beings, is the assemblage of individuals who have established a one-to-one relationship with the adult male proprietor who will govern it.[75]

It can be useful at this point to summarize the features of personal transactions, which allow Locke to set them apart from political ones. Individuals who perform them are supposed to have the competence to negotiate with another person about the terms of their relationship. Interaction within the family-household is statistically more peaceful than interaction among strangers, so that individuals can be left on their own, both in the state of nature and civil society, to institute and manage their relationships. There are limits to what can be negotiated between two and only two parties. Reason will tell us what those limits are, and we are entitled to defend ourselves from those who try to encroach upon those limits. Why then does one person have to assign power to the other at all, when becoming a wife or a servant? If people are rational enough to embark on the complex procedure described just above, why should one of them be subjected to the other? The synthetical answer is: because no *society* can exist if power is not assigned to someone, and the family-household is a *society*.

In particular, the nucleus of the family – the conjugal relationship between husband and wife – cannot perform its tasks if the two adults do not incorporate in one body. The family is a complex social structure, in which a contract for exchange and a social contract interweave.[76] Most personal contracts in modern society are ones in which the parties are concerned with the exchange of goods or services the other possesses or can perform. A person negotiates with another individual because the latter has access to, or possession of, something the former desires, and vice-versa. Locke maintains that husband and wife exchange access to each other's bodies, master and servant exchange services for wages, and two individuals exchange goods for money. The contract is instrumental to the exchange, and one's interest in interacting with the other individual is limited to obtaining what one possesses and the other wants.

In a social contract, individuals are not merely interested in exchanging, but aim at constituting an association in which they all share. Whereas, in personal contracts, individuals associate only to exchange, in the social contract, individuals exchange in order to associate. In instituting political society, Lockean individuals do not properly perform any exchange, because the latter can only take place where the parties have separate access to different goods in which they are mutually interested. Competent adults merely renounce their right to enforce the law of nature, and delegate it to the body politic. That is, all participants give up and acquire a thing of identical value. They all renounce their natural right to punish the transgressor, and they all gain the certainty that no private individual will retain that right.

Locke contends that the conjugal nucleus of the family is also a small society. A society composed of only two individuals presents particular problems, if it must pursue one over-arching end, and not only satisfy the individual needs of the parties. As Locke puts it, how can the family function as "one Body, with a Power to Act as one Body"? It is in fact "necessary to that which is one body to move one way," which to Locke means: "It is necessary the Body should move that way whither the greater force carries it, which is the *consent of the majority*."[77] This problem is faced by all types of associations, whether political or not. Where human beings form an artificial person, there must be a device allowing this person to make decisions and move in one direction or another. In political society, plurality permits the formation of a majority; and the majority will give more weight to one decision rather than another. The weight or force which will determine how the body will move is the *will*. It is the will of the majority that enables society to follow a course of action. Locke has a highly physical or material image of the working of a body politic. He in fact defines the will as a power (comprising faculty and energy):

> We find in our selves a *power* to begin or forbear, continue or end several actions of our minds, and motions of our bodies, barely by a thought or preference of the mind ordering, or as it were commanding the doing or not doing such or such particular action. This power which the mind has, thus to order the consideration of any *idea,* or the forbearing to consider it; or to prefer the motion of any part of the body to its rest, and *vice versa* in any particular instance is that which we call the *will*.[78]

The will is thus the faculty that can produce actual movement in our bodies or minds, by exerting a mental or physical force: the aggregation of these forces makes the body politic move. If the whole splits into two equal parts, the body will be immobilized, because the two forces applied to the body will be equal. Locke does not explore the possibility that a body politic splits in half, because it is highly unlikely that a plurality – and supposedly a numerous one – will not yield a majority, capable of pushing the minority in a given direction. Locke's insistence on the right of the majority to move the body politic can thus be explained by his conviction that the majority is what makes the body politic capable of moving at all.[79]

Conjugal society provides a clear example of a problematic case in this respect. In constituting a conjugal society, characterized by a purpose common to both spouses, the procreation and upbringing of children, man and woman must find a way of "moving" the association in one direction. But how can this direction be chosen if the component members are only two? How can a majority exist in such a situation? Given that there are only two people, as soon as they disagree, immobility and splitting are the two possible outcomes. The only solution to this *impasse* is to find a device by which a majority can be produced.[80]

Locke solves the problem of how to make decisions in conjugal society by assigning greater weight to one of the parties, thus creating a factual, although not numerical, "majority." Since Locke perceives the majority as a force which can move a body in one direction rather than another, he attributes the power to make decisions to the "weightier" party within the family.[81] Locke thus assigns greater weight to the husband because he cannot imagine an egalitarian society; that is, an institution in which the two members share power equally, without impairing the functioning of the association. As the decision-maker in conjugal society, the husband will therefore "have his Will take place before that of his wife in all things of their common Concernment."[82] His greater ability and strength are sufficient grounds to make Locke contend that the man's will counts more than the woman's. If the two individuals were equal *de facto*, and not only *de jure*, nothing could make them yield to one another. Only an objective situation of dependence and inferiority can explain why human beings accept to subject themselves to another, and grant the superior the right to make decisions for the association.

Locke's notion that the family is a "society" explains, even if it does not justify, the naturalization of asymmetrical positions which characterizes the relationship between man and woman. A servant too may still become part of his master's household, but his obligations are such that his contract can easily be reduced to a contract for exchange. The master and the servant do not have joint obligations toward a third party, as the husband and the wife do toward the child. The servant's subordination can easily be restricted to the activities and time-span of his job, while the rest of his life is under his personal control. But the woman's task of reproducing the species and educating the young ties her destiny to the institution that alone can, for Locke, satisfy the "intention of nature." The family can attain its ends only if the centrifugal forces present in every modern individual are controlled, and subjected to a principle providing cohesion and internal unity.

PRIVATE AND PUBLIC

Locke's conception of the domestic and political associations relies on the comparative approach, but it is also a decisive step toward the dissolution of that mode of analysis. Locke adopts the comparative strategy in order to rebut Filmer's conception, and to show that non-political and political forms of authority are radically different. The classical *topos* of the comparison of household and body politic was centered around the contrast between the power relations typical of each of the two institutions. The Aristotelian version opposed a naturally ordered household to a political association in which finding the proper order was the central issue, for nature did not dictate any uncontroversial allocation of power among heads of households who shared a condition of relative equality. Seventeenth-century Natural Law theorists, such as Suàrez, used the contrast between the natural and unquestionable power of the head of household, and the voluntary empowerment of the sovereign by adult free men, to emphasize the specificity of political authority. The individualistic premises of sub-sequent Natural Law theorists however undermined the distinction between the two realms as, respectively, the domain of natural hier-archy, and that of the artificial institution of power roles. Analogical arguments about household and body politic became more common, for members of the family were increasingly seen to perform the same operations as did citizens upon entering into civil society. In both cases, human beings negotiate their future condition of subordination with a prospective superior who is, at least juridically, their equal. Whether persons institute a political community, or not, depends solely on the type of negotiation which they undertake. If the attribution of the power of life and death is part of the bargain, the association born of the deal is political. And it is not, if individuals negotiate only the transference of lesser powers.

Natural Law theorists accomplished the dissolution of the *topos* by "politicizing," as it were, all power relations. For Grotius and Pufendorf, individuals who control their own capacities and resources are entitled to alienate that liberty completely, if they attain a greater good by engaging in that transaction. On the one hand, the homogenization of power relations is achieved by empowering *all* adults for the first time; a remarkable step forward from the long-standing assumption that household dependents are doomed to a perennial condition of subordination. On the other hand, however, the personal or political superior can legitimately acquire absolute power, for the alienation of one's own juridical person can well be complete and unconditional. Hobbes, who, on this point, as on many others, is the most consistent thinker of the century, openly declared that no society can survive if no one monopolizes the power of life and death. There is therefore no lasting association that is not political, and the ruler always enjoys a despotic power of sort.[83]

But it is an enemy of Natural Law theory, the patriarchalist Sir Robert Filmer, who spells out most clearly and boldly the implications stemming from politicizing all power relations. Filmer is radical and often incongruent, but he points to serious flaws in the theories of Natural Law writers. He is, therefore, a perfect polemical target for Locke, and an enemy whom he has to confront. But Locke also made him play the official knave, because he could attack the politicization of power relations, shared by Filmer and several prominent Natural Law thinkers, without having to attack the latter, with whom Locke had so much in common.

Since Filmer had flatly denied that any distinction existed between the domestic and political associations, Locke adopted the strategy of reintroducing the classical comparative approach in its most traditional form.

> To this purpose, I think it may not be amiss, to set down what I take to be Political Power. That the Power of a *Magistrate* over a Subject, may be distinguished from that of a *Father* over his Children, a *Master* over his Servant, a *Husband* over his Wife, and a *Lord* over his Slave.[84]

This rhetorically strong statement covers, as has been shown, a more nuanced conceptual argument, which upholds the contrast between the various types of power relations, without reintroducing a stark opposition of household and body politic.

First of all, Locke reduces the import of the contrast between a naturally ordered household and a voluntarily constructed political society. All power relations are a mixture of voluntary, traditional, and unreflective (in Locke's language, natural) dynamics. Reason, instincts, conscious decision, and the pressure of objective conditions of need combine in prompting people to accept rulers. Social relations are set on a continuum; various needs, aims, and the structural features of the group involved will determine what type of association will be instituted. The family, which, in principle, is a non-political association, can gradually and tacitly evolve into political society. By adopting the notion of tacit consent, Locke can justify more or less any historical transformation: from the transformation of the power of the head of household into political power, to the introduction of money to circumvent the prohibition to accumulate perishable resources.

Locke downplays the contrast between a naturally ordered household and an artificially constructed body politic, because that contrast assumed that domestic dependents were, by nature, inferior to heads of households who were relatively equal. Locke assumes that all are equal in the state of nature. Nonetheless, there are two notions of equality, one broader, and one narrower. According to the broader one, nature does not justify the exercise of political power. According to the narrower one, there are positions of superiority which have a "foundation in nature," but even these lesser forms of power must be consensually legitimated, and can be negotiated. In legitimating power, all persons perform the same operation, and must therefore have the same capacities and competence. Does that mean that all adults are equally competent? Does it mean that they are all political agents? Locke offers no clear answer to these questions. But even his narrower notion of equality is enough to undermine the distinction between a domestic order inscribed in nature and a voluntarily constructed political power. All power relations are, to a degree, constructed; as they are all, to a degree, the product of uncontrolled social mechanisms.

Locke's nuanced interpretation of the nature/convention contrast also supports his description of the state of nature as a relatively peaceful social condition. The capacity for contract-making turns out to be one of the ways in which rationally – or, at least, reasonably – interpreted experience enables individuals to live in peace with others, before they institute political authority. Compliance with natural duties and the uncritical acceptance of social practices produced through tacit consent[85] are the other two dynamics which maintain a non-antagonistic state of nature. Although family relations are far from being the only ones in which individuals engage, they occupy the center stage in Locke's description of the pre-political condition. This emphasis is partially a consequence of his polemical rejection of Filmer's assimilation. Locke talks so extensively about the family because he must show that politics are excluded from it. But familial relations are also central because, before civil society has come about, no other association is so lasting, important, and inclusive as domestic society is. If Locke can convincingly argue that the power of life and death is excluded from it, he has proved that no institution is political except the body politic itself.

Locke appears to contrast the world of the family with that of politics by relying on three criteria. The first is a "factual" observation: conflict plays such a minor role in domestic relations that the use of force can be ruled out from them. The second is a mixture of "factual" elements and normative assumptions: all the relationships present in the household are limited in the span of time, and in the range of actions that need to be controlled to fulfill the tasks of the association. The third is an openly normative prescription: contracts between two individuals may never regard the transference of the power of life and death.

I shall start considering the third point, for Locke's argument depends logically, if not rhetorically, on that normative assumption.

In asserting that individuals may not negotiate the transference of the use of force, when engaging in dual relationships, Locke applies the norm that prohibits self-enslavement.[86] Since all relationships between adults in the household are dual ones, the husband/master may not acquire the power of life and death by negotiating with a woman over the terms of their marriage contract; or by negotiating with a servant over the exchange of labor for compensation.

Family relations anyway regard only part of the life of the individuals involved. Both servants and wives retain control over their personal property, and over the time that they do not have to spend to carry out their tasks. This statement is a mixture of factual observations and normative preferences, for, especially for what regards women, it is very difficult to argue that the family does not take up the whole of their lives. Locke introduces the possibility of divorce on demand by each party, after children have grown, precisely to counter easy criticisms of his description of domestic relations.

Both these elements – the prohibition of self-enslavement, and the limited scope of the domestic association – would merely be wishful thinking if it could not be shown that individuals do abide by them. To use contemporary language, Locke's efforts would be ineffective if his account were completely counterfactual. If human beings were discovered to engage in negotiation over the use of the power of life and death when setting up the family, and to use that power to regulate it, the prohibition would be noble. But it would not help Locke to discredit Filmer's version, in which all normative preferences are presented as factual descriptions.

Locke therefore presents as a fact an image of family life from which lethal conflict has been expounded. Domestic relations, at least as they can be found in the male-centered Western family, are usually peaceful. Parents tend to love their children, husband and wife are united by affection and mutual care as much as by interest, and servants – well, servants are described as having an overriding interest in remaining on good terms with their masters. The alternatives available are unpalatable: death from starvation, or emigration to the distant forests of America. If household relations are ordinarily peaceful, to assign the power of life and death to the head is redundant. And human beings who are supposed to consult their reason to regulate their conduct and interaction would have no reason to propose an onerous arrangement which is not justified by their experience.

As seen, peace in the domestic association is ensured at the price of reintroducing asymmetrical power relations. But why should the wife assign a greater power to the husband? Why cannot we find another solution – for example, that the two rule "in turns"?

Locke reintroduces inequality, because he is convinced that equality is a source of conflict, as the transformation of the state of nature into a state of war shows. Individuals who are equal tend to go all the way if they disagree, and they are less willing to accept that the other is right and can have it his/her own way. In the Hobbesian (and Pufendorfian) state of nature, even between man and woman a war would have to be waged to decide "who gets what" in case the two disagree. Locke can avoid such a dramatic portrait of the state of nature, because his version has the solution already built into it. He assigns a limited power to the husband, so that conflict will be suffocated on the rising by the imposition of the superior's will on the will of his subordinate. Equality is renounced, so that domestic relations can be described as peaceful. And since domestic relations are peaceful, the head of household will not have to exercise political authority.

The surreptitious and indirect elimination of conflict, which is attained by reintroducing inequality in the family, generates new questions. Locke distinguishes domestic from political society by contending that the first does not require the exercise of the power of life and death, whereas the use of force is at the core of political rule. Even if we take Locke's argument at face value, one question remains open: since political society is a response to conflict, where and why does conflict arise? Pufendorf had openly contended that the growing complexity of social life, especially in towns, triggered enmity among heads of families, who consequently proceeded to institute political rule. But Locke never presents such an explicit portrait of the transition from the state of nature to civil society. And it is therefore legitimate to ask: can individuals who are personally subjected to a superior, but retain control over a part of their lives, engage in conflicts which will make the institution of political authority necessary? The question is crucial, because it is another way of asking: who enjoys political agency? Only heads of households, as all other Natural Law theorists openly declares? Or all adults, as in the state of nature? If adults may not alienate their political agency to a personal superior, should they not participate directly in the institution of political authority? Or does Locke tacitly assume that they are vicariously represented by the head of household?

Locke never answers these questions, and I believe that the text does not warrant any conclusive interpretation. By remaining silent on this point, Locke avoids a difficult issue, which other Natural Law thinkers more or less openly debated. But they had a way out of the predicament, for they accepted the notion that individuals were entitled to alienate their natural right to use force even in one-to-one transactions. By granting political authority to a personal superior, individuals could be assumed to have tacitly or explicitly granted him the right to negotiate the social contract on their behalf. But Locke rules out one-to-one contracts regarding the power of life and death, that is, political power, for such transactions amount to self-enslavement. And he indicates no other procedure through which the husband or master can have legitimately acquired the right to represent his dependents in the social contract. If he does that nonetheless, he is *de facto* usurping a power that Locke wanted to deny to him in the first place. Despite the far-reaching implications of ignoring this issue, Locke offers no solution to it in the *Two Treatises*.

Locke adopts a rhetorical strategy which makes the omission less noticeable. In contrasting domestic and political society, he relies on one of the features of the comparison, namely that of analyzing the two associations as institutions which are wholly independent of each other, and which can therefore be considered separately. Locke contends that, if we set household and body politic side by side, the first is not a political institution, while the latter is. But what happens when we consider the two as component elements of the same social structure – that is, when we think of households as the smaller and lesser units of society as a whole, and of political society, as what takes care of the concerns of the entire association? By reflecting upon the relationship between the family and the political domain, we can inquire into Locke's conception of the distinction between private and public.

Locke's model, as in the case of all Natural Law thinkers, is diachronic, and it describes the passage from the state of nature, where the family already exists, to civil society, as the exit from the natural condition. Although civil society supersedes the state of nature, it does not completely override it, for it is brought into being to ensure stability to social relations in which individuals have engaged independently of the state. This description of the state of nature is crucial for establishing the domain of legitimate intervention by the magistrate. In other words, Locke's description of the state of nature normatively bears upon the conduct of the state in respect of forms of interaction which originally preceded it, and which will continue to exist in the political condition.[87]

For Locke, social relations in the state of nature achieve a high degree of stability and predictability thanks to the human capacity for apprehending and complying with the law of nature. Locke therefore attributes to all adults autonomous agency, which enables them to regulate their conduct, and even to curtail their independence, in exchange for peaceful and harmonious interaction.

Locke's conception of agency is very similar to that of other Natural Law thinkers, and it is explicitly proprietary. Individuals are supposed to "own" the faculties and skills that allow them to function in the world – precisely because some of those faculties are the object of transactions with others. Each individual has a *"Property* in his own *Person,"*[88] and enjoys exclusive access to what is *proper* to him. Locke includes in his notion of property external goods, physical and mental faculties, and the capacity for autonomous action itself. We are proprietors of our own persons, both of things which can be separated from us, and of personal endowments. Property plays a crucial role in Locke's conception of power relations, because by alienating our property we alienate what makes us persons. If this extensive notion of property is kept in mind, only slaves are propertyless.[89]

An individual who has alienated all his property is no longer an independent agent, and, reciprocally, a fully autonomous human being retains control both of external goods, and of personal endowments.[90] In between non-agency and full agency, as it were, Locke conceptualizes also a minimal conception of agency. This focuses on the control over one's capacities, rather than external resources, as the crucial factor to determine whether a human being is an autonomous person.[91] The beggar who chooses to become a servant cannot be said to own anything, but he still retains control, that is, possession, of his body and mind. He can decide what to do with his own life, the very thing which the slave cannot do.

One can be less than a full agent either because one possesses no external resources, or because one has transferred control over one's personal capacities to another. Mere possession of material goods does not guarantee to the person that she will retain full control over her own actions. In domestic society, women proprietors will be subjected to their husbands as much as women who only control their own persons. The woman partially gives up her autonomy in subscribing to the authority of the man; he will make decisions for their association insofar as their common interest is concerned. The attribution of power to the husband impairs the wife's autonomy, even if she retains control over her own material property. As already remarked, it is not clear whether Locke thought that individuals who have somehow curtailed their capacity for agency enjoy political rights. It would seem intuitively correct to argue that for Locke only persons who retain their full agency can be politically active, although he offers no justification for excluding dependents from the public arena.

Locke's analysis of agency in proprietary terms has direct implications for the distinction between private and public. Locke's notion of the private domain includes both external and personal resources. The individual "owns" the faculties that constitute her as an agent, and what she acquires by exercising her faculties. Since each adult, in Locke's view, is an autonomous agent – unless mad, incompetent, or captive in a just war – each adult possesses and controls a private domain. There are differentials between the private domains of individuals, which correspond to the differential in agency noted above. By exercising their agency, individuals can expand their private domain, as well as narrow it. The private sphere of the head of household is broader than that of his servant or his wife, because his dependents have granted him control over some of their own personal resources. His property will therefore include both external resources – land, money, etc. – and the personal resources of those who have subjected themselves to him. Reciprocally, dependents will have lessened their private domains by all the personal capacities that are under the control of their superior.

Nonetheless, if agency may not be completely alienated, and each adult possesses a private domain, each individual will also enjoy a public status complementary to her private one. Do individuals who do not enjoy full personal agency have a public stand? Can Locke's contention that everyone has some degree of property be of any practical significance, if no public agency is recognized to less than full agents? If we assume that political agency is the prerogative of those who have maintained their independence, can we hypothesize that dependents have a public life, although one falling short of active political participation? How can women and servants avoid a *de facto* condition of enslavement, if they cannot utter their concerns and voice their demands in public?

In the absence of a clear answer in Locke's text, a few speculations appear permissible.

By rejecting the permissive interpretation of the law of nature, Locke has introduced the inviolability of each adult's private domain. This implies that if the state is instituted for defending individual property, the state may have to take care of all aspects of each adult's life that may be harmed by others. If compared with the public domain of the classical tradition, which began outside the walls of the household, Locke has "expanded" the public domain to include the concerns and entitlements of all adults. Locke does not specify which activities and relations may require the use of force, for any of them can. Any time a party tries to harm the person of another human being, to damage his external resources, or to violate the terms of a contract to which he has freely subscribed, the other party has the right to retaliate.

In fact, in a pre-political condition, each human being is responsible for managing her personal "property" as she "thinks fit, within the bounds of the Law of Nature." This means that each one can interpret the law of nature, conclude contracts, join various associations, and enforce the terms of those transactions, in case of disagreement. Human beings enforce the law of nature in defense both of their own persons and property, and of those of others who are in danger. Locke's portrait of the peaceful state of nature thus depends on a twofold argument. First, that adults are capable of complying with the law of nature when they engage in personal transactions. And, second, that individuals create a network of mutual control and support, that is, a non-institutionalized public domain. Abuse and trespassing can and should be punished by any third party who happens to witness the events. Human beings are not depicted as altruistic by Locke. But they are other-regarding, when someone disrupts the peaceful order which enables everyone to take care of his business undisturbed. Humankind thus forms a community, although one which is only held together by the shared capacity for consulting and applying the law of nature. As Laslett has put it, individuals in the state of nature practice "natural political virtue."[92]

The Lockean state of nature is therefore both a condition of institutional anarchy, and one in which an informal public domain has already come into existence. What defines the boundaries of this public domain? In other words, when does the informal network of control and support have to intervene? The obvious answer is: when the abuse and misuse of force are perpetrated or threatened. There are situations in which it is relatively easy to interpret the case at hand: for example, when we or others engage in unjustified physical aggression. But to use force, even for Locke, has a wider meaning. The prohibition to starve others to death, for example, implies that I have to take into consideration a wider and more nuanced range of consequences, if I want to know whether what I am about to do is legitimate or not, and if I have to pass judgement on other people's deeds. In appropriating this piece of land, am I appropriating the last plot available, perhaps reducing other human beings to starvation? In gambling my property away, am I endangering my children not yet of age? In deciding the type of marriage which I prefer, am I furthering the "intention of nature," which establishes the survival of the species, and the raising of the young, as the parents' natural duties? In trying to answer these questions correctly, individuals have to go beyond ascertaining the consequences of their actions for this or that person, and must think of their long-lasting and far-reaching implications for human beings in general.

We can therefore say that the interpretation of the law of nature has a private and a public side, as it were. We need to interpret the law of nature for concluding our personal transactions, and for assessing the import of our actions for others. We can analytically distinguish the two aspects of this activity. But can we distinguish them operationally? If a person can assess the private consequences of her actions, on what grounds could we argue that she cannot assess their public import? And since all adults can do the former, we must conclude that they can also do the latter. This means that, at least in principle, Locke's recognition that all adults can manage their private domain implies granting them public agency as well.

In an egalitarian state of nature, political participation of a kind is thus recognized to all. Both enforcement and interpretation of the law of nature are decentralized, and this is an unavoidable step, if the state of nature is to be a peaceful and self-regulated condition. Locke's account of the institution of civil society confirms that the interpretation of the law of nature is a kind of public activity, but it also brings to the fore Locke's negative attitude toward participatory practices.

Locke starts by contending that individuals who institute civil society aim to ensure the protection of their private domains.

> For all being [in the state of nature] Kings as much as he, every Man is Equal, and the greater part no strict Observers of Equity and

Justice, the enjoyment of the property he has in this state is very unsafe, very unsecure ... he ... is willing to joyn in Society with others ... for the mutual *Preservation* of their Lives, Liberties and Estates, which I call by the general Name, *Property.*[93]

But to attain this end, they transfer two powers to the community, and, consequently, to the magistrate: the right to enforce, and, to a degree, the right to interpret the law of nature.

The first *Power, viz. of doing whatsoever he thought fit for the Preservation of himself*, and the rest of Mankind, *he gives up* to be regulated by Laws made by the Society, so far forth as the preservation of himself, and the rest of that Society shall require; which Laws of the Society in many things confine the liberty he had by the Law of Nature.

Secondly, the *Power of punishing* he wholly *gives up*, and engages his natural force, (which he might before imploy in the Execution of the Law of Nature, by his own single Authority, as he thought fit) to assist the Executive Power of the Society, as the Law thereof shall require.[94]

These two passages confirm that Locke's view of what constitutes the public domain includes both the right to use force, and the right to interpret the law of nature. The transference of the use of force to the state is the indispensable step to ensure protection of a private domain managed autonomously by its possessor, and it is the logical complement of a theory in which political authority is limited. The notion of the state as guardian and protector of each individual's private sphere, and as enforcer of norms which neither the state nor the citizens may change justifies interpreting Locke's political philosophy as the first expression of modern liberalism.[95]

The transference[96] to the state of the right to interpret the law of nature is more problematic. For this right is precisely what defines the capacity for autonomous agency which marks the boundary of the individual's realm of autonomous action. Each person's private domain coincides with the set of personal and external resources which each one has been able to acquire and preserve. Locke's portrait of a peaceful state of nature served the purpose of showing that self-regulated individual agency did not lead to disastrous results, so that the state need not acquire absolute power to keep peace. But if the interpretation of the law of nature is, to a degree, assigned to the state, the activity through which individuals construct their own private domain is subjected to governmental control.[97] Locke's work thus lends itself to ambivalent interpretations. Is Locke a proto-liberal thinker, or is he a more conservative and traditional writer, who empowers human beings in the state of nature only to dispossess them in civil society, in the name of the common good?

Besides paving the way to two potentially conflicting views of Locke's political philosophy, the recognition that the interpretation of the law of nature is a public activity engenders questions about the nature and tasks of politics. The "liberal" bent of Locke's political philosophy supports the view that politics coincide with the enforcement of shared norms on trespassers. All that individuals have to do to develop peaceful social relations is to mind their own business, and to avoid harming others. They delegate to the state the power to use force, but they retain full control over their private agency. But the transference to the magistrate of the capacity to interpret the law of nature reveals a more complex picture. Locke's state of nature is peaceful because individuals are other-regarding, although not altruistic. They are "politically" active, and they express public agency in considering the consequences of their choices for society as a whole. Politics go beyond the enforcement of norms, and require the assessment of the social implications of personal choices and activities. This activity is a kind of political participation, although performed in an uncoordinated and informal way. When social relations grow in size and complexity, individuals become unable to take into consideration the needs of the group, and civil society is instituted. But does the interpretation of the law of nature need to be centralized? And if it is, can human beings retain full private autonomy, while delegating the public function of interpretation to the magistrate?

Locke's individualistic and egalitarian assumptions, coupled with the inviolability of each one's personal domain, are the premises of a democratic and participatory theory of politics. Locke himself backs away from it, and ultimately opts for a much more prudent view of the role of individuals in active politics. He backs away from the full egalitarianism of the state of nature, for household dependents see their public agency curtailed by their loss of personal independence. And he retreats from granting direct participation to heads of households in civil society.[98] As a consequence he also has to introduce restrictions on their private autonomy, and assign a broad power of interpretation and implementation of the law of nature to the political ruler.

Locke has however set the stage for inquiring further into one of the central problems of modern political philosophy: if we agree with Locke that each person is endowed with an inviolable personal domain, how can we ensure both safety of that personal domain, and social integration? If each one is on his/her own in governing his/her life, is not some form of direct political participation indispensable to find an agreement about what is shared? May not there be a necessary link between individualistic premises and the decentralization of the activity whereby shared norms are ascertained? Is it plausible to see a connection between a new conception of publicness and the characteristics of the social universe which is (in principle) politically active? Locke's *Two Treatises* justify extrapolating these questions, but it would not be fair to Locke to ask him for answers. It is to Hutcheson's work that we must turn to explore these issues in greater depth.

4 A new public

Francis Hutcheson

NATURAL SOCIABILITY

Locke develops a distinction between private and public which is grounded on the notion that individuals can regulate their lives as they think fit, within the boundaries of the law of nature. The Lockean state of nature is relatively peaceful, for individuals can order their relations without the intervention of political authority. But if peace is to be maintained, political activity of a kind is indispensable, consisting of protecting our fellows, and assessing the wider implications of our choices for the group at large. A public network thus comes into being, generated by the informal and decentralized activity of protection of, and care for, others. Human beings perform all these complex operations by discovering and applying the norms established by God for the species. In describing individuals who can recognize others' rights, and assume them as their duties, Locke ascribes to men and women a type of autonomous agency which is ethical and juridical at the same time. It is ethical, for in respecting other people's rights, a person does what is (morally) good. It is juridical, for it enables adults to conceive of specific instances of good or evil as enforceable claims, on the one hand, and as punishable transgressions, on the other.

Although Locke intertwines moral and juridical questions, the fundamental structure of his argument is juridical. He asks juridical and legal questions. What rights do human beings have by nature? How much power can they claim over others? What sanctions are appropriate against transgressors? And he upholds the view that the source of obligation is God as the supreme legislator, and the dispenser of punishment and reward.[1]

But in post-Lockean philosophy, the moral side of the issue, as it were, is increasingly emphasized. It is emphasized against politically-grounded interpretations of the origin of norms, such as the one which

Hobbes offered.[2] And it is emphasized against the idea that norms do not have to be "right" and "good" at all, but merely have to be effective, to hold society together and make it flourish, as Mandeville hypothesized. The point is therefore to show that only principles which are authentically "good" from an ethical point of view can ensure stability. Legal and political rules – and any rule issued by an authority – are binding because they are morally right, not the other way around.

The issues of the nature of norms, the primacy of morality, and the political function played by those norms come to the fore in the work of Francis Hutcheson, who develops these themes in reaction against Bernard Mandeville's *Fable of the Bees*.[3] Mandeville contended that the "cunning politician" ensures peaceful and thriving social relations by inventing rules which twist and manipulate the fundamentally antisocial drives of human nature. According to Hutcheson, only authentically virtuous conduct can avoid conflict. Hutcheson therefore develops his inquiry in two directions. First, he studies the nature of morality. And second, he shows what bearing morally approvable conduct has upon politics; and he contends that the practice of political virtue is indispensable to ensuring the "public good."[4]

These two distinct but related themes are central to an understanding of Hutcheson's distinction between private and public, and his conception of the nature and tasks of politics. I shall try to show that Hutcheson's moral theory is based on individualistic assumptions which reinforce the individualistic and egalitarian bent of his political theory. By intertwining moral, juridical, and political aspects of conduct, Hutcheson elaborates a model of universal political participation grounded in the voluntary compliance with moral/juridical norms. We are all political agents because we can all behave in a morally approvable way, understand what furthers the good of our fellows and what does not, and translate our notions of moral good and evil into the corresponding juridical notions of right and wrong. This does not mean that Hutcheson recognizes full political agency to all adults, if by this we mean the activity through which human beings found political institutions. As in previous Natural Law thinkers, heads of households vicariously represent the dependent members of the family. But Hutcheson does conceptualize a new informal public domain, from which nobody may be excluded.

At the basis of this new public domain, there lies, as remarked, the capacity to understand and fulfill our obligations. We are endowed with a specific faculty, the moral sense, which tells us whether actions and intentions are approvable or disapprovable. The moral sense produces sensory/emotional reactions to characteristics in persons and actions, which are apprehended as good. These reactions can neither be produced at will, nor be manipulated. Hutcheson contends that existing social relations embody and express the principles which are at the basis of an authentic morality. To the modern reader, this style of argumentation – which was the standard one at the time – generates two opposite impressions. On the one hand, the writer appears to rationalize and beautify social relations to fit the ideal model he has in mind. On the other, he appears to construct an ideal model which can be compatible with factual data. Hutcheson moves back and forth between normative reasoning and "sociological" observation, and the two types of evidence clearly carry the same weight in his mind.

This approach, ambiguities aside, allows Hutcheson to depict a society in which authentically virtuous individuals can maintain peaceful relations without being coerced, or manipulated, by cunning politicians. The moral sense enables human beings to understand the set of norms – laws of nature – that ensure harmonious coexistence. All that human beings must do to cohabit peacefully is to let their natural benevolence guide their choices. If humans were always capable of morally approvable conduct, political institutions would never be necessary.

The moral sense not only gives us perceptions of good and evil, but it also enables us to recognize natural entitlements and obligations. And it also enables us to add the conventional rights and duties through which stable social institutions can be erected and maintained. Hutcheson resorts to the seventeenth-century tradition of Natural Law theory, especially in its Pufendorfian version, in order to account for the juridical implications of morally shaped conduct. In a fully socialized state of nature, all sane adults institute complex associations, although each person maintains the right to exercise the power of life and death. Hutcheson depicts a state of nature which is more egalitarian and less antagonistic than that of Locke, and in which "natural political virtue" plays the fundamental role. The egalitarianism of Hutcheson's moral theory shows in his description of domestic relations, which is especially impressive for its anti-authoritarian tones. However, at the decisive moment, when political society becomes necessary, because peace is threatened, the traditional household ruled by the adult male reappears at the center of the stage.

On a first reading, Hutcheson appears to add little to the Lockean version of the relationship between the state of nature and civil society, and, consequently, to the distinction between private and public. As in Locke, the distinction must be understood in terms of jurisdictional domains, personal or political, and of the type of agency individuals practice in them, or through them. But the interest of seventeenth-century Natural Law theorists, Locke included, lay rather in the juridical aspects of agency. Hutcheson offers an ethical account of agency and social interaction; and he then draws its juridical and political implications. Since Hutcheson focuses on all the aspects of conduct that are morally relevant, he considers as crucial to social stability a broader range of features than the ones usually taken into consideration by a juridically minded writer. This means, on the one hand, that not all interaction relevant to social stability has a juridical counterpart. But on the other hand, it means that there are more aspects of human experience which require juridical recognition, than the ones which previous Natural Law theorists took into consideration. The list of natural rights, for example, grows longer. And the human capacity for compliance with moral norms makes the state of nature more fully social and more long-lasting than in any previous thinker.

Morality and legality[5] are both indispensable if the state of nature is to be peaceful, but institutional politics are not, at least for a long time. Hutcheson's belief in the self-sufficiency of a stateless, that is, non-political, condition leads him to hypothesize that anarchy can at times be preferable to oppressive political arrangements.[6] Civil society is an answer to the growing complexity of social relations, and its fundamental function is to secure a balance which once existed and was lost.

That balance requires us to harmonize the rights of individuals, expressed in subjective terms, with the common good. This tension between the "greatest happiness of the greatest number" and individual happiness is the *leitmotif* of Hutcheson's political theory. He appears to intertwine utilitarian and civic republican elements. But recently commentators have emphasized only the latter side of Hutcheson's thought, and labeled him a civic humanist or a classical republican.[7] The civic elements of Hutcheson's views should not allow us to forget that his theory points in less straightforward directions. In particular, we cannot offhandedly dismiss his individualism, which has important egalitarian implications, and decisively shapes Hutcheson's theory of politics.

The individualistic bias of Hutcheson's philosophy is closely connected to his acceptance of natural jurisprudence, and this bias looms large in both his moral and his legal theory. Hutcheson sees voluntary individual compliance with moral norms as constitutive of social relations. Therefore, every adult must be capable of morally approvable conduct, if non-political social relations are to exist and last. Moral dynamics must conversely be such that all adults are capable of them. We must translate certain moral norms into the corresponding juridical ones, and we must acknowledge that good (or evil) features of persons and deeds give life to the corresponding rights and duties. Therefore, every adult is an interpreter of the law of nature, she is a holder of rights, and she is capable of managing those rights.

The reader will have noticed that one of the consequences of Hutcheson's approach is that we have not mentioned the traditional contrast of domestic with political society. This theme plays nearly no part in Hutcheson's work, for two reasons. First, his description of associations in psychological/moral dynamics leads him to see an unbridgeable gap between non-political and political associations. What does a family based on physical attraction, affection, and love have in common with a political association which enforces the respect of individual rights and of the common good? Second, Hutcheson's individualism makes him emphasize the voluntaristic aspects of all societies, family included. Consequently, he abandons the contrast between a naturally given domestic hierarchy and a political order which ensues from an agreement among peers.

Nonetheless, Hutcheson's egalitarian tendencies have clear and serious limits, which become apparent in his treatment of political agency and political virtue.

Male proprietors express political agency and virtue in giving up their natural liberty and instituting civil society, thus entrusting rulers with the power to enforce the norms that were already operating in the state of nature. Heads of households incorporate dependents and represent them vicariously; they give precedence to the care of the common good over their selfish one to avoid corruption, and they bear arms. The tension between civic republican notions and utilitarian ones is apparent. Citizens must practice political virtue, in republican fashion. However, political virtue consists in the delegation of power to representatives, rather than in direct participation; the common good is defined arithmetically as the maximization of the happiness of all individuals; and the pursuit of social happiness is justified not only as an end in itself, but also as the means through which individual happiness can be attained. More important for this analysis, the public domain is defined in typical Natural Law fashion, as the sphere of the state which is in charge of protecting social relations already in existence. The state is a pacifier, and the citizen acts politically in instituting it and letting it do its job, rather than in acting directly.

Although full political agency is only granted to adults males, Hutcheson's individualism implies that political virtue can also be expressed in a different way. All adults express it in the morally/ juridically structured state of nature, in which their capacity for public agency permits peaceful social relations before the state has come into being. Natural political virtue enables each individual to see himself connected with all other individuals of the species. This ideal association is an abstraction which Hutcheson calls "society," "mankind as a system," or "the publick." Individuals express political virtue when they try to maximize their happiness, in such a way as to make it compatible with the happiness of all. This notion of political virtue is different from that of civic republicanism. Human beings practice it in a condition from which no adult can be excluded. And they use it to construct harmonious social relations, rather than to attain a common good which is defined independently of, but requires, as its material prerequisite, those social relations. A new conception of the public domain thus appears to be implicit in Hutcheson's work, as this final chapter aims to show.

THE MORAL SENSE

Hutcheson's account of natural social relations is shaped by his anti-Mandevillian stance. According to Hutcheson, if human beings functioned as Mandeville hypothesized, society would not exist. Manipulation, twisting of the instincts, and pursuit of the public interest through appeals to selfishness would not produce harmonious social interaction. Without the observance of truly moral principles, centrifugal forces would gain the upper hand. It is fortunate that human beings are capable of disinterested behavior, which is both ethically approvable, and conducive to the well-being of society. Natural sociability, that is, the innate desire and inclination to live with others, characterizes the species. Nonetheless, if we wish to have the company of our fellows we must sacrifice our selfish urges. Natural sociability points not merely to an instinctual drive, to a "fact" of human nature, but to the victorious struggle of altruistic against selfish motives, of generous against self-centered affections.[8]

We can thus consider existing social relations as the living proof that there exists in human beings a natural tendency to seek the company of others, and to comply with the norms that make coexistence possible. If natural sociability were not inscribed in human nature, stable social interaction would be unthinkable. But if we were unable to perform our duties, the social instinct would not be strong enough to overcome our selfishness.

For Hutcheson, the family is the institution that confirms these tenets. In contending that "the first relation in order of nature is marriage,"[9] Hutcheson summarizes the various elements at play in interaction. Marriage is first in order of nature because it springs from a basic instinct, that of propagation, which is common to humans and animals, and which ensures the survival of the species. However, this instinct is physiologically indiscriminate, or, in Hutcheson's words, "brutal." If we followed it blindly, we should not ensure the preservation of humankind. Children, in fact, depend on adults, and require care, love, and assistance for several years. Parents – as those appointed by nature to perform this task – ought therefore to remain together until their offspring can shift for themselves. The condition of children, thus, "plainly declare[s] the intention of nature, that they should be propagated by parents first united in mutual love and esteem, in an affectionate and lasting partnership, to assist each other in this most important duty toward our kind."[10] A third natural characteristic provides the link between the innate instinct for indiscriminate sexual intercourse, and the natural duty to provide for the young. This characteristic is natural modesty.

> Nature has wisely formed us in such a manner, that in all those who are under the restraints of the natural modesty, and of any sense of virtue, the inclination to procreate is excited, or at least generally regulated in its choice of a partner, by many delicate sentiments, and finer passions of the heart of the sweetest kind.... As we thus previously know the natural design of this impulse, and the obligations toward offspring thence to ensue, as we are endued with reason, we are obliged to restrain this impulse till we have obtained assurance of such harmony of minds as will make the long joint education tolerable to both parents.[11]

Hutcheson sets on a continuum three features of human nature: instincts (the sexual one), psychological characters which owe their existence to interaction (modesty, or the sense of honor and shame), and the rational faculty which allows us to recognize our obligations, and prompts us to moderate the instincts.[12] The juxtaposition of these characteristics raises problems. If it is spontaneous for us to choose the partner with whom we can establish a lasting relationship, why do we have to hypothesize an instinct contrary to our nature, which then has to be repressed? (Ockham's razor is violated here.) Even granted that there are two opposite drives in human nature – the brutal instinct, and modesty – why should we be under an obligation to restrain ourselves? Does not modesty effortlessly direct us toward the proper satisfaction of sexual desire, so that we can raise our offspring? The answer has to be in the negative, for human beings do ignore the promptings of their innate controlling mechanisms, and become prey to their own instincts.

If natural modesty does not operate constantly and infallibly, what makes human beings incline toward the right conduct? What bridges the gap between instinct and its acceptable satisfaction, if not coercion (or manipulation)? In order to avoid the latter solution, Hutcheson hypothesizes a further aspect of human nature, which participates both in nature as innate and given, and in nature as consciously elected because it promotes what is (morally) good. This feature is the moral sense, which justifies the assertion that human beings are naturally social, and capable of morally regulated conduct.

The moral sense – a notion which Hutcheson inherits from Shaftesbury[13] – is a faculty that makes us perceive the moral quality of intentions and actions.[14] According to Hutcheson, moral qualities are features of deeds and motives, which can be grasped only if we hypothesize a specific faculty. Hutcheson anchors in sensation all human responses to external stimuli. Or, to put it another way, he reads as sensory stimuli – which can only be registered by sense – all the relevant qualities of objects, deeds, and persons. The moral sense operates like the aesthetic sense. We perceive, through sensation, whether an object is beautiful or ugly, and whether an action or motivation is good or bad. Hutcheson transfers the empiricist assumption – which holds that information about the world can enter into our minds only through the senses – from the epistemological to the psychological and to the moral levels. The immediate consequence of this approach is that reason plays a merely instrumental role.

> This power judges about the means of the subordinate ends: but about the ultimate ends there is no reasoning. We prosecute them by some immediate disposition or determination of soul, which in the order of action is prior to all reasoning; as no opinion or judgement can move to action, where there is no prior desire of some end.[15]

The moral sense enables us to perceive whether actions and intentions are good or bad, morally approvable or disapprovable.

> The affections which excite this moral approbation are all either directly benevolent, or naturally connected with such dispositions; those which are disapproved or condemned, are either ill-natured, by which one is inclined to occasion misery to others; or such selfish dispositions as argue some unkind affection, or the want of that degree of the benevolent affections which is requisite for the publick good, and commonly expected in our species.[16]

The moral sense, therefore, plays the role of a judging or, in ethical terms, a justifying capacity. But it does not move us to act; in

Hutcheson's own terms, it is not an exciting reason.[17] What prompts us to act is desires (and aversions), which cannot be "raised at will," either by ourselves or by others.[18] Human beings are moved to act by the desire of a future pleasure, or by the aversion of a future pain. To act in our own self-interest obviously gives us pleasure. But we derive pleasure, according to Hutcheson, not only from things that maximize our happiness – and minimize our pain – but also from things that maximize others' happiness – and minimize their pain.[19] There thus exist two distinct types of actions, springing from two different psychological sources: selfish and benevolent.[20]

Performing morally approvable actions thus brings pleasure to the agent, but this does not mean, according to Hutcheson, that we can bring ourselves to feel benevolent because we desire the pleasure accompanying that affection. If we are not benevolent, our desire to be cannot by any means make us be. This is a crucial point in Hutcheson's moral philosophy, for, if it were possible to raise benevolent motives at will, human beings would be able to perform benevolent actions out of selfish motives. That is, they would be altruistic merely because they would maximize their own pleasure by doing the good of others.[21] This was precisely what Mandeville – and Hobbes before him – contended: human beings are selfish creatures, and it is only by playing with their selfish desires that politicians can induce them to behave in a socially constructive way. And it is also apparent that, if motivations can be produced at will, the door is open to that manipulation of natural instincts by which the Mandevillean politician could tame human beings.

Although we cannot be benevolent out of selfish concerns, we can become aware of the fact that performing authentically altruistic actions will ultimately give us pleasure, and a sort of pleasure much superior to any other we may experience.[22] The moral sense orders hierarchically the sources of pleasure, and makes us recognize the greater moral value of the pleasure ensuing from altruistic acts and intentions.

> This moral sense from its very nature appears to be designed for regulating and controlling all our powers. This dignity and command-ing nature we are immediately conscious of, as we are conscious of the power itself.... So we immediately discern moral good to be superior in kind and dignity to all others which are perceived by the other perceptive powers.[23]

The capacity for approvable moral conduct is at the core of natural sociability. As already quoted, actions deserving moral praise are motivated by benevolence. When we do others good, that is, when we are altruistic, we behave in a morally approvable way. Hutcheson thus ranks good actions according to the degree of altruism, as it were, characterizing them, and he expresses the highest-ranking moral value in the terms that utilitarianism will make famous, as the greatest happiness for the greatest numbers. This approach to morality makes it apparent why proper moral conduct is an indispensable element of natural sociability. If human beings can yield to benevolent rather than selfish urges, they can adopt the behavior that, by maximizing the welfare of the group, allows them to have a peaceful social life, without the intervention of a coercive and manipulative agency.

MORALITY AND SOCIAL WELFARE

Hutcheson's account of the working of the moral sense is also a portrait of self-regulated social interaction. Hutcheson makes morality play two roles. He employs it, as usual, to give an account of how a free, but error-prone, being can strive to attain the good. And he uses it to justify the assertion that the species is naturally social. The capacity for performing morally approvable actions becomes the ground upon which Hutcheson can defend the natural sociability of the species. And the existence of social relations proves that humans are authentically moral.

Through his account of the moral sense, Hutcheson has provided the element to bridge the gap between nature as instinctual and innate, and nature as what human beings should choose because morally approvable. We are endowed with characteristics – like the social instinct – that indeed make us capable of living peacefully with others. But whether we actually express that instinct or not is a matter of moral choice, and of the proper application of those normative sets of principles known as laws of nature. Hutcheson can thus contend that "the several powers, dispositions, or determinations above-mentioned are universally found in mankind, where some accident hath not rendered some individual monstrous, or plainly maimed and deficient in a natural faculty."[24] And he can at the same hold that

it must be obvious we are not speaking here of the ordinary condition of mankind, as if these calm determinations were generally exercised, and habitually controlled the particular passions; but of the conditions our nature can be raised to by due culture; and of the principles which may and ought to operate, when by attention we present to our minds the objects or representations fit to excite them.[25]

The interweaving of instinct and morality is nowhere more apparent than in the family. In comparison to looser and more distant social ties,[26] nature makes it relatively easier to express natural sociability with the members of one's family. Instincts make us desire the good of closely related persons, and overcome our selfishness for their sake, by prompting us to love them, that is, by making us feel more strongly the pleasure we derive from their happiness. In the case of the family, natural bonds are so strong that the moral charge, which is implicit in any action or intention having others' happiness as its target, nearly vanishes. That we are nevertheless confronted with a moral choice is apparent in the repression of the sexual instinct. If we did not choose the morally approvable conduct, and satisfied it indiscriminately, we should be unable to fulfill the intention of nature regarding the preservation of the species.

Hutcheson relies on the internal dynamics of eroticism to explain how fulfillment of our selfish desires – gratification of the sexual instinct – and compliance with our obligations can be harmonized. We indeed feel the "brutal impulse," but we feel an irrepressible urgency to satisfy it only when certain conditions are obtained. Virtue and wisdom, innocence of manner, complacence, confidence, and goodwill are the "natural incitements and concomitants of the amorous desire; and almost obscure the brutal impulse toward the sensual gratification, which might be had with persons of any character."[27] But this innate controlling mechanism would not operate, if we did not know that sexual desire must be satisfied to propagate the species, and if we did not know the obligations which we have toward those born of us. The education of children requires that we share our life with another person for several years, and we are therefore prompted to direct our desire toward the object which can satisfy all requirements. Instincts corrected by morality thus structure social relations.

By portraying how voluntary and involuntary factors shape approvable conduct, Hutcheson has given us an account not only of our moral faculty, but also of the sociological function which approvable conduct performs in maintaining social harmony. If we accept Hutcheson's moral theory, we can indeed conclude that conduct informed by the features which he describes would be socially beneficial. But this does not mean that all conduct that is socially beneficial springs from ethically approvable motives. In particular, human beings may end up by maximizing social welfare out of the selfish desire to receive approval from their fellows. To receive approval is undoubtedly a pleasant experience, and we can indirectly have that experience if we act out of benevolence. But to choose a line of conduct only because we have a desire to be approved cannot and should not receive moral approval, either from ourselves or from others.

It is in the working of a specific feature of human nature – the sense of honor and shame – that this problem becomes apparent. The sense of honor and shame makes us sensitive to the praise or blame which we receive from others in response to our conduct.

> By another natural determination, which we may call a sense of honour and shame, an high pleasure is felt upon our gaining the approbation and esteem of others for our good actions, and upon their expressing their sentiments of gratitude; and on the other hand, we are cut to the heart by censure, condemnation, and reproach. All this appears in the countenance. The fear of infamy, or censure, or contempt, displays itself by blushing.[28]

We have already seen this "natural faculty" at work in the form of modesty, which makes us repress the "brutal impulse" and defer its gratification until the proper partner is found. But the sense of honor and shame is responsible for a much wider range of deeds than the repression of sexual desire. It embodies our wish for approval, and our psychological dependence on others. We cannot live in their company without being concerned with their feelings toward us. We are thus led to behave in a way acceptable to them, because we fear the rejection which we should otherwise encounter. This natural sense – Hutcheson insists – is not the same as the moral sense. It is a further motive, an "incitement" to act in a way that others can approve. And what triggers their approval, if not those actions that are prompted by the desire to maximize others' – and not the person's – good?

If only actions motivated by benevolence must receive approval, actions performed out of fear of censure should not produce the same result. Fear of censure is a selfish, not a benevolent, motive, as Hutcheson admits. If the moral sense makes us approve only of actions springing from authentically altruistic motives, we should never receive approval for actions stemming from selfish ones, although these actions further the happiness of others.

The recognition that we can be motivated to act by the sense of honor and shame as well as by the moral sense is problematic for Hutcheson's theory. Hutcheson forcefully argues against Mandeville that only authentic benevolence can ensure a well-balanced society. But the concession that social harmony can ensue from selfish behavior brings

Hutcheson to a position not very dissimilar from that of Mandeville. Human beings take advantage of one·another's selfish passions in order to attain "public benefit." Hutcheson does not need the "cunning politician," for it is the reciprocal game of mirrors which human beings play for one another that does the trick. But in other respects his solution is dangerously close to that of the author of the *Fable*.

Hutcheson cannot avoid this predicament, for he has to pay this price in order to show that morality guarantees social order. It is his emphasis on the "sociological" implications of morality which shifts Hutcheson's – and our – attention from the strictly normative dynamics of his moral theory, to the descriptive account of the practical consequences of that moral theory. This entails a shift from the analysis of the phenomena relevant to an argument about the grounds of moral approval, to the analysis of the phenomena relevant to an argument about the effectiveness of ethics. If morality is socially consequential because it does ensure social welfare, then it is only by verifying whether social welfare has been attained that we can show the correctness of our assumption. But the latter operation encounters some epistemological problems, which prevent us from ever being sure that what we are observing is authentically moral conduct, rather than conduct motivated by selfish desires.

These epistemological facts – of which I shall say more in a moment – are a source of problems for Hutcheson's thought, but they are also an important symptom of the changing nature of moral discourse, and of the changing relationship between morality, legality, and politics. And it is Hutcheson's analysis of the difference between the moral and the social value of deeds that will provide the ground for the identification of a new public sphere.

The epistemological questions regard the inaccessibility of phenomena which are nonetheless central to moral evaluation. What is relevant to moral judgements is whether actions spring from benevolent motives, for we can only approve of those actions that stem from benevolence. We usually infer benevolent motives from actions that do others good, but, analytically, we should keep motives and actions distinct.

> An action is called *materially good* when in fact it tends to the interest of the system, as far as we can judge of its tendency; or to the good of some part consistent with that of the system, whatever were the affections of the agent. An action is *formally good*, when it flowed from good affections in a just proportion.... Actions materially good may flow from motives void of all virtue. And actions truly

virtuous or formally good may by accident, in the event, turn to the publick detriment.[29]

Hutcheson's distinction between formal and material aspects of actions illustrates the different points of view from which we look at moral phenomena. If we are concerned with the moral value of conduct, then intentions are indeed paramount. What makes our actions morally approvable is whether they stem from benevolent motives. But if morality is to be the pillar upon which natural sociability is built, can society work simply because people have benevolent motives? Do these infallibly produce actions maximizing the happiness of society? Can we infallibly judge intentions? By making morality so central to the proper working of social relations, Hutcheson has thus to answer some questions.[30]

The first is: can we know intentions? Hutcheson shows himself to be of two minds in this respect. Although he repeatedly contends that "we are led to approve or condemn ourselves or others according to the temper displayed," and that the moral faculty judges "all the motions of the *will*," he recognizes that "man cannot accurately judge about the degrees of virtue, or vice, in the actions of others, because their inward springs are unknown."[31] Intentions matter from an ethical point of view, but they are wholly private. How can we base the judgement of the social relevance of actions on the doer's intentions?

The second problem is that there is not a one-to-one correspondence between benevolent intentions and actions which do others good. We can cause disasters with the best intentions. In such a case, the action would be formally good, but materially damaging. If we had to infer intentions from actions with absolute certainty, all actions formally good would have to be materially good. Since this is impossible, to pass moral judgement on a person only from the result of her actions would imply that we hold her responsible for all the possible implications of her actions. Since no human being has thorough control over the chain of causes and effects, no one can be absolutely certain that an action performed with correct intentions will actually augment others' happiness. The result of our deeds cannot be the subject matter of moral evaluation – or, at least, not the only one.

> Our hearts approve us, and God promises rewards to us, not because others are in fact happy, but because we have such kind dispositions, and act our parts well in their behalf, whether in the event they are happy or not.[32]

And, third, in the same way as benevolent motives can result in harmful actions, so selfish motives can produce socially beneficial ones. The working of the sense of honor and shame shows that, out of the selfish desire for others' approval, we can be induced to perform actions that maximize welfare.

> 'Tis owned by all, that many actions, beneficial to others, may directly spring from selfish desires of rewards, of returns of good offices, of honour.... Nay, from the desire of our own happiness we may have an inward undissembled desire of another's happiness, which we conceive to be the means of our own.[33]

Since intentions are inaccessible, but the consequences of our actions are relevant to social welfare, conduct affecting society will be judged on the basis of its objective results, that is, the maximization of others' good. It becomes irrelevant to know what motivations prompt people to act. Insofar as social harmony is concerned, what counts is that the members of the group are induced to further the general welfare. Whether they do it out of genuine altruism, or out of selfishness, or some unconscious mechanism, the final result is not affected. The sense of honor and shame shows why people who are only interested in their own welfare are not harmful to society, and even benefit it: "And even men of little virtue are excited by it to such useful services as they would have otherways declined. The selfish are thus, beyond their inclination, made subservient to a publick interest; and such are punished who counteract it."[34]

The Mandevillean tone of these passages must not have escaped Hutcheson, for he tries to correct it by establishing a functional relationship between the sense of honor and shame and the moral sense. The sense of honor and shame is made a prerequisite, so to speak, for the rising of the moral sense. To understand how human nature works, Hutcheson contends, we must observe children, whose instincts and faculties are unhampered by the corrupting influence of the world. Children show from an early age that they are endowed with moral discernment, which reveals its presence in the form of the sense of honor and shame.[35] The occasion that leads to the expression of this sense is the emergence of sexual desire. Before that moment, children were innocent, because they perceived all actions as neutral and indifferent from a moral point of view.

It is not desire alone that triggers our sense of honor and shame, but the presence of other human beings – those who could satisfy our desire, and the "impartial spectators." Savages living in solitude – "in this unnatural state," according to Hutcheson – would not react to the sexual desire with the impulse to conceal it from others, and would not feel ashamed. But, once brought into society, "they would soon despise sensuality and selfishness. As soon as they knew how the race of mankind is preserved, they would desire marriage and offspring."[36] Social interaction thus becomes the occasion for the appearance of that very faculty – the moral sense – that makes us aware of the importance of benevolence as a motive for actions. And a specific type of social interaction – that leading to the satisfaction of sexual desire – starts the process through which human beings are made wholly human.

By establishing the functional interdependence between the sense of honor and shame and the moral sense Hutcheson emphasizes the continuity between psychological experience shaped by interaction, and moral evaluation of that experience. The story runs more or less as follows. The sense of honor and shame alerts us to the reaction which our actions provoke in others. We realize that we enjoy being approved, and dislike being disapproved. Out of the selfish desire for pleasure, we may thus decide to behave in such a way that can receive approval. But we also learn that if we listen to authentically altruistic motivations, we can experience pleasure out of the contemplation of those motives. That pleasure is much higher than any other, and feeling it makes us happy. We are thus induced to cultivate our moral sense, which, in turn, will induce us to enhance our capacity for feeling, and acting out of, benevolence. We shall also receive approval from others, because our benevolence will awaken their moral sense, and will prompt them to look favorably upon us.

This approach may explain how the individual engaged in analyzing his motivations can interpret the relationship between his selfish desire for approval prompted by the sense of honor and shame, and his altruistic affection of benevolence. But it does not help us to understand whether others act out of selfish or altruistic motives. There remains the possibility that we approve of others simply because they conform to our expectations: they have furthered social welfare, and this is what matters. But more interestingly, if we consider morality from the point of view of its effectiveness, we can ask: does it matter whether intentions are approvable or not? If we wish to attain social order, do actions have to be authentically moral? Or are we not more concerned with outcomes?

The epistemological problem of the knowability of intentions can thus lead one to adopt two solutions. The first emphasizes the continuity between psychology and morality, and their implications for social order, that is, in Hutcheson's language and framework, for legality and politics. In describing a condition of natural sociability, Hutcheson describes a state of nature: human relations not yet coordinated by a centralized political authority are regulated by a network of reciprocal rights and duties[37] which can generate claims and grievances, and require sanctions and redress.[38] Political institutions are, in classical Natural Law fashion, the answer to the growing uncertainties of the natural condition.

The second solution emphasizes the discontinuities between moral philosophy and social theory, and it leads Hutcheson, who pursues it alongside the first one, to inquire into the grounds of distinction between morality, legality, and politics. Hutcheson plays a very important role in conceptualizing the differences among these three ways of thinking about social practices. In particular, he carves a juridical space and mode in between morality and politics. This juridical mode lies not only rhetorically between the other two. It participates in both, for Hutcheson's view of the continuities between aspects of human experience prevents him from carrying the analysis of the discontinuities to its logical conclusion. In other words, from our point of view Hutcheson has "failed" to articulate fully the distinction between morality, legality, and politics. But if we consider it from another point of view, this "failure" means that Hutcheson has juxtaposed and intertwined the two motives, rather than opting for one over the other. It is this hesitation that provides us with interesting insights into the dynamics of a new public agency and public domain.

MORALITY, LEGALITY, AND POLITICS

Hutcheson sees important continuities between psychological experience shaped by interaction, moral evaluation of that experience, and juridical implications of those evaluations. As usual, Hutcheson faces two tasks. The first is to inquire into the nature of rights and obligations, and the second is to show the effectiveness of juridical norms in a pre-political state of nature. The moral sense gives us both notions of good and evil, and of right and wrong. There is no substantive difference between good and right, evil and wrong. But in speaking of good and evil we inquire into the supreme end of our conduct (and the one we should foremost avoid). In speaking of right and wrong, we specify what actions and intentions conform to that end.

> From the constitution of our *moral faculty*, above-explained, we have our notions of *right,* and *wrong,* as characters of affections and actions. The affections approved as right, are either universal good-will and love of moral excellence, or such particular kind affections

as are consistent with these. The actions approved as *right,* are such
as are wisely intended either for the general good, or such good of
some particular society or individual as is consistent with it. The
contrary affections and actions are *wrong.*[39]

"Right" and "wrong" can here be taken as the juridical counter-
parts to the ethical notions of "morally approvable," and "morally
disapprovable." In offering this definition, Hutcheson appears to have
looked at juridical phenomena from the point of view of an objective
theory of *jus.* But if we look at juridical phenomena from a subjective
perspective, we can see that "to have a right" to "x" or to do "x," is
not the same as to conform to what is good. We have rights to things, or
to do things which are simply "not bad." They are innocent, or
indifferent things and actions.

> Our notion of *right* as a moral quality competent to some person, as
> when we say one has a *right* to such things, is a much more complex
> conception. Whatever action we would deem either as virtuous or
> innocent were it done by the agent in certain circumstances, we say
> he has a *right* to do it. Whatever one so possesses and enjoys in
> certain circumstances, that we would deem it a wrong action in any
> other to disturb or interrupt his possession, we say 'tis *his right*, or
> he has a *right* to enjoy and possess it. Whatever demand one has upon
> another in such circumstances that we would deem it wrong conduct
> in that other not to comply with it, we say one has a *right* to what is
> thus demanded.[40]

Subjective rights are thus defined from the perspective of the individual
who wishes to know what she can and may do to further her happiness.
The set of individual legitimate claims does not merely include the
class of all that is conducive to the general welfare translated into
subjective terms. It includes claims to things and activities which are
innocent and therefore morally neutral from a social viewpoint, but
generate in others the obligation not to impair the exercise of those
rights. Indeed, we have an obligation to allow others to act upon them,
and to disregard that obligation is morally disapprovable.[41] According
to Hutcheson the term right thus denotes: a) a moral quality; b) the
competence to do something which is virtuous or innocent; c) the
entitlement to possession; and d) the reciprocal of a corresponding
duty.[42]

The emphasis on the subjective side of the theory of rights has led
Hutcheson to identify a set of phenomena which become morally and
juridically relevant only because the individual attaches value to

them.[43] There are thus two definitions of good and right. A positive one: good or right is what is conducive to universal well-being. And a negative one: good or right is what others have an obligation not to hinder. Individuals can value things and activities which are in themselves neither right nor wrong. But once an individual has claimed a right to "x," that claim has generated a new moral value. This does not reflect the moral value of "x" – after all, "x" is innocent or indifferent – but the moral value of having made a legitimate claim. This appears to be confirmed by the fact that that claim has generated in others an obligation to allow us to pursue "x," which cannot be disregarded without causing moral disapproval.

Since rights of individuals are not merely translations into subjective terms of what is objectively good, there may arise a tension between the two goals which society must attain: the good of the greatest numbers, and individual happiness. Individuals may decide to engage in activities which are not conducive to social welfare, even if they do not damage it.[44] Hutcheson does not directly explore the implications of this hypothesis. But he inquires into the broader issue of the relationship between individual and collective happiness. He relies on a cornerstone of his moral theory: the person is truly happy when she is benevolent. She discovers that maximizing social welfare makes her feel the highest pleasure of which she is capable. She will thus be inclined to claim as her right the pursuit of activities that maximize her own and the collective welfare at the same time. Hutcheson asserts that

> the *moral faculty* most approves and recommends such dispositions as tend most to the general good, and at the same time such as may give the noblest enjoyment to the agent upon reflection. And thus the two *grand determinations* of our nature, by a thorough examination of our constitution, may appear perfectly consistent, and be generally gratified by the same means.[45]

The criterion to order axiologically all sources of pleasure is that "the chief happiness of any being must consist in the full enjoyment of all gratifications its nature desires and is capable of."[46] Human beings strive for their perfection, and enjoy the expression of their higher capacities, the highest among them being the moral one. Although the individual is entitled to choose things and activities that may be neither conducive nor detrimental to social welfare, a proper assessment of what happiness really is will induce him to give priority to what is beneficial to all.

This attempt to join a concern for the welfare of society as a whole to a subjective theory of rights emphasizes the holistic bent of Hutcheson's political philosophy. We are happy when we exercise our highest faculties; and we do this when we "desire the greatest happiness and perfection of the largest system within the compass of [our] knowledge."[47] This formulation is the most direct expression of Hutcheson's leaning toward classical republicanism. But this conception is not merely a reformulation of the classical republican notion that the individual can only find happiness through the community. The subjective theory of rights casts a new light on that classical tenet. In particular, it establishes a reciprocal dependence between individual and collective happiness which was unknown even to the Aristotelian version of the nature and source of *eudaimonia*. The individual is happy when he recognizes that furthering the welfare of others allows him to express his higher faculties. But the welfare of society is ensured only if the individual claims that he has a right to pursue his personal happiness, even if the latter consists of doing the good of others.

The definition of the general well-being as the "greatest happiness of the greatest numbers" shows that Hutcheson may be moving even further away from classical republicanism. Can we take the arithmetical expression to be just a different and enticing formulation of the classical notion of the "common good"? Or should we take it at face value? If we do the latter, we may conclude that the reciprocal dependence between individual and collective welfare has led Hutcheson to interpret the latter in aggregative as well as holistic terms.

> In comparing the *moral Qualitys* of Actions, in order to regulate our Election among various Actions propos'd, or to find which of them has the greatest *moral Excellency*, we are led by *our moral Sense* of *Virtue* thus to judge, that in *equal Degrees* of Happiness, expected to proceed from the Action, the *Virtue* is in proportion to the *Number* of Persons to whom the Happiness shall extend: And here the *Dignity,* or *moral Importance* of Persons, may compensate Numbers; and in equal *Numbers,* the *Virtue* is as the *Quantity* of the Happiness, or natural Good; or that the *Virtue* is in a *compound Ratio* of the *Quantity* of Good, and *Number* of Enjoyers: And in the same manner, the *moral Evil,* or *Vice,* is as the *Degree* of Misery, and *Number* of Sufferers; so that, *that Action is best*, which accomplishes the *greatest Happiness* for the *greatest Numbers*; and *that, worst*, which, in *like manner*, occasions *Misery.*[48]

We can harmonize the aggregative and holistic definitions of the common good if we remember that individual happiness coincides with the condition in which the person has elected the welfare of others as the main aim of her activities. The happiness of the greatest numbers is ultimately the sum-total of conditions of happiness of individuals who give priority to their benevolent affections. Hutcheson can thus conclude:

> The grounds of suspecting a great opposition between one's private interest and the indulging of the social affections in all generous office of virtue, may be pretty well removed by what is already said of the high enjoyments of the sympathetick and moral kinds .... There is a natural subserviency of the private or selfish affections, while they are kept within certain bounds, not only to the good of the individual, but to that of the system; nor is any one compleat in his kind without them. And as the happiness of a system results from that of the individuals, 'tis necessary to it, that each one have the selfish affections in that degree which his best state requires, consistently with his most effectual services to the publick.[49]

The happiness of the individual – considered in both its selfish and altruistic dimensions – is the ground upon which valid claims are articulated, as perfect (and imperfect) personal rights. The protection of perfect rights becomes the first duty of other human beings and society itself. But in protecting these rights, society also protects the human capacity to care for the good of others. Hutcheson thus articulates even the balance between individual and collective happiness through the subjective theory of rights. Perfect rights include: life, a good name, the integrity of one's body, the acquisitions of one's industry, freedom (within the limits of the law of nature), freedom of conscience, and of marriage; but also the right to sacrifice one's own life for the good of others.[50]

The discovery of moral principles and their juridical implications does not require the initiative and direction of political rulers. The condition in which individuals learn to use and to refine their moral sense, and to interpret its injunctions in terms of rights and duties, is a state of nature. It is a state of liberty, without any common superior, where we are "obliged by the natural feelings of our hearts, and by many tender affections, to innocence and beneficence toward all.... 'Tis no fictitious state; it always existed and must exist among men, unless the whole earth should become one empire."[51] In his account, Hutcheson moves back and forth between the moral and juridical aspects of human conduct. Since what we perceive as morally good also leads to our perception of right and wrong, the "natural feelings of our hearts and tender affections" make us infer the specific rights to be recognized to each individual, in accordance with the law of nature. Natural sociability implies that our interaction with others is shaped by the recognition that we all have by nature certain rights and the corresponding duties. The state of nature is thus a condition of perfect reciprocity. "The *natural equality of men* consists chiefly in this, that these natural rights belong equally to all: this is the thing intended by the natural equality, let the term be proper or improper."[52]

According to Hutcheson, natural equality carries two fundamental implications. The first is that "no endowments, natural or acquired, can give a perfect right to assume power over another, without their consent." And the second is that all share the same right to dispose of their natural liberty and powers, in order to create real or personal adventitious rights,[53] that is, to modify their natural state. Hutcheson thus makes the twofold aspect of natural equality apparent. Equality means first of all civil equality: all are entitled to the use of their natural faculties, nobody excluded. Equality also means political equality, at least in the negative sense: no one has by nature a "perfect" right over someone else. In recognizing to individuals the capacity for the creation of adventitious rights and duties, Hutcheson accepts that we also have a right to curtail our natural liberty.[54]

In describing the family, Hutcheson intertwines all these elements. The family is the first and most important adventitious society, that is, it is an association voluntarily set up by man and woman with the purpose of reproducing the species. It is also the association in which natural feelings of affection are stronger than in any other group, and where natural good and moral good are nearly indistinguishable. Since love for spouse and children enhances the human capacity for compliance with moral obligations, coercion appears scarcely needed to regulate familial relations. Hutcheson makes this explicit in a passage critical of polygamy:

And hence we see in fact that where this practice prevails, the women are every way treated as slaves: no friendly regards had to their satisfactions; chains, and prisons, and guards must confine them, and not the bonds of love and friendship.[55]

By contending that man and wife can comply with the duties of their states, Hutcheson can depict a fairly egalitarian marriage. If each person spontaneously fulfills his/her natural obligations, why should power be assigned to one of the two? Hutcheson solves Locke's problem of how to harmonize potentially conflicting wills, by resorting to the human benevolence.

Hutcheson's egalitarian view of conjugal relations shows in his treatment of sexual mores. He condemns the double standard, and he asserts that rights and duties of the spouses are reciprocal: "Nature has designed the conjugal state to be a constant reciprocal friendship of two."[56] Hutcheson remarks on the injustice of prevailing practices, which burden the wife more than the husband. The wife can ask for a divorce, she retains control over her private property, she has, by nature, an equal share in the authority over children, and her husband must be faithful to her as much as she to him. And, as soon as serious disagreement occurs, the only acceptable solution is the intervention of an arbitrator. Hutcheson goes so far as to contend that the adminis-tration of the domestic patrimony ought not to be wholly entrusted to the husband, but managed jointly by him and the wife. Hutcheson seems unconcerned that the egalitarian marriage may endanger the stability of the family – one of the reasons that had induced Locke to assign authority to the man. After all, the "bonds of love and friend-ship" are chains strong enough to save the family from internal dissolution.

If the family well illustrates the dynamics of natural sociability and their egalitarian underpinnings, it also illustrates the limits of Hutche-son's egalitarianism, and how individual happiness can be subordinated to the good of the group. Although the family need not be hierarchical, Hutcheson accepts the male-centered type which has developed through-out history. The attribution of superior power to the male head is the doing of civil society. Hutcheson offers no justification for it. Positive laws have introduced an asymmetry where nature established none. This inegalitarian arrangement can even be imposed on the woman as what maximizes the welfare of the family rather than her own. By relying on her benevolence, and on her capacity to transfer part of her natural liberty through a contract, the inegalitarian family will once again be "legitimated."

Hutcheson's acceptance of the male-centered Western family should not lead us to ignore that in his account domestic society is losing its monolithic aspect. The household – which technically comprises husband/wife, parent/child, and master/servant relations – breaks down into its component parts: kinship and labor relations. The moral charge of strong emotional interaction of course holds true for those united by blood and kinship, which we now identify with the nuclear family. Husband and wife, and parent and child, are united by strong instinctual bonds. Erotic and affective dynamics explain and justify the existence of a highly cohesive group, but they also set the group against all other types of interaction which human beings may have, even within domestic society. Masters and servants living together may continue to develop attachments, sometimes strong ones, to each other. But emotional ties cannot account for their relationship, which is defined by the exchange of service for wages. A contract[57] regulates this exchange, which does not grant the master any power over the servant, but only power over his labor.[58] And a different transaction is required if the servant chooses to become a member of the master's house.

Hutcheson's concern with the moral and psychological aspect of social dynamics leads him to emphasize the specificity of each relationship, and to minimize the role which power plays in the regulation of social relations. Locke saw conflict as scarcely significant within the walls of the house, but he openly upheld a non-egalitarian view of domestic relations. Hutcheson barely mentions the possibility of conflict, and opts for a more egalitarian approach to interpersonal relations, for he contends that morally shaped interaction guarantees harmony better than coercion.[59] In other words, Hutcheson has begun the analytical process of differentiation of social relations, which will later become the focus of sociological thought.

The second reason why domestic society tends to dissolve, as a social group and a juridical subject, is the recognition of juridical autonomy to all individuals composing it. Hutcheson accepts the universalistic assumptions of Natural Law theory, and asserts them vigorously. A social universe not yet regulated by political rules is the outcome of discrete choices and actions. Civil equality is the juridical counterpart of a shared moral sensitivity.[60] Hutcheson rejects the double standard in sexual matters on the ground that the moral sense is the same in all human beings. If we accept this tenet, we must also accept that individuals should all react in the same way when a similar moral problem arises, and they should equally curb the instincts that violate the principle of natural sociability. And since they are all equal from a juridical point of view, they are entitled to the same treatment in similar matters; when they commit a crime against the laws regulating sexual matters, for example, they should all be treated with uniform severity.[61]

Hutcheson's detailed account of psychological, moral, and juridical dynamics allows him to assert that human beings are naturally fit for a society distinct from a political union. Social relations, especially marriage and family, spring from immediate instincts, while political institutions are not something immediately desired. Why does political society come into life at all? Why do human beings abandon a state of liberty and peace, sufficiently regulated by their natural capacity for assuming natural obligations and for expanding them, through the creation of adventitious rights? Hutcheson resorts to concrete examples of stateless societies in order to prove natural sociability. His emphasis on this point lends new weight to the question: when does the state

130   *Private and Public*

come about? If the state is no longer the prerequisite of life in society, the institution of political power must be justified otherwise. In order to answer these questions, Hutcheson resorts to the classical argument of Natural Law writers that human beings decide to abandon the state of nature when inconveniences and dangers become acute, but he offers a revised interpretation of it.

Hutcheson combines the effects of historical change and human failure in implementing benevolence. Historically, people found the state of anarchy tolerable "while simplicity of manners continued, but when corruptions encreased they found it necessary to contrive civil polity."[62] And morally, the problem arises from human beings' limited capacity to comply with their duties.

> If all mankind were perfectly wise and good, discerning all the proper means of promoting the general happiness of their race, and inclined to concur in them, nothing further would be wanting; no other obligations or bonds than those of their own virtue and wisdom.[63]

But why do human beings, who have shown themselves able to accept those bonds in so many ways, become incapable of doing so? What is the nexus between corruption and a decline in morality? If the latter is the cause of the former, how can we account for this degeneration?

The moral sense performs its function at its best when it makes the individual sensitive to the happiness of the largest possible number. It is easy to be benevolent with those close to us, especially when connected by ties of blood. Benevolence extends concentrically from smaller to larger groups. But the further we move from the individual and the larger the group becomes, the harder it becomes for the moral sense to exercise its influence on the person. Closer relationships in fact have a stronger and more violent effect than more distant ones. Even when driven by generous motives, human beings can fail to comply with their duties because they do not realize that the good of the larger community, although felt more weakly, must be preferred to the good of the smaller one.[64] When we prefer the good of those dear to us to that of the larger society, we have become "corrupt," even if we do not behave selfishly. When growth and refinement replace the simplicity of manners typical of small and poor societies, the mechanisms of adjustment between selfishness, limited generosity, and universal benevolence break down, and the introduction of political authority becomes inevitable.

Hutcheson's account of the foundation of political society shows the insufficiency of a purely ethical account of social relations, as well as the limits of his egalitarianism.

The dissolution of the household as a juridical entity embodied in the adult male occurs only at the level of social relations. All are endowed with independent juridical personalities, but only insofar as action in the non-political realm is concerned. When we deal with matters political, domestic society is resurrected. Hutcheson has hinted at the possibility that the woman renounced her rights in favor of the husband, and this arrangement turns out to be the most common. Hutcheson depicts a state of nature composed of independent households which, through their heads, incorporate in a body politic. Heads of households *de facto* exercised the power of life and death before the state was instituted,[65] and they were therefore the only ones entitled to institute political authority. Nonetheless, Hutcheson is induced by his individualistic assumptions to account for the supposed consent which all family members gave to the institution of the political ruler.

> The parent in uniting with others in this political body stipulates protection, and the advantages of a civilized life, not only for himself but for his family, and this in any tolerably constituted states is a *negotium utile gestum*, or a transaction most beneficial for them.[66]

The distinction between fully and partially autonomous agents is juridically so relevant that Hutcheson classifies the members of civil society as either citizens or subjects, depending on whether they have a direct or a mediated relationship with the holders of political authority. At the end of the century, Kant will express the same distinction by adopting the even more explicit labels of active and passive citizenship.[67]

A NEW PUBLIC

Hutcheson's conception of morality is also the foundation of his view of legality. Both moral and juridical notions are expressions of our perception of what the good is, and of what is conducive to its realization. But the interpretation of human deeds and motives through a juridical rather than moral framework defines a specific set of phenomena as being relevant to juridical questions. Not all that is morally relevant can be translated into rights and duties: we do not have any legal obligation to have approvable intentions. Not all that is juridically relevant stems from what is morally approvable: we have an obligation to allow others to pursue activities which are morally innocent. Not all that is morally relevant can become the source of a claim to a perfect right: we have a moral, but not a legal, obligation to charity. At a more general level, we can say that a juridical framework reifies, as it were, features of deeds and relations to objects which are, from an ethical point of view, purely abstract normative qualifications of those deeds and relations. Rights and duties can be institutionalized, or made the objects of transactions and negotiations. In particular, (perfect) rights and duties can and must be enforced. I owe money to a friend: my natural benevolence prompts me to return it, and I experience a feeling of moral approval for my action.[68] If I do not comply with my duty, I may experience moral disapproval, and maybe even social rejection, but nothing more. But if I think of the same situation in juridical terms, the friend has a perfect right to be repaid, and I have an obligation to repay the loan. Compliance with that obligation can be forced upon me, by another person in the state of nature, or by the magistrate in civil society.

The juridical interpretation of phenomena is thus a two-faced enterprise. It looks at morality for its foundations, and at politics for its implementation. However, for Hutcheson legality does not merely lie in between the other two, but it participates in both. To think in juridical terms means to use one's moral capacity to identify rights and duties. And to act as a juridically minded person means to enforce the respect for those rights.

What makes Hutcheson's conception of legality of particular interest to this essay is the fact that it contains a new version of the distinction between private and public. This new version is constructed around the notion that every adult's capacity for moral evaluation enables her to be a legal and political agent as well. As in Locke, moral/juridical agency has a private and a public side. As we can assess the moral and legal consequences of choices regarding our private lives, so we can assess their consequences for society as a whole. Public agency of a kind is the inevitable complement of a theory that empowers individuals at the personal level.

Two conceptions of the distinction between private and public and of personal agency are present in Hutcheson's work. The first basically reproduces the Lockean one. The distinction between private and public regards two jurisdictions. Hutcheson holds that all adults are competent to perform the actions through which they give life to social institutions. All are endowed with the same perfect rights, all can enrich their set of natural rights with adventitious ones, as they can curtail them by transferring part of their liberty to another.[69] The private domain of each adult therefore includes the capacities that allow her to function as an autonomous agent in the social realm, and the personal and external possessions acquired through voluntary transactions. But not all adults enjoy the correspondent political agency, although in the state of nature everyone can supposedly exercise the power of life and death. Women and servants delegate this function to heads of households, and only the latter institute political authority. Domestic society reappears as a juridical unit, represented by its head, and incorporating dependents who have lost their full independence.

This conception is well illustrated by one of Hutcheson's classifications of phenomena to which the laws of nature apply. It is offered in *A Short Introduction to Moral Philosophy*, in which Hutcheson distinguishes between private rights, rights of economics, and rights of politics. Private rights regard each individual in the state of natural liberty. Rights of economics refer to domestic society. Rights of politics refer to the government and its possible forms.[70] This triad summarizes the conception of agency elaborated by Natural Law theorists and shared by Hutcheson. There is a condition of natural liberty in which all are equal; adults are entitled to dispose of their endowments as they think fit, including the partial transference of independence; and those who are fully autonomous are active political agents. Although Hutcheson's classification does not reproduce Pufendorf's two-staged state of nature, the implications are the same.

However, in the same work Hutcheson proposes a second classification: there are rights of persons (or private), of societies and corporations (or public), and of mankind (or common to all).[71] Rights of persons concern each individual; rights of societies and corporations concern all possible associations, political and not; and rights of mankind concern all human beings conceived as a totality without any institutional embodiment.[72] The two classifications do not coincide, and the difference is not irrelevant, for the latter points to the second conception of the distinction between private and public at which I have hinted above.

Rights of persons are, as seen, those accruing to individuals in the state of nature, abstracting from any social interaction. Rights are translations into juridical language of morally perceived notions of good (and evil). As these perceptions are innate in each individual, so is the notion of right.

Indeed in many objects of our desires, this consistency [of desires with higher principles] is so obvious, or there is so little presumption of any opposition, that we are convinced of our right to them at once without much reflection or more extensive interests; nay in many cases we seem to have an immediate sense of right along with the natural desire.[73]

Every adult has these perceptions, and operates accordingly, for everyone is a moral agent, including slaves.[74] Since juridical principles are inferred from moral evaluations, Hutcheson's universalistic moral individualism has direct juridical implications: every adult is a subject of rights. Rights include, as they always do in seventeenth-century Natural Law theory, both the capacity for claiming and enforcing them, and the endowments that can become the objects of transactions with others. Each person's private domain comprises all that each person does with what is her own, without harming others. The private domain expands to include all relationships and possessions that are consensually established or acquired. But, strictly speaking, the private domain coincides with the person herself and her original set of rights, for every transaction may result in a threat to the safe enjoyment of each individual's rights.

If the enforcement or defense of one's rights characterizes public activity, the public domain corresponding to this narrowed private sphere potentially includes all relational activities in which the person chooses to engage. This is confirmed by Hutcheson's notion of harm, which is much broader than Locke's. Perfect rights include very immaterial things – reputation, right to marry the person of choice, etc. – which supposedly make up each person's happiness. One can affect others in ways that require protection much more easily than Locke had supposed.

But this is not the only implication of granting a personal domain to each adult. This personal domain is centered around a capacity for moral evaluations, and their articulation in juridical terms. In performing this operation, individuals engage in a complex activity: they recognize what they can claim as perfect rights, by evaluating the compatibility of those claims with general welfare. Thus, even in the state of nature, human beings recognize that they have an obligation to further the good of others while pursuing their personal interests. According to Hutcheson, a condition of institutional anarchy does not entail the absence of the "public sense." Historically, this has meant that human beings have been able to maximize the good of more or less large societies – families, small communities, etc. – which have not yet attained political incorporation. But behind the historical – or sociological – exemplification, there lies a more interesting analytical point.

Human beings' correct choices in relating to others are those that are guided by the criterion of maximizing the general welfare. As in Locke, there exists a "public" which does not coincide with the political institutions of civil society. But Hutcheson goes much further than Locke in conceptualizing the features of this new public. He calls it "mankind as a system," and he contends that rights can be predicated of it as of natural persons. Through this abstraction, which has no institutional embodiment, humankind is seen as an aggregate, endowed with perfect rights.[75] But rights against whom, if all are members of it? Against each person, considered separately from it, and potentially in conflict with it.[76] Hutcheson also calls this abstraction "the publick," and the label is not merely rhetorical. We can recognize in it a new species of public person, and public domain. It is a public person, for Hutcheson presents it as capable of holding rights, and making demands on its members. It is a public domain, because all are members of it, because it collects what human beings share in common, and because individuals express in it a new kind of political virtue.

"Mankind as a system" has no institutional personification. It is the name with which Hutcheson identifies the abstract connection of each individual with all other members of the species. Although "mankind as a system" is an abstraction, its role as the regulator of human conduct is very concrete.[77] By assigning perfect rights to it, Hutcheson implicitly accepts that those rights can be enforced. This means that, after political society has been instituted, the state will be responsible for imposing compliance. But what happens in the state of nature, where no political institution exists? Arguably, each individual, enabled by his moral sense to identify those rights, can enforce them. This ensures that the state of nature is not a state of war. Hutcheson insists on this point especially in relation to the right of punishing transgressors:

> 'Tis also the right and duty of the system which each one should execute as he has opportunity, to assist the innocent against unjust violence, to repel the invader, to obtain compensation of damage done, and security against like attempts for the future.... This is the foundation of the right of punishing, which, as we said above, men have in natural liberty, as well as in civil polity.[78]

When someone encroaches upon the perfect rights of humankind, someone else is entitled to punish him. If it is clear how this works in relation to the violation of the perfect rights of an individual, what does it mean to impose compliance of norms that are only significant for the community, in a situation in which there is no community and no public institution? Does each individual become the interpreter and defender of the abstraction called "humankind" and its rights? It is not surprising that Hutcheson does not explain in detail what he means by assigning enforceable rights of humanity in the state of nature, because it is difficult to see how his principle could inform actual interaction.

What is important in this description is that human beings can identify an abstract collective subject out of their experience of discrete social relationships. "Mankind as a system" is a notion which plays a normative function in guiding individual conduct. It helps each adult to choose the behavior that is compatible with the welfare of all human beings, rather than granting her the right to act against those who do not comply with those norms. In fact, Hutcheson presents the rights of humankind as duties of individuals. These duties differ from the duties which each one has toward one's fellows in that there is no specific recipient of them. No natural or artificial person can claim the right corresponding to the duty. Since complying with those duties will lead to greater social welfare, the beneficiary will be society itself, and the individual who behaves responsibly, as a member of that society.

"Mankind as a system" is thus an abstraction from a sociological as well as a juridical point of view. It is a notion which expresses the outcome of the process whereby individuals understand that the happiness of the greatest number is the highest ethical value. It is a name given to the awareness that there is no individual happiness without social welfare. Hutcheson even hypothesizes a "public sense," which gives us our "determination to be pleased with the *Happiness* of others."[79]

The most interesting feature of this new public is that individuals practice in it a new kind of political virtue. Both the adjective and the noun are crucial. "Virtue" points to the ethical foundation of Hutcheson's conception of agency: human beings are virtuous when they act out of benevolence. "Political" points to the fact that by being virtuous human beings here do not only strive to act out of intentions which are morally approvable, but they try to do what is conducive to the welfare of all, to recognize the juridical implications of that choice, and to accept the enforcement of the rights and duties ensuing from it. This activity is political in both its effects and dynamics. In its effects, because in practicing it individuals make personal choices which have implications for all the members of the group, and, in principle, the species. And in its dynamics, because it entails participation of a kind in the interpretation of the norms that ensure the integration of the group.

The ground for universal participation in the interpretation of norms lies in Hutcheson's individualistic assumptions. These are relevant from a psychological/moral and a juridical/political point of view. At the psychological/ethical level, the process of refinement of the moral sense can only occur within each individual's psyche. Hutcheson's rooting the apprehension of moral values in sense implies that there exists no deduction of moral principles from reason. Feelings of pleasure and pain are private, and therefore, by definition, subjective. Whether they are the same in different human beings is contingent, not necessary. We can assert that there exist shared criteria to evaluate actions only if we have empirically verified the overlapping of individual emotional/sensory responses.

However, this psychological/ethical individualism does not in itself justify the assertion that human beings must all participate in verifying whether they hold the same moral principles, with their juridical and political implications. As the later development of classical utilitarianism shows, if we verify that statistically human beings do operate in a similar fashion, we can then impute to all the "proper" sensory response, and extrapolate a sensory criterion, which is however universally valid. This solution is already present in Hutcheson. He assumes the uniformity of human nature, which allows him to impute to individuals uniformity of sensory responses to stimuli. He then verifies this assumption by analyzing actual behavior. The "sociological" side of Hutcheson's social theory thus plays the role of confirming that human nature does indeed function homogeneously, thus allowing us to extrapolate universally valid principles of moral good and evil.[80]

But unlike classical utilitarians, Hutcheson combines his psychology of morals with a subjective theory of rights. Individuals are sources of valid claims, which the community must respect and enforce. Social welfare is thus not merely the common good, as in the republican tradition. And it is not the maximum level of pleasure attainable, measured by compounding the total level of pleasure and pain in all members of society considered as an aggregate, as classical utilitarianism maintains. Social welfare is ensured when every individual's self-defined balance between pleasure and pain is positive, rather than negative. The calculation is made at the individual, not directly at the aggregate, level. Thus, if the main motivational force in human actions must be benevolence, every individual must have developed a moral sense which tells him that the greatest source of personal happiness is contemplating actions done for the good of others. But translated into the language of rights, this means that each person will assert her right to do what is conducive to her welfare – even if this turns out to be performing actions which spring from benevolent motives. This complex operation cannot be replaced by the paternalistic imposition on each human being of the task to attain general welfare, with the argument that ultimately that will be the source of individual happiness. Happiness derives from contemplating the proper motivation. And motivations, as Hutcheson repeats over and over again, cannot be raised at will. Only the individual can cultivate his moral sense so that benevolence will become his basic motive for acting.

Last but not least, each of us can make valid claims to the pursuit of innocent things and activities. Those claims must be compatible with the principle of maximization of general welfare, but they must not necessarily be conducive to the good of others. There is a gray area, between what is good for the individual, but detrimental to society, and what is good for the individual because it is the individualized side of social good. This gray area is that of the pursuit of innocent things or activities – what classical moral theory would have called things indifferent. As morally neutral, those things and activities do not engender any corresponding duty or obligation. But our right to pursue them does generate an obligation in others to allow us to pursue them. The individual is thus a spring of claims which generate the corresponding obligations because the person has attached values to things indifferent.

Each individual engages in all these activities in deciding the legitimacy of his course of action, thus acting in both his private and his public capacity. It is when confronted with the question: is my choice compatible with, or conducive to, the general welfare? that the person both asserts her rights, and evaluates the implications of that assertion for others. But the process of interpreting whether I am performing the correct action is not merely decentralized, as in Locke's state of nature. It is also shared with others, for it is social interaction that enables us to perform that activity in all its aspects. In particular, social interaction shapes the human capacity for proper moral responses, and therefore, indirectly, for the assessment of their juridical and political implications. And it also shapes what specific content the principle of the maximization of the general welfare will have in a concrete historical setting. Hutcheson in fact contends that

the laws of nature are inferences we make, by reflecting upon our inward constitution, and by reasoning upon human affairs, concerning that conduct which our hearts naturally must approve, as tending either to the general good, or to that of individuals consistently with it. These inferences we express in general precepts: They are discovered by us sometimes immediately, sometimes by induction, when we see what conduct ordinarily tends to good. Now 'tis impossible for us to have all possible cases and circumstances in view, so that we could discern that the inference holds in them all. We form our general rule or precept from what we see tends to good in all ordinary cases. But should we see that in some rarer cases a different conduct would in the whole of its effects do greater good than the following the ordinary rule in these cases also, we then have as good a law of nature perceptive or permissive to recede from the ordinary rule in those rarer cases, as we have to follow it in ordinary cases. These exceptions are parts of the law, as well as the general rule.[81]

Social interaction is essential to awaken our moral sense. This cannot be manipulated or twisted, but it can be stimulated and refined. As the example of the savage brought into society illustrates, without interaction the individual would remain unaware of the ethical import of his motivations. True human nature is for Hutcheson socialized nature. We learn the moral value of our actions from the response which we obtain from our fellows. Approval or disapproval excites first of all the sense of honor and shame, and this in turn excites the moral sense.

The sense of honor and shame is the structural psychological trait that makes us desire the approval of others. It is the selfish principle which induces us to behave so that others can give their approval. By making us sensitive to the reactions which we trigger in others, the sense of honor and shame alerts us to the moral value of our actions. If we do something which others deem a violation of their rights, we shall receive disapproval. Hutcheson calls the sense of honor and shame a "social" feeling, which makes us desire excellence in a public spirit.

The role attributed by Hutcheson to interaction may raise questions about the consistency of his anti-Mandevillean polemic. If we depend on social approval in order to learn to behave in a morally approvable way, what ensures that we receive approval because our motivations are the correct ones, and not because we have benefited others, out of selfish motives? In principle, others should approve us only when they have received a benefit which has made them feel moral pleasure. But we know from Hutcheson himself that others cannot always recognize what intentions we had when acting; and that society is more concerned with the result than with the intention of the doer. We may receive approval because we have obtained good results, independently of our intentions. And those who have benefited from our deeds may be happy because we have satisfied their desire for natural, rather than moral pleasure.[82] We may thus be approved simply because we have benefited others, even if our intentions were selfish, and even if we have satisfied the selfish desires of others. Society can thus play on selfish desires to make us do what increases the natural good of all. As in Mandeville, a set of pseudo-moral norms can thus be brought into being, through the interaction of individuals who react to being approved or censored by their fellows out of a selfish desire for a natural pleasure.

But even if we accept Hutcheson's contention that actions which spring from benevolence will raise in spectators a specific type of pleasure, which alerts them to the fact that the action is formally, not only materially, good, interaction remains crucial. For the dynamic of approval and disapproval is indispensable for attuning the individual to the moral value of his actions. Interaction is also indispensable to enable us to learn what we must do to make others happy at a specific time and place. Once again, the gap between intentions and their consequences is crucial. We may live in a society which sees common property as conducive to general welfare. If we are not aware of this fact, our benevolent intentions may lead us to consider certain things as the private property of some members, to deem a crime the appropriation of those items by another, and rush to the help of the seemingly injured person. It is only interaction which can tell us what is materially comprised in the general welfare of that society.

The interpretation of the general laws of nature, which allows human beings to live in peace before "mankind as a system" incorporates as a body politic, is thus both decentralized and socialized in Hutcheson's account of juridical agency. Each adult can and must assess the general implications of his choices for the public at large, for only the personal and voluntary compliance with norms can ensure peaceful social relations. Since the dynamics of refinement of the moral sense are individual in nature and operation, social interaction is essential to coordinate individual evaluations and choices. To compare the effects which our actions have on others, and consequently, whether the norms which we employ are intersubjectively valid, is constitutive of the applicability of those norms. Only others' reactions of approval or disapproval can tell us whether we have done what promotes their welfare and happiness. Participation in this activity of intersubjective comparison enables us to assign a specific content to be assigned to the principle establishing the maximization of the general welfare.

I have presented this complex activity as a form of political virtue, and the core of a new public domain. It is an abstract public, for it only lives in people's minds when they think of their connection to a wide human community. But it bears all the features of a public domain, because all, as moral agents, can participate in it; because it is concerned with issues which regard all; because it develops norms binding all; and because it aims at ensuring the cohesion and integration of the "system." And in thinking of herself as being connected to others of the same species through a network of mutual rights and obligations, each person does think of society as a non-institutionalized artificial person, integrated by shared values and norms.

But I should not feel entitled to label the participation in the elaboration of specific norms as a political activity if that elaboration were to remain merely ethical. It is its juridical aspect that enables me to qualify Hutcheson's practice of political virtue as a form of political participation. By employing our moral sense, and comparing our reactions to the reactions of others, we elaborate enforceable rights and duties.

Enforceability brings up the issue of the institutionalization of those practices. In the state of nature, political participation translates into the personal enactment of norms. In the long run, this will cause the usual problems to which Natural Law theorists have alerted us. Abuse, growing complexity of social relations, and human inability to embrace large societies of strangers in their moral/juridical reflection make incorporation into a body politic inevitable. After civil society has been instituted, the norms regarding "mankind as a system" are enforced by the state, which will be, at least from a juridical point of view, the holder of the rights of society against each member. But this should not mean that the activity of elaborating those norms can be transferred to the state itself. Hutcheson seems to agree with this conclusion, for the regulatory function of "mankind as a system" continues even in political society.

> The offices indefinitely due to mankind are ever incumbent on all while the system remains, however they are subdivided into several distinct states or polities. The duties are not taken away in a civil state, but the exercise of them may be limited as far as the political relation and the interest of the state may require.[83]

The state becomes the official interpreter and administrator of those "rights," but it cannot replace the activity whereby those rights are identified and accepted as valid claims. Only the individuals composing a community can perform that function, by assessing the moral value of their social experience. Nor can it be argued that the specific content of those rights is established once and for all, since the progressive refinement of our moral sense can make us sensitive to new morally problematic aspects of social relations.

However, the institution of the state is momentous not only because a formal, concrete, centralized public structure replaces the informal, abstract, and decentralized public person which Hutcheson has labeled "mankind as a system." By institutionalizing aspects of politics that were decentralized and informal in the state of nature, human beings have changed the boundary between non-political and political activity. As the enforcement of norms is subtracted from individual jurisdiction, and becomes the mark of public authority, the moral/juridical activity which I have identified as a type of political participation loses one of its crucial political qualifiers. Individuals renounce not merely the right to punish transgressors, but, more generally, the right to translate their moral perceptions into the corresponding rights and duties. The state is the official interpreter of the law of nature, and it promulgates the rules which we must follow in order to maximize personal and social welfare. Individual reflection upon the collective implications of personal choices appears no longer necessary, for it is replaced by the centralized issuing of written laws.

Nonetheless, if the refinement of the moral sense and of the norms that enable us to attain the maximization of the good is an activity which can only come about through the direct participation of individuals in a socialized process, that activity will continue, but as an expression of private agency. Those engaged in it will read it as a privatized reflection upon how to lead the good life, rather than as a form of political participation. Hutcheson's distinction between morality, legality, and politics is the ground upon which this different interpretation of the same activity can plausibly be maintained. In the state of nature, the political quality of the refinement of moral norms is apparent, in that morality is joined to legality as two distinct but intertwined modes of ordering human conduct. But once the state comes about, juridical inquiry will become an aspect of institutional politics, and morality will be seen as the separate foundation of both.

The second important consequence of political incorporation is the reduction of the universe of full citizens to heads of households. Sociologically, the informal public of the natural condition includes a wider universe than that of political society. Hutcheson's distinction between citizens and subjects illustrates the different relationship which a human being can have with the state. Only adult males are active, both in instituting political authority, and in retaining the right to control how power is exercised. But all participate in the moral activity through which individuals look at themselves as members of humankind, and elaborate norms. Nobody can be excluded, because that activity is the same that allows human beings to express natural sociability. Since there is no operational difference between becoming aware of the rights of a prospective husband, and of humankind, the capacity for the elaboration of moral norms regarding "the publick" must be recognized to all. All can express this type of political virtue, and be members of the non-institutionalized public. Insofar as this activity continues in civil society, although perceived only as ethical reflection upon the legitimacy of political decisions the new public is open to all adults.

The delegation to the rulers of juridical and political functions, the reduction of the refinement of norms to its ethical dimension, and the restriction of the universe of the politically active are the consequences of the foundation of civil society. Conceptually, the first two ensue from Hutcheson's attempt to elaborate a theory of morality which is the foundation of politics, and not vice versa. The third is the outcome of Hutcheson's acceptance of the alienability of personal rights, even if he does not share the proprietary approach to natural rights elaborated by Grotius and accepted by Locke. It is noteworthy that the distinction between morality, legality, and politics enables Hutcheson to escape the democratic implications of his description of the new "publick," in both sociological and conceptual terms. Individuals must be moral agents in civil society, where practicing political virtue has come to mean merely to conform to the decisions of elected representatives. And since what must be saved of direct participation is only its ethical aspect, most adults can be deprived of public agency, without being deprived of privatized moral agency, which is crucial to ensure social harmony.

Hutcheson does not confront the implications of his moral and political theory. But some further reflections are suggested by his work, and the work of the other thinkers analyzed in this essay, which I shall present in the next and final chapter.

Conclusion

At the beginning of this essay I told my readers that I wished to clarify the origins of the liberal distinction between private and public, and the implications which that distinction has for a theory of politics. I have adopted the jurisdictional definition of the pair offered by the *Corpus juris*, and I have explored its articulations in the work of modern Natural Law theorists, in particular Locke and Hutcheson. This is by no means the only way of inquiring into the meanings of the notions private and public. But I have chosen the jurisdictional approach because it has allowed me to focus my attention on the question: who can do what? Natural Law theorists adopt a definition which distinguishes between private and public in terms of the domains of competence of individuals and body politic. And the attribution of jurisdictions depends, in turn, on answering the question: what enables and entitles individuals and body politic to exercise control over their respective domains? The inquiry has thus moved from an analysis of the private and public realms, to a study of the type of agency exercised in each.

Given the individualistic and anti-organicist assumptions of seventeenth-century Natural Law theorists, the agency that they attribute to the body politic is merely the collection of capacities and powers which were originally in each individual. I have slightly changed the question once more, and asked: what does it mean to act in one's private or public capacity? If I am granted private agency, can I be denied public agency? And what theory of politics is implied in the answers to these questions?

If we look for answers in the works of Locke and Hutcheson, a shared view emerges. They contend that every adult has jurisdiction over personal capacities which enable her to claim and defend her rights, that is, the integrity of her person and possessions. Every adult can interpret the law of nature, in order to ascertain what she may claim, and what obligations she has toward others. And every adult can judge whether others' interpretations of the law of nature are correct. For Locke "correct" means "rational" or "reasonable," and for Hutcheson it means "maximizing the general welfare." But the basic structure of their arguments is the same. This approach allows them to contend that the state of nature is peaceful rather than antagonistic, because human beings can comply with the obligations dictated by the law of nature, and punish transgressors.

Individual agency thus has a private and a public side. If we wish to draw a line between the two, we can say that an individual's actions are private, when he pursues his interests without endangering others. But what is "endangering"? For Locke and Hutcheson, "endangering" means to harm or damage someone's perfect rights. We know what those rights are: we can list them one by one; and we also know what it means to be prevented from enjoying them. The public side of agency will thus include defending oneself and others, even through the use of force. It is this activity which the state will inherit when human beings abandon the state of nature. In this view, the line separating private and public agency, private and public domains, appears to be clear and steady. Locke and Hutcheson can be considered proto-liberal thinkers. Politics are concerned with the defense of a secure space for self-regulated private activities. Political participation is scarcely relevant, undesired by modern individuals who value their privacy, and unwelcome to elected representatives.

But if we analyze what "endangering" may mean, we can say that, even for Locke, a more complex interpretative activity is necessary to ensure that what one does conforms to the dictates of the law of nature. If I may not starve anyone to death, must I not ascertain whether my accumulation of land still leaves enough for others to survive? If I have to ensure the optimal reproduction of the species, what type of family should I choose? The issue becomes even more complicated for Hutcheson. If I can only fulfill my obligations by maximizing the general welfare, what does that concretely mean at any specific point in time? This interpretative activity appears to be essential for maintaining a peaceful state of nature. In fact, the growing complexity of social relations will strain the human capacity for doing so successfully, to the point that the institution of political authority becomes necessary.

This interpretative activity brings to the fore a dimension of politics which is quite different from the enforcement of already existing norms. To put it bluntly, to consider enforcement as the fundamental feature of politics means that we know what needs to be done, and the problem is: who should do it? And: can she do it? But if we consider interpretation as the crucial aspect, the question becomes: what should we do? And: who can decide what we should do? It may appear unjustified to separate two activities which are clearly indispensable not only in politics, but in any human endeavor. If I do not know what needs to be done, I shall engage in random behavior, rather than purposeful action. It is thus quite obvious that, when we transfer the power of enforcement to the political ruler, we also transfer the right to take decisions for the body politic. As Locke himself defines it at the beginning of the *Second Treatise*,

> *Political Power* then I take to be a *Right* of making Laws with Penalties of Death, and consequently all less Penalties, for the Regulating and Preserving of Property, and of employing the force of the Community, in the Execution of such Laws, and in the defence of the Common-wealth from Foreign Injury, and all this only for the Publick Good.[1]

But my contention that interpretation and enforcement may be the focus of two very different theories of politics is justified by two considerations: the consequences for the distinction between private and public; and the role and import of citizens' direct participation.

Considering the interpretation of the law of nature as an aspect of politics is relevant to the distinction between private and public, as we can already surmise from Locke. The capacity to consult and apply unwritten norms through reason is constitutive of our autonomous private agency. It is because we can assess the implications of our actions, and choose those that do not harm others, that we are granted a personal jurisdiction over activities and possessions. When we employ this capacity in the state of nature we both take care of our personal interests, and do it in such a way as not to break the peace. Where does the boundary lie between the private and public aspects of this activity? If we keep harm as the criterion of distinction, what counts as "harm," "damage," and "injure"? This is not a trifling issue, for Locke's distinction between private and public becomes blurred if we focus on this aspect of agency. This is confirmed if we look at the implications of the transference of the interpretation of the law of nature to the ruler.[2] Suddenly, not only is our public agency curtailed, but our private agency as well, for in regulating what can ensure the "common good," the state will limit our personal domain of competence. The clearest example offered by Locke regards the management of property in things, for this is a central issue for him. The state will set limits to the private appropriation of resources. But was not this a fundamental expression of private agency? Is not civil society instituted because we

want to defend our property? If the state monopolizes both interpretation and enforcement of the law of nature, how can we claim an
inviolable private domain? As I have pointed out, these questions
indicate a potential contradiction in Locke's political philosophy, and
they have justified diverging interpretations of its meaning. I wish to
leave aside the historiographical debate, which may well be insoluble,
and focus my attention on a possible answer which can be inferred from
Locke's text.

This answer hinges on a restrictive interpretation of what "harm" is.
In describing household relations, Locke gives us an illustration of how
much latitude we can recognize to individuals in handling their
personal endowments. The limits which human beings must respect in
order not to harm others leave quite a lot of room for maneuvering. The
rich proprietor does not harm the beggar who accepts to become his
servant because he is hungry, for the latter can choose whether to
become a servant, or to die. The prospective husband does not harm the
woman who accepts a lower position in the family, for she can choose
not to marry, and may even negotiate the terms of the marriage
contract. The accumulator of land does not starve the poor, since there
is such an abundance of unused land in America. If these reasonings
represent correct interpretations of the law of nature, and all the state
has to do is to continue along these lines, a broad private domain is
ensured to adults. But the price paid is twofold. First, only a minority
will enjoy that private domain, and the majority will actually curtail it
to a great degree. Second, and implicit in the first, we can dismiss
certain activities and relations as harmless and non-antagonistic, only
because the asymmetrical distribution of power enables one of the
parties to ignore the complaints and grievances of the other. The perfect
reciprocity which characterizes free and equal individuals in the state
of nature is abandoned. Through their personal transactions individuals
transfer some of their endowments to others, and authorize them to
make decisions on their behalf. The state will thus be in charge of
interpreting the law of nature only to avoid conflict between the
beneficiaries of those personal transactions. But the state will not
intrude into the management of the adult male proprietor's broadened
private domain. (Except, of course, if serious physical harm is
threatened against, or inflicted on, the dependent.)

We can thus say that Locke offers a sociological rather than a
conceptual solution to the problem opened by the recognition that the
interpretation of the law of nature is an aspect of both private and
public agency. Heads of households will retain their private agency by
dispossessing servants and women of theirs. It is in handling their

relationships with subordinates – women, children, and servants/ labourers – that independent men act as private persons, entitled to regulate their interaction with others by autonomously interpreting the law of nature. And they will delegate to the magistrate the right to interpret the law of nature on their behalf, only for what regards their relationships with their peers. Not only is Locke's solution an exercise in finding a sociological adjustment to a theoretical problem; it is also an example of the qualitative implications of quantitative considerations. Locke can contend that a *minority* of adult male proprietors retain control over their inviolable private domains, because, by including in these private domains a *majority* of dependents, their resources, and their endowments, he has excluded them from the public domain, and from the care and protection provided by the state.

What happens if we reflect on the qualitative consequences of thinking in quantitative terms, but we expand the universe of those entitled to see the integrity of their private domains secured? In other words, what happens if we contend that all are equally entitled to see their private domains protected?

It is already possible to find an answer in Hutcheson. Hutcheson's account of conjugal relations is more egalitarian than that of Locke. He establishes substantive reciprocity of rights and duties between husband and wife, at least for what concerns intrafamilial affairs. The patrimony of the family should belong to both; each spouse should exercise authority over some aspects of domestic life, and should not meddle in the jurisdiction of the other. The double moral standard in sexual matters is rejected, and so forth. The logical consequence of this egalitarian approach is that an arbiter has to intervene every time the two argue, so as to prevent one from violating the other's rights.[3] (Whereas Locke's solution was to assign power to the husband.) All other things being equal, this means that public intervention becomes more frequent, for all the issues which could be autonomously decided by the husband in Locke's model have to be decided by an external authority according to Hutcheson. If every adult is authorized to present her case, rather than yield to the will of the superior, problems and questions which were not public concern for Locke become public concern for Hutcheson. This finds a confirmation in Hutcheson's longer and more detailed list of perfect rights. The notion of what constitutes "harm" is being modified to include psychological and moral types of injuries, which must be prevented or punished by the magistrate.

The analysis of the interpretation of the law of nature as an activity in which private and public aspects are intertwined calls into question the possibility of establishing a sharp separation between private and public jurisdictions. In deciding how to manage my personal relations, a consideration of their public import is indispensable and inevitable. But if I transfer this activity to elective representatives, can I still declare that I retain autonomous control over my personal jurisdiction? In Locke and Hutcheson, that personal jurisdiction is based on inviolable natural rights, which precede any political concern and institution. But if it is the state that decides about their compatibility with the public good, are they still inviolable? Does not the private domain ultimately tend to coincide with the Hobbesian space left by the *silentium legis*? On the other hand, are not public monopolization of that activity and intrusion into everyone's private domain necessary if every citizen has to see her rights protected? Even if we assume that these rights limit the discretion of the ruler, is not the public domain expanding, albeit with the purpose of protecting a supposedly sacred private sphere?

It would seem that this paradoxical conclusion informs much of the current literature on the pair private/public, and the assessment of its descriptive and normative functions in social and political theory. Many welcome the acknowledgement of the internal inconsistencies of the liberal distinction as a positive development. Feminist critics, in particular, call for abandoning that distinction altogether, at least at the prescriptive level. Others have seen in the decline of the separation between a private and a public domain a sign of the victory of administration over politics, of instrumental over critical rationality, and of social conformity over the genuine sharing of authentically personal experiences.[4]

All these critics – albeit coming from very different quarters – share two features in common. They emphasize, first of all, what we might call an antinomy of practical reason which they consider typical of modernity. Right at the historical moment when the axiological primacy of private over public values has been asserted vigorously, the socialized public has known an unprecedented expansion, and threatens, or promises, to wipe out the private sphere.

Second, they appear to share the view that in strong models of the distinction, the private domain is seen as a prerequisite for life in public. This structural relationship between the two domains is quite independent of their axiological ordering. Thinkers as distant from one another as Aristotle and Locke consider life in public as subsequent to, and based on, the world of personal experience. In private, individuals express and satisfy what is basic and indispensable to human beings. In the liberal version, they also express what is essential to them. This private experience is what enables them to operate and function autonomously in the public domain.

I believe that there exists a logical connection between arguing that the private domain is a prerequisite for public life, and contending that we are witnessing a progressive weakening of the distinction in contemporary society. I wish to suggest that we sense a progressive erosion of the private domain, and a blurring of the boundary-line separating it from the public, because we can no longer consider the private sphere as a prerequisite for life in public.

In considering the private a "prerequisite for," we perform two distinct but related intellectual operations. First, we assume that the experiences, activities, and relations labeled by the term are "prior to" the experiences and relations which we have in public. "Prior" here points to both the temporal and structural location of the phenomena taken into consideration. The raising of children is an example of the temporal gap between personal and public life. There is a time-lag between birth and becoming a full member of the body politic, which is lived mostly in the family, or its equivalent, and its supporting institutions, and is mostly filled with privatized relations. But "prior" also means that certain activities are the structural precondition for public engagement: the satisfaction of physiological needs – the Arendtian realm of necessity – comes before any public activity.

On the basis of this seemingly descriptive account, we then perform the second operation, which is overtly normative, and is, in its turn, composed of two steps. The first is to contend that those activities and relations ought to be separated, and shielded from public control and intrusion. This is quite independent of the value attached to them. Aristotle may exclude them from the public arena, because they do not deserve to be seen and shared. Locke contends that the state must defend them, because they constitute the core of an inviolate personality. But in both cases, essential features of the human condition – which are supposedly common to all – are individualized and personalized on the ground that sharing them in common would alter them, or even destroy them.[5]

The second step is to assume that, without the experiences of the private world, individuals are unable to perform in public. The private thus becomes a prerequisite in the full sense of the term. The enjoyment of a private life becomes the structural precondition for public engagement. Slaves, who do not have a private persona, cannot have a public one. The women and servants of seventeenth-century Natural Law theorists disenfranchise themselves, as it were, by having less than full personal autonomy.

The final consequence of this procedure is that, as the bedrock of public life, what happens in private becomes more stable and rigid. I do not wish to rule out that there may be factual grounds which account for this outcome. Certain physiological activities, for example, appear to be preconditions of intellectual or moral ones, and are therefore considered more basic. But I wish to suggest that the allocation of those activities in the private rather than the public domain, and the seemingly obvious ordinal sequence established between them, are informed by often implicit normative preferences.[6] In other words, it appears to me that the stability, certainty, and unalterability of private life ensue from the type of intellectual operation performed in distinguishing between a private and a public domain, an operation shaped by the broader normative aims which guide the drawing of the distinction.

If we look more closely at Locke's conception, we can see that his model already undermines the stability and inalterability of the private sphere. I do not find any better way to express this development than by pointing to the metaphors which we employ in talking of the pair. The basic, recurrent, ineliminable metaphor is spatial. The notions of domain, sphere, realm, dimension, and so on, all refer to space. The conceptual criterion of distinction between private and public is described as a boundary-line – another spatial metaphor. We speak of invasion and intrusion. I need not continue. Spatial metaphors tend to reinforce the notion that the objects or phenomena in question occupy a definite place(!), stable and well marked.

But if we analyze Locke's conception of the distinction, a temporal metaphor is more accurate. Human activities remain private as long as they do not harm others. Negotiating with a seller is my private concern as long as I do not try to cheat him. Family affairs are my personal concern until I threaten my spouse's life. We cannot allocate activities to specific places once and for all, because they move from one "place" to the other, depending on whether they are harmless or harmful. We cannot rule out the possibility that harm is done even in relations which appear to be regulated by affection, love, or trust. Parents kill their children, husbands squander their wives' dowries, business partners run away with their associates' money. If harm is the criterion for deciding what is of personal, and what of public concern, even Locke's narrow notion of harm leads us to adopt a flexible attitude toward the allocation of activities and relations to either "domain."

The tendency to destabilize the boundaries of the private domain, and consequently of the distinction, becomes more evident if we look at both the historical and conceptual developments of the pair. Historically, the actualization of the normative liberal tenet which postulates that every human being has an inviolable private domain has meant that traditionally sheltered institutions have been opened to public scrutiny and control. This seems to have happened to labor relations, to conjugal ones, and it is a phenomenon which is now reaching children, whose welfare requires heavy intrusion into the domain of parental decisions and actions.

Conceptually, the broadening of the notion of "harm," already noticed in Hutcheson, and emphasized by John Stuart Mill, has meant that more aspects of life have been added to the list of those in need of protection by public authority. Nothing shows that the boundary-line between private and public has become indeterminate better than the criterion which we now mostly use to articulate the distinction: private is what is self-regarding, public what is other-regarding. From a logical point of view, this is a tautology, which reproduces in a new formulation the formal definition of the *Corpus juris*: private is what concerns the individual, public what concerns the community. But what is self-regarding, and what is other-regarding? Smoking, which was until very recently self-regarding, has dramatically stepped over into the realm of the other-regarding. Euthanasia may be on its way to make the journey in the opposite direction.

This last remark should alert us to the possibility that we are taking the part for the whole, that is, in this case, that we are mistaking one tendency in historical development – the publicization of certain aspects of life and social relations – for the only and dominant tendency. The overall picture may be more complex: privatization may well occur at the same time as publicization does. The decreased autonomy of the adult male has meant that the autonomy of laborers and women has increased. Sexual preferences and reproductive decisions are becoming personal concerns.[7] But polluting air and water has turned into one of the central issues of contemporary politics. Do these developments then point unerringly toward the elimination of the distinction between private and public, and to the creation of an undifferentiated social realm? It seems to me that a more balanced assessment of the historical tendencies of modern society can lead us to emphasize the instability of the distinction between private and public, rather than a steady movement toward its obliteration.

If this is correct at the sociological level, what are the theoretical implications of acknowledging the instability of the boundary between private and public? If the assumption that the private domain is a prerequisite of public life was the starting point of a conception that ensured stability to the private, what has undermined the plausibility of this assumption? I think that part of the answer already lies in the subjective theory of rights shared by both Locke and Hutcheson. In their vision, individuals are able, and entitled, to make claims to personal and material resources. In other words, this means that human beings define their own private domain. The latter, except for the capacities which constitute human agency, and are the same for all, is not a given, accruing to the person according to his/her status in life. It is the outcome of self-regulated activities, which can lead an individual to increase as well as decrease her original stock. A public authority is instituted to mend a situation of conflict, caused by relative scarcity of resources combined with human partiality.

This way of looking at the relationship between individuals and body politic is based on a conceptual loop, so to speak, which proceeds as follows. Individuals are autonomous agents in the state of nature. Their uncoordinated activity leads to the state of war, and therefore to the need for enforcement of rules by the magistrate. Once the latter has been instituted, we can say that the public sphere is in charge of protecting an already existing private domain. But if we consider the diachronic approach of Natural Law writers from a synchronic perspective, we can see that individuals engage in a never-ending process of definition of their private realms within civil society, and, consequently, of the boundary between private and public.

This dynamic is appropriately reflected in the private and public aspects of agency. When making a decision about my personal life, I have to take into consideration the implications of that decision for others, and, in principle, for society as a whole. I have to assess whether my action will, or may, affect my fellow citizens in such a way as to require public regulation. In interpreting whether my action conforms to the dictates of the law of nature, I indirectly weigh the compatibility of my rights with the rights of the other citizens.[8] And since everybody is supposed to do the same, society is the outcome of the balancing of all claims made by the members.[9] In performing this activity, individuals reciprocally define the boundaries and content of their private domains. It would thus appear that the boundary between private and public is not something which we can take for granted, or as given once and for all. It is itself the result of everyone's attempt to assert her rights, and to verify their compatibility with everybody else's claims. This implies that we can no longer assume the private sphere as a prerequisite for life in public, but we proceed to define its content and boundaries while deciding what requires control and regulation by the public.[10]

I have argued that the activity which enables us to distinguish between a private and a public domain is a form of political participation, which appears to be the logical complement of a theory of politics based on a subjective conception of rights. Lockean individuals practice it in the state of nature, thus making it possible to consider the state of war a historical contingency, rather than a natural necessity. However, when civil society is instituted, the transference of the interpretation of the law of nature to the magistrate means that direct participation is no longer acceptable, apart from extreme cases. But in Hutcheson, participation in the refinement of the law of nature continues even after the political ruler has been established as the institutional interpreter of that law.[11]

The development of an informal public is the outcome of a moral/ juridical activity of reflection upon the relationship between one's own and others' welfare. Thanks to morality we discover what our aims should be, and we assess whether deeds are informed by ethically approvable motivations. And thanks to juridical analysis, we reach an understanding about which morally approvable (or disapprovable) features of experience may be and should be translated into rights and obligations. In principle, the latter activity is transferred to the magistrate, together with enforcement, when civil society is instituted. But Hutcheson's conceptualization of "society," or "mankind as a system" as an informal public, shows that individuals continue to engage in the interpretation of the law of nature, despite the official monopolization by the state. Monopolization may be both undesirable and unattainable. It may be undesirable, for it means to assign to the "cunning politicians" a constitutive role in the refinement of the norms ensuring social cohesion. And it may be unattainable, given the psychological and moral dynamics on which Hutcheson relies in order to explain how human beings can harmonize individual and collective happiness.

If the interpretation of the law of nature is solely the task of the magistrate, the primacy of morality over legality and politics which is the cornerstone of Hutcheson's theory is called into question. In different ways, both Hobbes and Mandeville emphasized the central role of the sovereign and the politician in ensuring social integration through the creation and enforcement of norms. How can Hutcheson avoid an omnipotent or manipulative ruler, if he entitles the magistrate to be the only authority who can interpret and specify the very general law of nature? Are institutional devices such as frequent elections and accountability of representatives, and extreme remedies such as the right of resistance, enough to protect the citizens?

Even if we answer in the affirmative, there are structural aspects of

Hutcheson's thought which make it problematic for the individual to divest himself of that interpretative activity.

Hutcheson's individuals are ethical individualists. With the phrase ethical individualism I here refer to the fact that only uncoerced individual motivations can lead the person to do what is morally approvable. The "morally approvable" is what stems from benevolence, and aims at maximizing the general welfare. But it is only when the pursuit of general welfare becomes a source of individual happiness that social harmony can be attained. There is therefore a relationship of reciprocal determination between personal and social happiness. For it is only when each and every member of society is happy in doing the good of others that the general welfare is maximized. Formally this is all we need to know in order to understand how to avoid conflict between individual and society. But substantively, we must ascertain that aim "a" rather than "b" is what will maximize everyone's, and therefore society's, welfare. Who makes this assessment? An impartial spectator, who provides a universally valid interpretation of what makes everyone happy?[12] Or do we all participate in determining what makes both others and ourselves happy?

It would appear that the latter solution is the only one available if we join this ethical individualism to a subjective theory of rights, as Hutcheson does. Each of us is capable of translating, and entitled to translate, her moral perceptions into rights and obligations. In other words, each person can claim as her right what maximizes her own welfare. We know that there are basic aspects of life which everyone deems crucial to her welfare, and are therefore going to constitute their set of perfect rights. But each of us is also entitled to see as her right the pursuit of things and activities which are morally indifferent. Once we have attached value to them, those things and activities become morally loaded, for others have acquired an obligation to allow us to enjoy them. Individuals thus become "sources" of rights, in the sense that they can specify the law of nature in ways which escape the knowledge and competence of an impartial spectator, or a centralized political authority.

It is thus Hutcheson's theory of agency which becomes an obstacle to the full transference of the interpretation of the law of nature to the magistrate. The continuum between moral and juridical reflection calls into question the possibility that human beings stop articulating their moral perceptions in juridical terms, even in political society. An indirect confirmation that the interpretation of the law of nature is only partially, if at all, transferable comes from Hutcheson's focus on

private judgement as the faculty which constitutes the core of autonomous agency.

> Our rights are either *alienable,* or *unalienable.* The former are known
> by these two characters jointly, that the translation of them to others
> can be made effectually, and that some interest of society, or
> individuals consistently with it, may frequently require such transla-
> tions. Thus our right to our goods and labours is naturally alienable.
> But where either the translation cannot be made with any effect, or
> where no good in human life requires it, the right is unalienable, and
> cannot justly be claimed by any other but the person originally
> possessing it. Thus no man can really change his sentiments,
> judgments, and inward affections, at the pleasure of another; nor can
> it tend to any good to make him profess what is contrary to his heart.
> The right of private judgement is therefore unalienable.[13]

Direct individual interpretation of the law of nature structures the
informal public arena which outlasts the institution of the official
interpreter, that is, the state. Hutcheson offers an account of this
activity which sees it as the expression of political virtue, but can also
pave the way for its privatization.

Privatization is a possible outcome of Hutcheson's distinction
between morality, legality, and politics. In the state of nature, individuals elaborate moral evaluations, formulate some of them in juridical
terms, and enforce them, while the state will be the only official
interpreter and enforcer in civil society. Hutcheson's crucial step is to
separate enforcement and interpretation. This move turns individual
judgement on a problematic issue into the expression of personal
opinion, rather than the assertion of a right (or a duty). The state may as
well as not take that opinion into consideration in issuing norms. But
judgement is privatized also in the sense that it is no longer seen as the
outcome of the balancing between individual and social welfare. It is
considered as the expression of particularistic and self-centered concerns. It is only the state which will subsume all particular judgements
under general rules, and will then enforce them on all members of the
body politic.[14]

However, Hutcheson also presents participation in the informal
public as an expression of political virtue. The purely ethical reflection
on problematic issues gives life to a set of unwritten norms which guide
individual choices, and embody the human capacity for thinking of
one's welfare in connection with the welfare of society. Although
enforcement is no longer in the hands of citizens, ethical evaluations
are still formulated in the language of rights and obligations. This

means that they create a type of obligation different from a purely moral one. And it also means that juridical norms will regard a particular set of events, deeds, and personal features, namely those in which the balance between individual and collective happiness is at stake.

These two possible models of the relationship between morality, legality, and politics can lead us to construct two conceptions of the nature and tasks of politics. The first, in which readers will recognize a classical version of liberalism, emphasizes the division of labor between the citizens and the state along the lines of the distinction between unenforceable moral evaluations and enforceable legal claims. If enforceability is what distinguishes morality from legality, ethical reflection remains the concern of citizens, while enforcement of legal norms is the concern of the state. And since in transferring the power of life and death to the magistrate citizens have created the political association, politics are essentially defined as the exercise of the legitimate use of force.

But is enforceability the only feature distinguishing morality from legality? What do citizens attain by analyzing the moral values of deeds and persons? Do they merely identify the norms which will allow them to pursue the (moral) good? Or do they not reach an agreement on what issues are relevant to the welfare of the association, and what norms are necessary to ensure that welfare? Do they not attempt to harmonize individual needs and concerns with collective ones? The interpretation of this activity as an essential aspect of politics tries to deal with a crucial question regarding early modern society which was common to all Natural Law theorists, but expressed most clearly and cogently by Hobbes.

If we start from the assumption that society can only be explained as the outcome of individual choices and actions, and can only be justified by appealing to individual preferences and motivations, cohesion and integration will always be in question. Hobbes accepts that assumption for both historical and philosophical reasons. He describes seventeenth-century England as a society in which ascriptive social roles are no longer strong enough to keep people "in their place." Human beings whose only certainty is their own perceptions, needs, and desires lead lives marked by isolation and fear. For Hobbes, the solution to the problems arising in a natural condition characterized by epistemological and moral subjectivism is political. That is, only by consciously developing shared norms and institutions can human beings avoid the pitfalls of an atomized condition. As is well known, Hobbes holds that only a centralized political authority can produce the shared language, moral norms, and judicial sanctions which ensure the survival and flourishing of civil society.[15]

If we agree with Hobbes that, in modern society, we can no longer rely on traditional and unchallenged shared values and norms, how do we go about providing that shared ground? Does this search have to be a matter for politics, and if it is a matter for politics, does it have to be centralized in the hands of the sovereign? Can it be centralized, if only through the voluntary participation of each individual can a balance between particularistic desires and universalizable norms be attained?

As I have tried to show, Hutcheson indirectly offers at least a partial answer to these questions, by hypothesizing an informal public domain which precedes and supersedes the state. But Hutcheson is concerned with reading the activity whereby "the publick" is brought into being purely as moral reflection. He thinks that by subtracting enforcement from these moral assessments, he has purified that activity of its political component. But this is true only if politics are identified with the use of force. If politics in modern society regard the identification of what we share in common with strangers, so that centrifugal forces will not prevail, then Hutcheson's account of the activity shaping the new public is the description of a political enterprise.

Considering this enterprise political appears to me the only way of understanding some historical developments, and providing a normative view of politics suitable to contemporary concerns.

Only by recognizing the political dimension of moral/juridical reflection have I been able to make sense of some practical antinomies of our society. The one from which this inquiry has sprung is the dynamic of exclusion and inclusion which has affected disenfranchised groups in the last three centuries. These groups were initially cut off from institutional politics as they had always been, but they have finally won access to them. For at the sociological level, the privatization of morality has meant that even disenfranchised citizens could play a role in the informal public domain. Their moral competence, recognized to them because personal autonomy was indispensable to a healthy society, indirectly legitimated their limited and unwelcome, but relevant, presence in participatory activities, and has thus enabled them to impose on the political agenda the question of their access to full citizenship.

The second antinomy is the rather puzzling dynamic between private and public domains, as a significant part of the literature emphasizes. How can we explain why the assertion of the inviolability and axiological primacy of the private realm has coincided with an unprecedented expansion of the public? I have argued that it is the attempt to view the private as a prerequisite for life in public that induces us to ask a question which is by now meaningless. If there is no traditional and given public domain, into which full citizens step by leaving behind their private spheres, it may well be that the distinction between the two is the result of the participatory activity through which we identify what is and should be shared, and what is or should be personal. It should come as no surprise that the instability and mutability which characterize contemporary society call for a constant renegotiation of the boundary, thus engendering a feeling of confusion between what can pertain to private, and what to public, jurisdiction.

From the perspective of a normative theory of politics, the view suggested here tries to address two concerns. The first is expressed by writers who have been lamenting the disappearance of life in public from modern society. Indeed, we engage in a political life which is significantly different from that of classical Athens, republican Rome, or even eighteenth-century Britain. Are we still capable of transcending our particularity, and going beyond the mere bargaining for the allocation of resources through pressure groups? Can we overcome the neo-corporatist tendencies which lurk below the surface of radical political demands of disadvantaged groups? I cannot claim to have even begun to offer an answer to these questions. But I wish to suggest that this inquiry has taught me in what direction I can begin to look for an answer.

From a theoretical point of view, the question which haunted writers at the dawn of modernity remains the crucial one. If we consider individuals as able and entitled to define their rights, we face problems of coordination and integration which were transcendentally or traditionally solved in other societies. Politics thus come to regard the attempt to define the shared set of norms and values which ensure peaceful cohabitation. In participating in political life, individuals think of their common fate at a given time in a given place, and of the conditions which are necessary to make that fate tolerable. In being present in the modern public arena, citizens aim at influencing the elaboration of the principles whereby society functions. They may do so while attempting to reap benefits for themselves, or to obtain access to material and non-material resources. But without an agreement on the question of principles, any decision about the allocation of resources becomes problematic and illegitimate.

I have reached the conclusion that this "background activity," as it were, which enables us to agree on the prerequisites of life in the same association, is an activity *sui generis*, which I identify as politics. With regard to the modern distinction between morality and legality, the notion of politics which I am suggesting here carves out a conceptual space, modes of operation, and criteria of validity of its conclusions, which lie in between morality and legality.[16] Politics borrow from both moral and juridical thinking, but do not coincide with either, and they take into consideration only those phenomena which are relevant for balancing individual and collective welfare.

Political participation is what turns a "multitude," as seventeenth-century writers called it, into one body, capable of looking at itself as a unified institutional entity.[17] In acting politically, our principal aim is to create and maintain the association, and only derivatively do we use the association as an instrument to attain other ends. Family and church, economic enterprise and cultural institutions are supposed to be instrumental to the satisfaction of specific needs, and concerned with their own survival and welfare only as a means to fulfill those needs. On the contrary, the political association has first and foremost itself as its object of concern and care.[18] The loss of metaphysical certainty and historical continuity which appears to shape experience in contemporary Western societies has left the citizens in full charge of distinguishing between political and non-political, private and public, particularistic interests and universalizable norms. We now stand on the boundary-line between these modalities, and it is only through political participation that we can exercise control over the social forces which are shaping and moulding our lives.

Notes

INTRODUCTION

1 Among the few who have devoted their attention to the dynamics of the pair, I wish to emphasize the following contributions. M.L. Goldschmidt, "Publicity, Privacy and Secrecy," *Western Political Quarterly*, 1954, vol. 7, pp. 401–16; H. Arendt, *The Human Condition*, Chicago, The University of Chicago Press, 1958; H.J. McCloskey, "The Political Ideal of Privacy," *Philosophical Quarterly*, 1971, vol. 21, pp. 301–14; J.H. Reiman, "Privacy, Intimacy, and Personhood," *Philosophy and Public Affairs*, 1976, vol. 6, pp. 26–44; H. Van Gunsteren, "Public and Private," *Social Research*, 1979, vol. 46, pp. 255–71; N. Bobbio, "Pubblico, privato," in *Enciclopedia, XI: Prodotti-Ricchezza*, Torino, Einaudi, 1980, pp. 401–15; H.F. Pitkin, "Justice. On Relating Private and Public," *Political Theory*, 1981, vol. 9, pp. 327–52; J.B. Elshtain, *Public Man, Private Woman*, Princeton, NJ, Princeton University Press, 1981; S.I. Benn and G.F. Gaus (eds), *Public and Private in Social Life*, London, Croom Helm, 1983; M. Walzer, "Liberalism and the Art of Separation," *Political Theory*, 1984, vol. 12, pp. 315–30; J. Habermas, *The Structural Transformation of the Public Sphere*, Th. Burger (tr.), Cambridge, MA, The MIT Press, 1989; and J. Weintraub, "The Theory and Politics of the Public/Private Distinction," presented at the 1990 meeting of the American Political Science Association, San Francisco.

2 S.I. Benn and G.F. Gaus, "The Public and the Private: Concepts and Actions," in S.I. Benn and G.F. Gaus, *Public and Private*, p. 4. The concepts are stable in that their notational range is the same over time. Private refers to what is singular or hidden, public to what is shared or visible. At this notational level the concepts are formal and general, so that their meaning is partial or incomplete, for we do not know what empirical contents are connoted by them. In fact, we can associate very different empirical contents to the terms "singular," "hidden," "shared," and "visible," or to the terms of reference of the *Corpus juris*: "individual," "interest," and "commonwealth." And we can change the evaluative implications of the pair. As is well known, "private" is a derogatory term, in both Greek and Latin. It still is in the Renaissance, for example, in Thomas More, as Professor Skinner has reminded me. Whereas modern liberalism has often reversed the axiological order, or, at least, it has seen

private life as being as worthwhile as public life. Only the interweaving of the more formal and historically stable level with the more concrete and historically variable can determine the full meaning of the concepts in each specific case. Professor Skinner has remarked to me that, in his opinion, the formal level can be said to carry the notational *meaning* of the terms, while the empirically and evaluative substantive levels express the *uses* of the concepts, and these can be very unstable. (This is the view he has expressed in a series of methodological articles on these issues. See especially his "Meaning and Understanding in the History of Ideas," *History and Theory*, 1969, vol. 8, pp. 3–53.) I prefer to think of the formal level as a partial "meaning," and the substantive one as the full "meaning," rather than seeing in these two levels the contrast between "meaning" and "use." In other words, I am reluctant to consider "use" as a specific source of "meaning." But this is a complex problem, and I realize that I am not doing justice to Professor Skinner's remark, for which I wish to thank him.

3   *The Digest of Justinian*, Th. Mommsen, P. Krueger, and A. Watson (eds), Philadelphia, PA, University of Pennsylvania Press, 1985, bk II, ch.i, 1, 2. The translation here quoted has been corrected, because the Latin term *spectare,* which means "to regard," "to pertain to," "to concern" (someone), was incorrectly rendered as "to respect," which has in English a completely different meaning.

4   A. Erh-Soon Tay and E. Kamenka, "Public Law – Private Law," in S.I. Benn and G.F. Gaus, *Public and Private*, pp. 88–9.

> The three great, original characteristics of Roman private law as a living system up to the time of Justinian were firstly, a complexity which enabled it to cover the main social relationships of human life; secondly, a degree of abstraction enabling many of its principles to apply to a wide range of social relationships and over long periods of time without major change; thirdly, an autonomy of structure and development which gave law an independent role in the development of society as a whole.

5   The term community does not carry any specific meaning in this case, and does not point to, although it does not exclude, a conception of the body politic as being different from, and more than, the sum of its parts.

6   And to the secret domain of conscience, which is, however, insofar as kept secret, irrelevant in Hobbes's opinion. R. Koselleck analyzes the implications of this concession in *Critique and Crisis*, Oxford, Berg, 1988, ch. 2, pp. 23–40.

7   The regression in the hermeneutic cycle need not stop here, and we can ask: what explains each thinker's preference for a particular conception of politics? But this further step is not necessary to the purposes of this inquiry.

8   The phrase "Natural Law" is here capitalized to convey the difference between the Latin notion of *jus* and *lex,* which overlap in the English term "law." I prefer not to translate *jus* as rights, for *jus* includes both rights and duties, whereas "rights" evokes more specifically the modern notion of subjective (vs objective) rights.

9   Attacks on the hierarchical structure of the family are not absent from the

history of Western political thought. The Cynics in antiquity, and radical sects in the English Civil War, to name only two cases, provide good examples. But it is the first time that a revision of the grounds of that natural hierarchy is adopted by thinkers who occupy the centre-stage in Western thought.

10 P. Laslett has called it "natural political virtue." "Introduction" to J. Locke, *Two Treatises of Government*, New York, Mentor Books, 1965, pp. 122–3.

11 On the Marxist side, C.B. Macpherson's *The Political Theory of Possessive Individualism*, Oxford, Oxford University Press, 1962, is the text which has prompted the debate. From a liberal perspective, K.I. Vaughan accepts the centrality of the problem of scarcity of resources in Locke. The ultimate cause of the institution of government is "scarcity of land brought about both by ownership of private property and by increasing populations." *John Locke, Economist and Social Scientist*, Chicago, The University of Chicago Press, 1980, p. 94. A more general interpretation of Natural Law theory as centered around the issue of material possessions pervades the most recent contributions to the discussion. J.G.A. Pocock, "Virtues, Rights, and Manners. A Model for Historians of Political Thought," in *Virtue, Commerce and History*, Cambridge, Cambridge University Press, 1985, pp. 37–50:

> I am allowing my language to become Arendtian because I am interested in the possibility that jurisprudence can be said to be predominantly social, concerned with the administration of things, as opposed to a civic vocabulary of the purely political, concerned with the unmediated personal relations entailed by equality and by ruling and being ruled.

J. Tully, *A Discourse On Property: John Locke and his Adversaries*, Cambridge, Cambridge University Press, 1988, focuses on the role of distributive justice in Locke; and I. Hont and M. Ignatieff, "Needs and Justice in the *Wealth of Nations*," in I. Hont and M. Ignatieff (eds), *Wealth and Virtue*, Cambridge, Cambridge University Press, 1983, pp. 1–44, offer interpretations along that line for Smith.

12 H. Arendt, *Critique of Judgement: Lectures on Kant's Political Philosophy*, Chicago, The University of Chicago Press, 1982; J. Habermas, *Legitimation Crisis*, Boston, MA, Beacon Press, 1975; and H.G. Gadamer, *Truth and Method*, New York, Crossroad, 1989.

13 On this point, although with different intents, see S. Benhabib, "Judgment and the Moral Foundations of Politics in Arendt's Thought," *Political Theory*, 1988, vol. 16, p. 46:

> It is possible to go one step further in exploring the topic of a political ethic without altogether collapsing the distinction between the right and the good. This additional step would involve the encouragement and cultivation of a public ethos of democratic participation. Between the basic institutions of a polity embodying principles of the morally right and the domain of moral interactions in the life world, in which virtue often comes to the fore, lie the civic practices and associations of a society in which individuals face each other neither as pure legal

164   *Notes*

subjects nor as moral agents standing under ties of ethical obligations to each other, but as public agents in a political space.

14   J.B. Elshtain contrasts the world of the family as the world of privacy, and the social realm as the world of publicity, in *Public Man, Private Woman*. This view is shared by C. Pateman, in her recent book, *The Sexual Contract*, Oxford, Polity Press, 1988, pp. 3–4.

> Patriarchal civil society is divided into two spheres, but attention is directed to one sphere only. The story of the social contract is treated as an account of the creation of the public sphere of civil freedom. The other, private, sphere is not seen as politically relevant. Marriage and the marriage contract are, therefore, also deemed politically irrelevant.... The public realm cannot be fully understood in the absence of the private sphere, and, similarly, the meaning of the original contract is misinterpreted without both, mutually dependent, halves of the story.

She makes the same point more explicitly and extensively in "Feminist Critiques of the Public/Private Dichotomy," in S.I. Benn and G.F. Gaus *Public and Private*, pp. 281–306.

15   C. Pateman appears to oscillate between two interpretations of the condition of women in Natural Law theorists, especially Locke. See *The Sexual Contract*, p. 52. On the one hand, she claims, for Locke,

> women are excluded from the status of 'individual' in the natural condition. Locke assumes that marriage and the family exist in the natural state and he also argues that the attributes of individuals are sexually differentiated; only men naturally have the characteristics of free and equal human beings. Women are naturally subordinate to men and the order of nature is reflected in the structure of conjugal relations.

But Pateman acknowledges that "Locke suggests that a wife can own property in her own right, and he even introduces the possibility of divorce, of a dissoluble marriage contract." Pateman does not tell us how women can do all these things if they are not considered *prima facie* free and equal human beings. Pateman fails to explain how Natural Law theorists manage to grant equal capacities to all only to take them away, although she tells us why, in her opinion, they do it. See pp. 180–1.

16   H. Warrender has expressed this idea in a slightly different form in his "Political Theory and Historiography: A Reply to Professor Skinner on Hobbes," *Historical Journal*, 1979, vol. 22, p. 933:

> A serious difficulty in matching historical material against political theory is that theorists make interlocking statements for which the appropriate historical *scale* would appear to alter significantly, even in the course of the same argument. If historical evidence is to set limits to legitimate theoretical interpretation, some clarification of the crucial historical scale is therefore imperative.

(Italicized words and sentences in quotations are so in the original, unless otherwise noted.)

17   C.B. Parekh, "The Nature of Political Philosophy," in Preston King and C.B. Parekh (eds), *Politics and Experience*, Cambridge, Cambridge University Press, 1968, pp. 153–207, analyzes the differences between

identification and interpretation, and between a mode of analysis which uses interpretation in order to "identify" or "recognize" an object, and another which uses identification with the aim of "understanding" that object.

18 In comparing the task of the historian and that of the philosopher, J.G.A. Pocock writes:

> The history of political thought ... has in this way a tendency to become the history of mutations in the cardinal assumptions (perhaps unconscious ones) on which it can be shown to have been based. If the term "philosophy" may be used for thought which leads to the establishment or modification of cardinal assumptions, the history being written will be philosophical history.

"The History of Political Thought: A Methodological Inquiry," in P. Laslett and W.G. Runciman (eds), *Philosophy, Politics and Society*, Oxford, Basil Blackwell, 1975, pp. 182–202.

19 Even scholars who emphasize the separation between present and past ages cannot avoid agreeing that there must exist a homogeneous structure of a kind in us and past writers which allows us to understand them at all. Q. Skinner, *Meaning and Context*, Cambridge, Polity Press, 1988, pp. 257–8, and A. MacIntyre, "The Relationship of Philosophy to its Past," in R. Rorty, J.B. Schneewind, and Q. Skinner (eds), *Philosophy in History*, Cambridge, Cambridge University Press, 1984, p. 42:

> It is these schemes of belief which provide the framework of continuity through time within which the transition from one incommensurable body of theory to its rival is made; and there has to be such a framework; for without the conceptual resources which it affords we could not understand the two bodies of theory as rivals which provide alternative and incompatible accounts of one and the same subject-matter and which offer us rival and incompatible means of achieving the same set of theoretical goals.

I must confess that I do not understand why we should share "beliefs" with our ancestors, but not "ideas," and why incommensurability has to be introduced and then overcome.

20 The notion of "consent," as used by seventeenth-century writers provides a good example. As we shall see, Natural Law theorists consider a lot of activities, or lack thereof, as signifying that a person has given her consent. They also hold that we keep being "free to consent," even if under material pressure to accept the other party's proposal. A woman, for example, is free to accept subordination to her prospective husband (provided he does not physically force her), even if the alternative is death from starvation. As is well known, Hobbes goes so far as to say that even a direct physical threat does not impair our freedom.

21 M. Weber, *Economy and Society*, G. Roth and C. Wittich (eds), Berkeley, CA, University of California Press, 1978, vol. I, p. 53.

22 This also explains why, for stylistic reasons, I have used power and authority interchangeably, although the two concepts can carry different connotations. H. Arendt presents a view of their differences in *Between Past and Future*, New York, The Viking Press, 1961, ch. 3, "What Is Authority?" pp. 91–141.

1 DOMESTIC SOCIETY/POLITICAL SOCIETY

1   I am referring here to Western societies.
2   "Jurisdiction" and "competence" are partially overlapping terms in British juridical language. I therefore use them interchangeably. See "Jurisdiction," F. De Franchis, *Dizionario giuridico, Inglese–Italiano*, Milano, Giuffrè, 1984. I wish to warn the reader that in the seventeenth century, however, the term jurisdiction was always used as a synonym of political power. On the contrary, I employ it to denote both personal and political domains of competence.
3   On the type of discourse made possible by the vocabulary one employs, see the essay, already quoted, by J.G.A. Pocock, "Virtues, Rights, and Manners. A Model for Historians of Political Thought," in *Virtue, Commerce, and History*, Cambridge, Cambridge University Press, 1985, pp. 37–50, and his "Cambridge Paradigms and Scotch Philosophers," in I. Hont, and M. Ignatieff (eds), *Wealth and Virtue*, Cambridge, Cambridge University Press, 1985, p. 248.

> It is hard to find juristic terminology or assumptions in Machiavelli, Guicciardini or Harrington – though the second was a doctor of laws and the third lived in the iron age of the common law mind – and the reason is not far to seek: so at least the premises of the civic humanist paradigm strongly suggest. The basic concept in republican thinking is *virtus*; the basic concept of all jurisprudence is necessarily *ius*; and there is no known way of representing virtue as a right. [Virtue] becomes a quality of the relations between persons equal in citizenship, and between them and the republic, *polis* or *vivere civile*, which is the form of that equality. It pertains so directly to those relationships that it does not require that they be mediated through the proprietorship of things; property is the precondition of virtue, but not the medium in which it is expressed.

4   Q. Skinner has contended that in Machiavellian republicanism participation in public life is becoming the means through which the enjoyment of private life can be secured. "The Idea of Negative Liberty: Philosophical and Historical Perspectives," in R. Rorty, J.B. Schneewind, and Q. Skinner (eds), *Philosophy in History*, Cambridge, Cambridge University Press, 1984, pp. 193–221.
5   The classical example of misinterpretation is Aquinas's translation of *political* as *social*, which will become standard in the literature. H. Arendt comments on this point in *The Human Condition*, Chicago, The University of Chicago Press, 1958, p. 23. I first encountered two of the main themes which I explore in this chapter in an article by N. Bobbio, "Il modello giusnaturalistico" (1973), now reprinted in *Thomas Hobbes*, Torino, Einaudi, 1989. (My translation of this book is about to appear from the University of Chicago Press.) These themes are: the contrast of the Aristotelian conceptions of the family and the conception developed by Natural Law theorists; and the implications which conceptions of the family have for conceptions of politics.
6   Aristotle, *Politics,* E. Barker (tr.), Oxford, Oxford University Press, 1958, Bk II, 1263b, pp. 50–1; 1264b, pp. 54–5.
7   ibid., 1261a, p. 41.

8 ibid., 1253b, p. 12.
9 ibid., 1252a, p. 1.
10 ibid., 1259b, p. 32.
11 William J. Booth, "Politics and the Household. A Commentary on Aristotle's *Politics* Book One," *History of Political Thought*, 1981, vol. 2, pp. 203–26.
12 Aristotle, *Politics*, 1252a, p.2.
13 ibid., 1255b, p. 17.
14 ibid., 1259b, p. 32.
15 But what should we call the human groups in which ruling is permanently assigned to one or a few? Are they political bodies as well, or are they more similar to big households? Should an association guarantee participation to all citizens to deserve to be called political? In other terms, what are the minimal requirements to identify a *political* association? Why do we consider monarchy and aristocracy political forms of government, but we label Oriental kingdoms despotic? Aristotle struggles with these questions throughout the *Politics*, without offering completely satisfactory answers. It however appears that the criteria to distinguish a political ruler from a *de facto* despot are whether the interests of the governed are kept distinct from the personal interest of the governor/s, and whether the ruler furthers the good of the community or only his own. If these are the minimal criteria to identify a "political" community, then even the household can be considered a political association. In the *Nicomachean Ethics*, Aristotle appears to have already applied this reasoning, in contending that "the association of husband and wife is clearly an aristocracy. The man rules by virtue of merit, and in the sphere that is his by right; but he hands over to his wife such matters as are suitable to her." J.A.K. Thomson (tr.), Harmondsworth, Penguin Books, 1976, 1161a6, p. 276. This "minimal" conception of politics leads J.M. Blythe to explore the relevance of the Aristotelian analogical themes between household and body politic for medieval writers. But he tries to reconcile Aristotle's assertion that family and body politic differ in quality with his analogical motifs, rather than seeing them as the elements of two different conceptions of politics, which I have briefly sketched above. "Family, Government, and the Medieval Aristotelians," *History of Political Thought*, 1989, vol. 10, pp. 1–16.
16 Slaves are considered items of private property like things. The head of household will automatically promote their welfare when properly taking care of his own. A good father will try to further the good of his children as well as his own. Aristotle, *Politics*, 1253b, p. 10; 1254a, p. 11. Women are not mentioned in this respect, because their condition is problematic for thinkers. (*De facto* they are treated like children.) They are adult and free, but they are denied autonomy. The arguments to defend this position always read implausibly, and Aristotle well knew that some thinkers (among them Plato) had admitted that women could perform the same tasks as men.
17 Thomas Aquinas, *On Kingship*, Toronto, The Pontifical Institute of Medieval Studies, 1949, pp. 9–10.
18 What Aristotle considered mere livelihood, attainable even by the household.

19   The term "body politic" is amphibolic, in that it indicates both the part and the whole. Our term "state" does the same.

20   Q. Skinner, in *The Foundations of Modern Political Thought*, Cambridge, Cambridge University Press, 1978, vol. I, p. XIV, has emphasized the role played by Stoic notions in the elaboration of the modern vocabulary of politics.

21   For an analysis of the evolution of the notion of *jurisdictio,* see M.P. Gilmore, *Arguments from Roman Law in Political Thought, 1200–1600*, Cambridge, MA, Harvard University Press, 1941.

22   F. Suàrez, *De Legibus*, Madrid, Consejo Superior de Investigaciones Cientificas, Instituto Francisco de Vitoria, 1971, vol. I, pp. 122–3. The translation of excerpts from Suàrez's work is mine, as there is no complete English version of the *De Legibus*.

> A private home, which is ruled by the father of the family, is called imperfect in an absolute rather than relative sense.... For people do not join in it as fundamental members of a body politic, but inferiors only exist in the interest of the master, and are all in various ways subjected to his power.

And pp. 151–2:

> And from this the second difference [between domestic and political association] follows, for there is much more coercive power in political than in domestic authority. For public power is much greater than private power, also because more coercion is necessary to rule a perfect community and keep all its parts in order, than to rule a private home and private persons.

23   Which Suàrez attributes to Aristotle himself: "The reason of which can be found in Aristotle, for such a community possesses neither political authority, nor the coercive power which is properly required in a legislator." ibid., I, p. 123.

24   By distinguishing between affirmative and negative precepts of the law of nature, and contending that affirmative precepts may be altered by human beings to provide for the needs of social life, Suàrez offers a hypothesis to explain how men gave up their natural equality and submitted to a ruler. It is permissible to renounce one's natural liberty, as heads of households do in choosing a sovereign, servants or slaves in subjecting themselves to a master, women in confirming through a free choice their natural subordination to their husbands. Although power ultimately comes from God, only human beings can actualize it through their actions and their active interpretation of the law of nature. ibid., IV, pp. 31–2.

25   J. Bodin had already developed this argument. *The Six Bookes of a Commonweale*, R. Knolles (tr.), New York, Arno Press Reprints, 1979, p. 9.

> For albeit the maister of the family haue three hundred wiues, as had *Salomon* King of the Hebrews; and six hundred children, as had *Hermotimus* king of the Parthians by his multitude of wiues; or fiue hundred slaues, as had *Crassus*; if they bee all vnder the commaund of one and the same head of the familie, they are neither to be called a people, nor a citie, but by the name of a family onely: Yea although hee

haue many children, or seruants maried, hauing families themselues
children also; prouided alwaies, that they be under the authoritie of one
head, whom the law calleth father of the family, although he yet crie in
his cradle.

26 Which does not mean, to seventeenth-century writers, that they exchange
things of equal value, but merely that each party must gain something in
the transaction. On the definition of reciprocity, see A. Gouldner, "The
Norm of Reciprocity: A Preliminary Statement," *American Sociological
Review*, 1960, vol. 25, pp. 161–78.

27 His most important work is *Of the Law of War and Peace*, published in
1625. K. Haakonssen writes about Grotius:

> Grotius's influence was, of course, vast and varied, and a history of
> social and political thought in the seventeenth and eighteenth centuries
> might well be written that takes as its Leitmotiv the role of the modern
> school of natural law which he, despite all scholarly qualifications
> about his originality, must still be said to have founded (if for no other
> reasons than because he was thought to have done so).

"Hugo Grotius and the History of Political Thought," *Political Theory*,
1985, vol. 13, pp. 239–65. R. Tuck offers a good illustration of the
contemporary and subsequent interpretations of Grotius as the "first of the
modern," in "The 'Modern' Theory of Natural Law," in A. Padgen (ed.),
The Language of Political Theory in Early Modern Europe, Oxford,
Oxford University Press, 1985, pp. 99–119. R. Tuck here reports A.
MacIntyre's view that Grotius's theory is a "later development of
Aquinas' view of natural law into a law for the nations."

28 H. Grotius, *Of the Law of War and Peace*, A.C. Campbell (tr.), New York,
M.W. Walter Dunne, 1901, bk. I, ch. II, i, p. 33.

29 "His" survival, as it is unclear whether Grotius included women,
although the capacities which he recognizes to them – to conclude
contracts, to get redress against their husbands when the latter trespass,
etc. – seem to imply that women too are endowed with the faculties
necessary to take care of their own preservation.

30 R. Tuck, *Natural Rights Theories*, Cambridge, Cambridge University
Press, 1981, p. 67.

31 H. Grotius, *War and Peace*, I, I, iii, p. 18; iv, p. 19; ix, p. 20. The third
meaning clearly recalls Aristotle's discussion of justice as both a specific
virtue, and the synthesis of all virtues, in *Nicomachean Ethics*, 1129b30–
30a18, pp. 173–4.

32 H. Grotius, *War and Peace*, I, I, iv, pp. 19–20.

33 At least in the sense that we have no trouble in understanding what form
that relationship may take.

34 Pufendorf partially makes this point, as we shall see below. P. Riley
remarks this logical distinction in discussing Locke, in "Locke and the
Dictatorship of the Bourgeoisie," *Political Studies*, 1965, vol. 13, pp. 219–
30.

> The sense in which food must belong to a man before it can do to him
> any good is a biological one – namely he has to eat it; and the sense in
> which an Indian's nourishment is *his* is a logical one – namely that we

can only identify nourishment by identifying the man nourished. This is not to talk of rights at all, and particularly not to talk of absolute rights. It is a very dangerous way of talking, for it swiftly confuses the "his" of identification with the "his" of ownership or rightful possession.

I agree with Riley that we ought not to confuse the two senses of "his." But I am afraid that seventeenth-century thinkers, Locke included, did "confuse" them. For they, especially Grotius and Locke, treated the faculties which identify a person as being her property.

35   Not power over oneself, which is an endowment we receive from God. The faculty to dispose of oneself, which is the base for exercising rights, thus assumes this double feature of being constitutive of human personality as such – of identity, as we would say today – and of being something detachable from us and alienable. This ambivalence is partially responsible for the awkwardness of Grotius's text on this point, and of the present interpretation.

36   H. Grotius, *War and Peace*, II, III, ii, p. 103.

37   ibid., II, XI, iv, p. 134.

38   ibid., II, XVII, ii, pp. 195–6.

39   All, excluding only idiots, madmen, and infants. ibid., II, XX, vii, p. 226.

40   In Grotius's proprietary model. We should probably prefer to say "inhere in," or "are constitutive of," a person.

41   ibid., II, XII, ii, p. 144.

42   ibid., II, XXV, iii. p. 287.

43   Or to no one, as is the case with *res nullius*. But personal resources always belong to someone.

44   Grotius specifies that "services accompanied with mutual obligation are those where the use of a thing is allowed to any one without a complete alienation, or where labour is given in expectation of some valuable consideration." ibid., II, XII, ii, p. 144. The proprietary model thus also holds for transactions through which resources are not permanently transferred to others. These types of transactions do not permanently impair one party's personal capacities, thus leaving the two parties in a condition of equality.

45   Although Grotius emphasizes that sovereignty can literally be acquired as property.

> Some sovereigns hold their power by a plenary right of property; when for instance it comes into their possession by the right of lawful conquest, or when a people, to avoid greater evils, make an unqualified surrender of themselves and their rights into their hands.

ibid., I, III, xi, pp. 71–2.

46   Be they personal, or political, regarding material or personal resources.

47   ibid., II, II, xviii, p. 99; III, I, ii, p. 291.

48   Although radical libertarians contend that we can voluntarily dispose of ourselves entirely.

49   ibid., I, II, i, p. 33.

50   ibid., I, II, i, p. 33; III, III, ii, pp. 315–16.

51

> The moral power then of governing a state, which is called by Thucydides the civil power, is described as consisting of three parts

which form the necessary substance of every state; and those are the right of making its own laws, executing them in its own manner, and appointing its own magistrates.

ibid., I, II, vi, pp. 60–1.

52 In other terms, individuals transfer to the ruler the power of life and death. But since only a superior can be sure that his commands will be obeyed, the transference is meaningless unless the transferor at the same time recognizes the superior's right to dispose of the transferor as he thinks fit. The transaction regards the right to punish transgressors, but the procedure entails the alienation of much more than that right. Tuck remarks that Locke found the obvious solution of having individuals transfer that right without alienating their personality. *Rights Theories*, pp. 172–3. It is however interesting to observe that even in Locke's case the procedure is consequential for the distribution of power, as the people, in transferring only the right to punish, retain that position of superiority that the ruler acquires in Grotius's case.

53 H. Grotius, *War and Peace*, III, XXV, i, p. 285. It is on the basis of statements such as this that Haakonssen, in "Hugo Grotius," p. 256, offers a "liberal" interpretation of Grotius's theory of the location of sovereignty.

> For him [Grotius] sovereignty can only exist in both [people and rulers] taken together (i.e. in the politically organized society as a whole).... The ruler is the special agent for the sovereignty of which the state alone is the common agent. In other words, sovereignty is not a power that rulers have over subjects, but one that they exercise on behalf of the corporate body.

If it were not so, says Haakossen, how could Grotius contend that citizens continue to enjoy individual liberty, although not political liberty, under an absolute government? I wish to offer two remarks on this view. The first regards the interpretation of the ruler as the caretaker of the corporate body. The comparison with the domestic association is helpful here, for the Grotian ruler performs the same role as the head of household. The latter does indeed take care of the good of the family, but he does so by ruling over the other members. How can he ensure the welfare of the group, if everyone goes his own way, and if democratic participation in the decision-making process has been rejected? (As Grotius rejects it.) The second remark addresses the question of the possibility of enjoying individual, we should say civil, but not political liberty. It seems to me that Grotius can contend that personal liberty is safe under an absolute government, because I am secure in the enjoyment of my property from invasion and harm not so much from the sovereign, as from other fellow-citizens. (Which is the reason why the political community was instituted in the first place, and it is Hobbes's strong reason to support absolute political power.) It is true that for Grotius, unlike for Hobbes, there is a preexisting natural order which the ruler should implement. But as I shall try to show below, who interprets the details of that order, after civil society has been established? If it is the ruler, and without appeal, citizens have *de facto* alienated their agency. It seems to me that the ambiguities in Grotius's text are addressed in a more balanced way by R. Tuck, in *Rights Theories*, pp. 77–80.

54   This dynamic is also reflected in the debate over the nature of justice, to
which Grotius gives a significant contribution. As Tuck has well illustrated, Grotius abandons Aristotle's conception of distributive justice in
favor of commutative justice, which requires that people be given what
legitimately belongs to them. The law of nature however comprises what
is proper, besides what is just. And it is by enforcing "propriety," not
merely justice, that the sovereign can take care of the public good. "But
we have said, the law obliges us to do what is proper, not simply what is
just; because, under this notion, right belongs to the substance not only of
justice, as we have explained it." *War and Peace*, I, I, ix, p. 20. Grotius is
aware of the implications of his conception. In rejecting the traditional
argument that the pursuit of the common good implies to recognize a
superiority to the people over the sovereign, he says:

> But it is not universally true, that all power is conferred for the benefit
> of the party governed. For some powers are conferred for the sake of the
> governor, as the right of a master over a slave; in which the advantage
> of the latter is only a contingent and adventitious circumstance.

Since a people can enslave itself to the sovereign, the latter is not
necessarily obliged to give priority to the good of his subjects over his
own. I, III, viii, p. 67.

55   S. Pufendorf, *Of the Law of Nature and Nations*, London, 1717, bk I, I, vii,
p. 5.

56   ibid., I, I, xix, p. 12.

57   ibid.

58   ibid., I, I, iii, p. 3.

> We may define our *Moral Entities* to be *certain Modes superadded to
> Natural Things and Motions, by Understanding Beings; chiefly for the
> guiding and tempering the Freedom of voluntary Actions, and for the
> procuring of a decent Regularity in the Method of Life.*

59   ibid. II, V, iii, p. 48. And about the correlation of rights and obligations, he
writes: "For these two Moral Qualities have such a mutual Relation and
Dependence, that whenever there is produced an *Obligation* in one Man,
there immediately springs up a Correspondent Right in another." Bk III,
V, i, p. 47.

60   ibid., III, V, vii, p. 50.

61   ibid., II, II, iii, p. 106.

> Every Man is concern'd to be perfectly in his own Power and Disposal,
> and not to be controlled by Pleasure or Authority of any other. On
> which account too, every Man may be this acknowledg'd *equal* to every
> Man, since all Subjection and all Command are equally banish'd on
> both sides.

62   ibid., VI, III, vii, p. 385. Pufendorf contends that even the slave and his
property are not at the complete disposal of his master.

63   ibid., VI, I, ix, p. 333. Nearly the identical passage can be found in
Hobbes:

> And whereas some have attributed the Dominion to the Man only, as
> being of the more excellent Sex; they misreckon in it. For there is not

always that difference of strength or prudence between the man and the woman, as that the right can be determined without War.

Leviathan, C.B. Macpherson (ed.), Harmondsworth, Penguin Books, 1980, XX, p. 253.

64

If, then, we suppose all Mankind thus plac'd in a Condition of Natural Equality and Liberty, it may happen that a Woman as well as a Man, shall desire Issue peculiarly for herself, over which she may preside and command. Now to accomplish this End, it is necessary, that a Covenant pass between a Man and a Woman, for their *Mutual Assistance in Serving Posterity.* If this Covenant be *Simple,* nor join'd with an Agreement about constant Cohabitation, but respecting barely the Procreation of Children, it confers on neither Party any Sovereignty, or Right over the other, except they may challenge, on either side, the *promised Alliance,* with regard to *Posterity.* And, in this Case, if it was expresly intimated in the Covenant, that the Woman desir'd issue properly for her self and her own Management, the Children shall be under the Government of the Mother.

S. Pufendorf, *Nature and Nations,* VI, I, ix, p. 333.

65   ibid., II, II, iv, p. 108.

66

For though the diversity of Sex, and Number of Years, are not of external Imposition, yet in the method of a Social Life, they involve some kind of a Moral Notion; in as much as different Actions are becoming in different Sexes, and Persons of various Ages require a various Treatment and Application.

ibid., I, I, xii, p. 6.

67

For all Men enjoy a *Natural Liberty* in the same Measure and Degree, which before they suffer to be impair'd or diminish'd; there must intervene either their own Consent; Express, Tacite, or Interpretative, or some Fact of theirs, by which others may obtain a Right of Abridging them of their Liberty by Force, in case they will not part with it by a voluntary Submission.

ibid., III, II, viii, p. 184. We find it hard to believe that human beings doomed to subjection are anyway free. But Pufendorf's view that rights and obligations are constituted through agreement, by imposing a "moral quality" on a relation, for example, explains why he insists on the requirement of free consent to a position of subjection. In commenting on the work *De Civitate* by the German writer J. Friedrich Hornius, who remarks that the woman's consent is reduced to accepting the man who asks her for marriage, since the man's power is unquestionably established by God, Pufendorf affirms that her free consent is constitutive of that power, since man and woman are equal by nature.

And that the Woman, for this reason, lies under no Obligation to obey, before she hath by her own Consent, submitted to the Rule and Authority of an Husband. And though that she should thus submit

herself, be indeed agreeable to the Divine Will, yet this doth not hinder,
but that her own Covenant and her Subjection consequent upon it, are
the *immediate* and *nearest* Cause productive of *the Husband's Power.*

ibid., VI, I, xii, p. 337.

68   The term *jus* signifies *"that Moral Quality by which we justly obtain
either the Government of Persons, or the Possession of Things, or by the
Force of which we may claim somewhat as due to us."* ibid., I, I, xx, p. 12.

69

I acquire a *Right* over a Person, if he either expresly or tacitly
consents, that I shall prescribe to him what he ought to do, to suffer, or
to forbear; by Virtue of which Agreement he both obliges himself,
voluntarily to study Obedience to my Pleasure, and at the same time
grants me a Right of compelling him, in case of default, to his Duty, by
proposing some considerable evil, which I shall otherwise bring upon
him.

ibid., III, V, iv, p. 48.

70   ibid., III, II, ix, p. 186.
71   Pufendorf never mentions unmarried women as independent adults.
Although women's consent to the exercise of power over them is
necessary, Pufendorf is convinced that women cannot be, in the world as
we know it, independent human beings.
72   ibid., VII, I, iv, p. 456.
73   Human beings are all equal; at least normatively, as we should say today.

Since the Human Nature agrees equally to all Persons, and since no one
can live a sociable life with another, who does not own and respect him
as a Man; it follows as a Command of the Law of Nature, that every
Man esteem and treat another as one who is Naturally his Equal, or who
is a Man as well as he.

ibid., III, II, i, p. 178. Pufendorf specifies that the equality he is talking
about is "an Equality of Right." ibid., III, II, ii, p. 180.

74   ibid., VII, I, xi, p. 336.
75   Although all adults are in principle endowed with political agency, the
alienation of personal capacities curtails their independence, and leaves
only heads of households to give life to civil society. It therefore becomes
irrelevant whether dependents had assigned the power of life and death to
their personal superior. If they had, the head of household would anyway
transfer to the ruler that power together with his. If they had not, they
would at any rate be virtually represented by the head of the family, and
their active participation would thus be excluded.
76   Pufendorf emphasizes that a convention is not sufficient, and that a formal
agreement is necessary. He however uses the two terms synonymously.
77   ibid., VII, II, vii, p. 469.
78   ibid., VII, III, i, p. 484.
79   ibid., VII, III, vi, p. 488. Pufendorf mentions that size is not enough to
transform a household into a body politic. In Pufendorf, it might be a
reference to Hobbes, who hypothesizes both a commonwealth by acquisition and a commonwealth by institution. Since for Hobbes fathers acquire
their power over children as over anyone else, a family is for Hobbes a

small commonwealth, in which political power is exercised. Hobbes retains only one difference between household and body politic, which directly refers to size: whether the association can be conquered without engaging in a war. *Leviathan*, XX, p. 257.

80   With all the consequences for public agency.
81   H. Grotius, *War and Peace*, I, I, vi, p. 20.
82   S. Pufendorf, *Nature and Nations*, VII, VI, vii, p. 523.
83   ibid., VII, VI, vi, p. 522.
84   Except for the law of nature itself, which is enforced only by God. The sovereign, of course, had better follow the prudential rule that depriving his subjects of their private property, or endangering its secure enjoyment, is counterproductive. But subjects are not entitled to hold the sovereign accountable if he does not follow that prudential rule. For Pufendorf, therefore, as for Hobbes, the private domain coincides with whatever is not regulated by the law. Property is

> frequently distinguish'd into *Plenary* and *Diminutive*. The former is either join'd with that they call *Eminent Property*, in which manner Civil States, or the Heads and Governors of them possess their Goods; or else disjoin'd from it, and term'd *Vulgar*; by which a private Man enjoys a full Power of disposing of his Goods, except so far that the Use of them be not Under the Direction of the Municipal Laws.

> ibid., IV, IV, ii, p. 146.

85   ibid., VII, VI, xvii, p. 534.
86   ibid., VI, II, xi, p. 375.
87   ibid., VII, III, i, p. 484.

2   PATRIARCHALISM

1   If the differences between analogy and assimilation are not kept in mind, it becomes impossible to understand what sets Filmer apart from other writers, who may describe the king as a father, but would never contend that their power is the same. For example, R.W.K. Hinton, in "Husbands, Fathers, and Conqueroros, I," *Political Studies*, 1967, vol. 15, pp. 291–300, interprets Bodin as a patriarchalist – which he is not – because he uses analogies between the care of the family and of a kingdom; and he then contends that Filmer uses the family/kingdom identity only as a metaphor.
2   Hobbes contends that families are small kingdoms, for a person acquires political power by institution or by acquisition. Fathers are rulers by acquisition, as their children are *de facto* under their authority, which they will legitimate *a posteriori* by giving their consent once they have grown. Household and body politic are thus the same type of association, at least from the point of view of the nature of the power relations structuring them. Hobbes abandons the traditional criterion of distinction, which pointed to a difference in "essence," either grounded metaphysically, as in Aristotle, or based on the nature of the actions of the members. But, significantly enough, Hobbes retains the criterion of size to maintain a distinction between the two groups. "But yet a Family is not properly a

Common-wealth; unlesse it be of that power by its own number, or by other opportunities, as not to be subdued without the hazard of war." *Leviathan*, C.B. Macpherson (ed.), Harmondsworth, Penguin Books, 1980, XX, p. 257.

3   It should be remarked that the public has always, at least functionally, precedence over the private. Even if we hypothesize, as mature liberalism has done, that the public must preserve and defend the sanctity of the private sphere, privileged access to it has to be granted to the public so that protection can be ensured.

4   As Grotius's distinction between private and public law, mentioned in Chapter 2, makes clear.

5   S. Pufendorf, *Of the Law of Nature and Nations*, London, 1717, bk VI, III, vii, pp. 385–6.

6   Patriarchalist themes are pervasive in seventeenth-century British political discourse. See G.J. Schochet, *Patriarchalism in Political Thought*, New York, Basic Books, 1975.

7   This approach is adopted by Plato, in *The Statesman*.

Are we then to regard the statesman, the king, the slavemaster, and the master of a household as essentially one though we use all these names for them, or shall we say that four distinct sciences exist, each of them corresponding to one of the four titles?... Furthermore, is there much difference between a large household organization and a small-sized city, so far as the exercise of authority over it is concerned?

The Statesman, in *Collected Dialogues*, E. Hamilton and H. Cairns (eds), Princeton, NJ, Princeton University Press, 1985, 258e, p. 1021; 259b, p. 1022.

8   Filmer bluntly summarizes his position in discussing Suàrez:

Suàrez proceeds, and tells us that "in process of time Adam had complete economical power." I know not what he means by this *complete economical* power, nor how or in what it doth really and essentially differ from political. If Adam did or might exercise in his family the same jurisdiction which a King doth now in a commonweal, then the kinds of power are not distinct. And though they may receive an accidental difference by the amplitude or extent of the bounds of the one beyond the other, yet since the like difference is also found in political estates, it follows that economical and political power differ no otherwise than a little commonweal differs from a great one.

R. Filmer, *Patriarcha*, in *Patriarcha and Other Political Works*, P. Laslett (ed.), Oxford, Basil Blackwell, 1949, p. 78. All other works by Filmer are quoted or cited from Laslett's edition. Laslett edits the 1653 manuscript of *Patriarcha*. Prof. Wallace discovered an earlier version, written between 1628 and 1631, which omits the critique of *De Jure Belli* and *Mare Clausum*, and does not quote Selden's *Titles of Honour*. R. Tuck, "A New Date for Filmer's *Patriarcha*," *Historical Journal*, 1986, vol. 29, pp. 183–6. I learned too late of the new edition of Filmer's works by Johann P. Sommerville (Cambridge, Cambridge University Press, 1991) to be able to consult it.

9   R. Filmer, *Directions for Obedience to Government in Dangerous or Doubtful Times*, p. 232.

10   R. Filmer, *Patriarcha*, p. 63.
11   R. Filmer, *Observations upon Aristotle's Politiques Touching Forms of Government*, p. 241. About the domesticization of politics implied by the lack of the distinction between private and public, see J.B. Elshtain, *Public Man, Private Woman*, Princeton, NJ, Princeton University Press, 1981, pp. 319–23.
12   The proprietary view of sovereignty is typical of medieval political thought, and starts to be questioned primarily by Bodin in *The Six Bookes of a Commonweale*. What we read in Grotius and Natural Law theorists until Locke is therefore the end of the story and not its beginning. M.P. Gilmore, *Arguments from Roman Law in Political Thought*, 1200–1600, Cambridge, MA, Harvard University Press, 1941, describes the development of a non-proprietary conception, and considers Bodin crucial in rejecting the medieval view. Otto Gierke, in his still important work on Natural Law, contends that the construction of the independent personality of the state, aside and above the person of the ruler, is one of the crucial and indispensable elements of the modern theory of the state. *Natural Law and the Theory of Society, 1500 to 1800*, Cambridge, Cambridge University Press, 1934, p. 161.
13   R. Filmer, *Observations on Mr Hobbes's Leviathan: Or His Artificial Man – A Commonwealth*, p. 241.
14   G. Parry, "Individuality, Politics and the Critique of Paternalism in John Locke," *Political Studies*, 1964, vol. 12, pp. 173–4:

> To extend paternalist rule into the age of discretion is therefore to maintain individuals in the backward condition of children. Far from being analogous to politics, paternalism contradicts its very bases. Paternal rule is not the secondary activity of umpirage or compromise between individual interests and self-chosen activities but is over those incapable of such choices.... The very vocabulary of paternalism betrays its anti-political character. It is not the language of individuality – "choice," "liberty," "industry" – but of childhood – "protection," "tutelage."

15   R. Filmer, *The Anarchy of a Limited or Mixed Monarchy*, pp. 289–90. The moral categories of "things necessary" and "things indifferent" do not apply in a situation where human beings do not "know," according to Genesis, the difference between good and evil.
16   Filmer's use of the concept shows that the issue is shifting from the definition of proper ecclesiastical and political jurisdiction, to a problem of jurisdictions within the realm of politics. J. Locke will use the same categories to discuss the issue of toleration. By redefining what belongs and what does not belong to the realm of "things indifferent," and by contending that government cannot interfere with this realm, he will both elaborate a very strong defense of toleration, and also redefine the boundaries between the sphere of individual discretion, and that open to government intervention. *An Essay Concerning Toleration*, in *Scritti editi e inediti sulla tolleranza*, C.A. Viano (ed.), Torino, Taylor, 1961, pp. 82–6.
17   In arguing against democratic procedures, Filmer contends:

> Mankind is like the sea, ever ebbing or flowing, every minute one is born another dies; those that are the people this minute, are not the

people the next minute, in every instant and point of time there is a variation: no one time can be indifferent for all mankind to assemble; it cannot but be mischievous always at the least to all infants and others under age of discretion; not to speak of women, especially virgins, who by birth have as much natural freedom as any other, and therefore ought not to lose their liberty without their own consent.

Anarchy of Mixed Monarchy, p. 287.

18   R. Filmer, *Observations upon Aristotle's Politiques*, p. 224.

19   R. Filmer, *Observations on Mr Hobbes's Leviathan*, p. 241.

Mr Hobbes confesseth and believes it was never generally so, that there was such a *jus naturae*; and if not generally, then not at all, for one exception bars all if he mark it well; whereas he imagines such a right of nature may be now practised in America, he confesseth a government there of families, which government how small or brutish soever (as he calls it) is sufficient to destroy his *jus naturale*.

G.J. Schochet agrees with Filmer's critique of Hobbes's description of the state of nature, and analyzes the possible implications of a social natural condition for Hobbes's political theory. "Thomas Hobbes on the Family and the State of Nature," *Political Science Quarterly*, 1967, vol. 83, pp. 427–45. On the analogies between family and commonwealth in Hobbes, see R.A. Chapman, "*Leviathan* Writ Small: Thomas Hobbes on the Family," *American Political Science Review*, 1975, vol. 69, pp. 76–90. In "Husbands, Fathers, and Conquerors, II," *Political Studies*, 1968, vol. 16, pp. 55–67, R.W.K. Hinton contends that Hobbes was Locke's true enemy, because he intertwined patriarchalism and contractualism.

20   R. Filmer, *Anarchy of Mixed Monarchy*, p. 287.

21   R. Filmer, *Patriarcha*, p. 58.

It is a common opinion that at the confusion of tongues there were seventy-two distinct nations erected. All which were not confused multitudes, without heads or governors, and at liberty to choose what governors or government they pleased, but they were distinct families, which had Fathers for rulers over them.

22   The Hobbesian solution of hypothesizing a contract *a posteriori* is for Filmer merely a confirmation that human beings are not born free.

23

And yet for all this every Father is bound by the law of nature to do his best for the preservation of his family. But much more is a King always tied by the same law of nature to keep this general ground, that the safety of his kingdom be his chief law.

ibid., p. 96.

24   If on the surface this conception reads identical to that of Hobbes, the difference lies in the fact that Hobbesian individuals can use their reason to find a solution, whereas Filmer's heads of households can only actualize in the person of the monarch a political authority which has always been among them *in potentia*.

25   R. Filmer, *Directions for Obedience to Government*, p. 233. By Filmer's own admission, to prevent fathers from exercising their power – as

happens when a monarch rules – "destroys the frame of nature," or, in other terms, violates another of his fundamental principles, that the law of nature cannot be altered.

26 The monarch's rule, moreover, is absolute and arbitrary. (Except for compliance with the laws of God and nature, which can only be enforced by God.) Unlike for Hobbes, who contends that the sovereign's will must be made known through written laws, for Filmer the sovereign can rule by issuing idiosyncratic commands. He declares his will (or has it directly executed), and no redress is possible, as happens between a father and his dependents.

27 R. Filmer, *Patriarcha*, p. 96.

28 R. Filmer, *Observations upon H. Grotius*, pp. 268–9.

29 Translated into the language of Natural Law theory, this problem reads: can the law of nature be changed?

30 A. Ascham, *Of the Confusions and Revolutions of Governments*, Delmar, NY, Scholars' Facsimiles & Reprints, 1975.

31 E. Gee, *The Divine Right and Originall of the Civill Magistrate from God*, London, 1658, V, p. 146. At this time, *Patriarcha*, which was published posthumously in 1680, only circulated in manuscript. But other works by Filmer where he presents his position were already available. For example, *The Anarchy of a Limited or Mixed Monarchy*, 1648; *The Necessity of the Absolute Power of all Kings*, 1648; *Directions for Obedience to Government in Dangerous or Doubtful Times*, and *Observations upon Aristotle's Politiques Touching Forms of Government*, 1652; *Observations Concerning the Originall of Government*, 1652; and the *Freeholder's Grand Inquest Touching the King and His Parliament*, 1647; all in *Patriarcha and Other Political Works*.

32 E. Gee, *Divine Right*, I, pp. 34–5.

33

> And amongst men, in Natural power, that is, strength, or might of body, the family is greater than the Master, the Subject excel their Sovereign, the Soldier overmatch their Leaders; whereas the Moral power in relation to each of these is in the Master, the Sovereign, the Leader.

ibid., I, p. 16.

34 ibid., III, p. 79. And on the contract:

> Thus by their own contract persons become associates in private traffique, fellow-citizens are incorporated in one Common-wealth, and Nations become confederates in one league: thus two by marriage become man and wife.... Thus freemen make themselves servants; and thus Common-wealths, or bodies politique come under this or that form or constitution of Government.

ibid., III, p. 83.

35 It might be more correct to say that human beings do not merely legitimate authority, but are the efficient cause of its coming into being. I employ an Aristotelian terminology because it seems to me that Gee still relies on a teleological view of the relationship between God's commands and human implementation of them. Power roles exist *in potentia* in God's mind and will, and human beings give them actuality. Gee is in this very close to Suàrez, whose metaphysics is Aristotelian rather than Stoic. Gee is

however on the watershed between teleologism and mechanism, as he also sees human intervention in terms of the application of general rules (the law of nature) to specific cases. Laws of nature establish general principles, and we are responsible for subsuming concrete instances under them.

36   ibid., V, p. 145.
37   J. Tyrrell, *Patriarcha, non Monarcha,* London, 1681, and *Bibliotheca Politica,* London, first published 1691–2. As is well known, Tyrrell and Locke were well informed of each other's work, to the degree that authorship of specific points in both thinkers is uncertain. I therefore feel entitled to discuss Tyrrell's *Bibliotheca Politica,* which was published after Locke's *Two Treatises* were in 1689–90, before discussing Locke. Despite the similarities of their conceptions, Tyrrell fails to give as complete a treatment of the relationship between individual rights and political power as we can find in Locke, who can be seen, theoretically if not historically, to have offered a "solution" to the problems left open by Natural Law theory and Filmer's attack on it.
38   J. Tyrrell, *Bibliotheca Politica,* 1718 edn, dialogue I, p. 26.
39   J. Tyrrell, *Patriarcha, non Monarcha,* vol. I, p. 35; *Bibliotheca Politica,* dialogue I, p. 10:

> You and I agreed, that even before the Fall Adam was superior over his Wife and Children, and that they owed him not only Gratitude and Respect as a Parent, but also Obedience in all indifferent things: Yet I deny that this Power or Superiority of Adam over his Wife and Children was at all a Despotical or Civill Power, but meerly Oeconomical, for the Good and Convenience of Adam, and the well ordering and Preservation of his Family; which you will easily grant, if you please to consider what are the essential Differences of Civil Government from Oeconomical. Now the essential Properties of Civil Government consist in preserving and defending the Subjects, both in War and Peace, from foreign Enemies, and intestine Injuries, and Invasions of Men's Persons and Properties, and in revenging and punishing all such Transgressions by Death, or other Punishments, and consequently in making Laws concerning Property, and for restraining Robberies, Murders, and the like.

40   It is noteworthy that the state of nature replaces the state of innocence as a *topos* at a certain point in *Bibliotheca Politica,* when slaves are introduced into the picture. (Supposedly because there were no slaves in the Garden of Eden.) This rhetorical move from the one to the other however shows that the state of nature is the laicized version of the Biblical rendering of human origins.
41   Seventeenth-century writers are not yet fully distinguishing between descriptive and normative levels of analysis.
42   J. Tyrrell, *Patriarcha, non Monarcha,* vol. I, pp. 24–5.
43   ibid., vol. I, pp. 102–3. Servants, slaves (as in Pufendorf), women, and children. Vol. I, p. 110: "But it does not therefore follow, that he has such a despotic power over her, that she [the wife] may in no case judge when he abuses his fatherly or husbandly power." J. Tyrrell, *Bibliotheca Politica,* dialogue I, pp. 14, 30, 32, 33.

44 ibid., dialogue I, p. 38.
45 J. Tyrrell, *Patriarcha, non Monarcha*, vol. I, p. 109.

> But suppose he [the husband] is able to govern her [the wife], and the family, the question is, what kind of power he has over her, as a husband, in the state of nature? I grant, that if she made it part of her bargain to be absolutely subject to him, as that he might command her in all things a slave, and make her do what work he pleased to appoint, and that he may either turn her away, or put her to death, if he find her imbezilling his goods or committing adultery; the woman in this case is bound by her contract, as another servant, who makes her self so by her own consent.

46 ibid., vol. I, p. 109. It must also be remarked that Tyrrell, like Pufendorf, contends that the woman is made subject to the man by God, as a punishment for her sin. Locke will also accept this interpretation of Genesis.
47 The same reasoning is present in Pufendorf, but Tyrrell makes it fully explicit.
48 ibid., vol. I, pp. 73–4.
49 I wish to emphasize once more that this does not necessarily mean that that power has naturalistic foundations. The head of the family leads the group not because of intrinsic superior capacities, but because he has somehow won the trust of his subordinates. When naturalistic elements are reintroduced – as by Locke in the marriage contract – writers do state that explicitly.
50 ibid., vol. I, p. 14. "I see not why it might not be so agreed by the Contracts, that the father should not dispose of the children without the mothers consent."
51 Especially in *Patriarcha, non Monarcha*. In *Bibliotheca Politica*, possibly because of his exchanges with Locke, Tyrrell advances a less permissive conception, which is the one adopted by Locke, and which will therefore be fully explored in the analysis of the *Two Treatises of Government*.
52 In the Roman/Thomistic version too, the natural inequality of dependents insulates the family from the public arena; politics only occur among equal adult male proprietors who "walk out of the domestic association into the public domain," as Bodin puts it.
53 J. Tyrrell, *Patriarcha, non Monarcha*, vol. I, p. 111–12. The sentence is ambiguous: do members of the family get together because they only fear an external enemy? If that were the case, civil society too would only have to face that task, and we know that that is not the case. Tyrrell is here trying to defend his view – that family relations are intrinsically different from those typical of a body politic – without rejecting the possibility that a head of household may acquire political authority.

3 PRIVATE/PUBLIC

1 Peter Laslett has proved the relevance of Filmer to the development of Locke's own conception in his 1965 critical edition of the *Two Treatises*.
2 M.A. Butler emphasizes Locke's anti-patriarchalism in "Early Liberal

Roots of Feminism: John Locke and the Attack on Patriarchy," *American Political Science Review*, 1978, vol. 72, pp. 135–50.

3   As Pufendorf and Tyrrell stress.
4   If this conceptual move is decisive in setting family relations apart from political ones, other associations, churches, economic enterprises, academies, clubs, can be seen as falling between the two. And, in fact, economic enterprises can easily transform into political associations, as the case of the American colonies shows. Locke also has to admit that the family as well can become a political association, where the head of household has monopolized the power of life and death. But can it become a *civil* society? On these matters, see my remarks in note 66 below.
5   At least in discussing the nature of political authority in modern European society. The *topos* continues to enjoy favour in the discussion about Oriental despotism; the best example is of course Montesquieu's *Lettres persanes*.
6   I say "appears" because nowhere does Locke explicitly say that only heads of households are full citizens. As we shall see, however, his theory of incorporation – and the family requires incorporation – justifies assuming that only heads of households are politically active.
7   J. Locke, *Two Treatises of Government*, P. Laslett (ed.), New York, Mentor Books, 1965, I, 52, p. 214; I, 55, p. 216; I, 65, p. 225; I, 64, pp. 223–4; I, 69, p. 229.
8   ibid., I, chs III-VI.
9   Locke summarizes the same point in par. 96 of the *First Treatise*, but in the *Essays* he treats it more extensively.
10   J. Locke, *Two Treatises*, I, 96, p. 250.
11   J. Locke, *Essays on the Law of Nature*, W. von Leyden (ed.), Oxford, Clarendon Press, 1964, p. 183.
12   J. Locke, *Two Treatises*, I, 63, p. 223.

> I agree with our A——, that the Title to this *Honour* is vested in the Parents by Nature, and is a right which accrews to them, by their having begotten their Children, and God by many positive Declarations has confirm'd it to them: I also allow our A——s Rule, *that in Grants and Gifts, that have their Original from God and Nature, as the Power of the Father* (let me add *and Mother*, for whom God hath joyned together, let no Man put asunder) *no inferior Power of Men can limit, nor make any Law of Prescription against them*, O. 158.

13   ibid., I, 53, p. 215.
14   ibid., I, 47, p. 209.
15   ibid., I, 88, p. 244.
16   ibid., II, 77, p. 362; 65, p. 353.
17   ibid., I, 47, p. 210.
18   ibid., I, 63, p. 223.
19   ibid., I, 29, p. 196.
20   John Dunn has emphasized the central role assigned to God in Locke's political thought, and the Christian origins of Locke's concept of equality, which explains its limits. Dunn offers a very restrictive interpretation of the application of that notion, by asserting that equality before God can very well accompany an uncritical acceptance of social inequality. *The*

Political Thought of John Locke, Cambridge, Cambridge University Press, 1969, pp. 225–7. As I try to show in this study, a more complex dynamic between egalitarian assumptions and inegalitarian conclusions is at work in Locke's conception.

21 P. Laslett, "Introduction" to J. Locke, *Two Treatises*, p. 98.

22 J. Locke, *Essays,* p. 161.

23 J. Dunn, "Consent in the Political Theory of John Locke," *Historical Journal*, 1967, vol. 10, pp. 153–82. According to Dunn, Locke's use of consent in social relations must be interpreted as merely the juridical confirmation of non-negotiable ascriptive positions of superiority and subjection.

24 J. Locke, *Two Treatises*, I, 43, p. 206.

25 ibid., I, 67, pp. 226–7.

> If all this be so, as I think, by what has been said, is very evident, then Man has a *Natural Freedom* ... since all that share in the same common Nature, Faculties and Powers, are in Nature equal, and ought to partake in the same common Rights and Priviledges, till the manifest appointment of God, who is *Lord over all, Blessed for ever*, can be produced to shew any particular Persons Supremacy, or a Mans own consent subjects him to a Superior.

26 See the Introduction to this volume, especially note 11.

27 From now on, I shall consider as "personal" resources those that cannot be separated, either physically or analytically, from the body of the possessor. External resources are thus primarily "material" goods: land, money, etc. It is noteworthy that labor, which is in itself a personal resource, was being moved from the category "personal resources" to that of "external resources" right in the period here taken into consideration. In other words, labor started to be seen as externalizable. Locke already distinguished between the servant who joins the master's family, and therefore accepts his rule in all non-political matters, from the laborer who only sells his services for wages, and who must obey his master only to the extent that their contract establishes. But for Locke, the servant is anyway in a position of dependence, for he has granted his master control over his own body, at least to a degree. Subsequent historical development will prompt people to see the sale of labor as a transaction over a resource which can be considered like a "material" one, through which individuals do not assign any power to the buyer.

28 D. Hume, *A Treatise of Human Nature*, P.H. Nidditch (ed.), Oxford, Clarendon Press, 1980, pp. 487–8.

29 Thomas Hobbes is the Natural Law theorist who considers *power* as the resource over which individuals have conflict. Power comprises any form of eminence, material, physical, and intellectual. Even in Hobbes's case, however, only adult males, mostly heads of households, are considered when the sovereign is instituted. For Hobbes too, and despite his egalitarian assumptions, families are formed in the state of nature in which servants and women will be incorporated before political society is brought about.

30 J. Locke, *Two Treatises*, II, 77, pp. 361–2.

31 The problem of the nature and source of moral obligation is very important

in Natural Law theory, but it does not directly bear upon the central themes of this essay. For a detailed account of how seventeenth-century Natural Law theory and eighteenth-century British moralists discussed this issue, see S.L. Darwall, "Motive and Obligation in the British Moralists," *Social Philosophy and Policy*, 1989, vol. 7, pp. 133–50.

32   J. Locke, *Two Treatises*, II, 79, p. 362.

33   ibid., II, 56, p. 347.

34   "For Law, in its true Notion, is not so much the Limitation as the *direction of a free and intelligent Agent* to his proper Interest, and prescribes no farther than is for the general Good of those under that Law." ibid., II, 57, pp. 347–8.

35   ibid., I, 86, p. 242.

36   ibid., II, 6, p. 311.

37   ibid., II, 11, p. 314.

38   ibid., II, 23, p. 325.

39   ibid., II, 6, p. 311.

40   ibid., II, 56, p. 347.

41   ibid., II, 58, p. 349.

42   ibid., II, 118, pp. 391–2. Locke is here concerned with the right of children to leave their father's body politic once they have grown, and with excluding that the magistrate annuls the duties of parents and children. However, the exclusion of the magistrate also works the other way around.

43   J. Locke, *An Essay Concerning Toleration*, in *Scritti editi ed inediti sulla tolleranza*, C.A. Viano (ed.), Torino, Taylor, 1961, p. 86:

> I say all practical principles, or opinions, by which men think themselves obliged to regulate their actions with one another; as that men may breed their children, and dispose of their estates, as they please; that men may work or rest when they think fit; that polygamy and divorce are lawful or unlawful, etc. – these opinions and the actions following from them, with all other things indifferent, have a title to toleration; but yet only so far as they do not tend to the disturbance of the state, or do not cause greater inconveniences than advantages to the community.

44   J. Locke, *Two Treatises*, II, 65, p. 353; 77, p. 362.

45   ibid., II, 78, p. 362.

46   ibid., II, 23, p. 325.

> This *Freedom* from Absolute, Arbitrary Power, is so necessary to, and closely joyned with a Man's Preservation, that he cannot part with it, but by what forfeits his Preservation and Life together. For a Man, not having the Power of his own Life, *cannot,* by Compact, or his own Consent, *enslave himself* to any one, nor put himself under the Absolute, Arbitrary Power of another, to take away his Life, when he pleases. No body can give more Power than he has himself; and he that cannot take away his own Life, cannot give another power over it.

J. Feinberg analyzes the differences between alienable and defeasible rights in seventeenth- and eighteenth-century political theory, and he maintains that inalienability did not exclude voluntary transfer. Only indefeasibility did. "Voluntary Euthanasia and the Inalienable Right to Life," *Philosophy and Public Affairs*, 1978, vol. 7, pp. 93–123. A.J.

Simmons, "Inalienable Rights and Locke's *Treatises*," *Philosophy and Public Affairs*, 1983, vol. 12, pp. 175–204, analyzes this issue more in detail in Locke's theory.

47 Real rights regard the control of goods and possessions, whereas personal rights regard the performance of actions and services.

48

> *Conjugal Society* could subsist and obtain its ends without it; nay, Community of Goods, and the Power over them, mutual Assistance, and Maintenance, and other things belonging to *Conjugal Society*, might be varied and regulated by that Contract, which unites Man and Wife in that Society, as far as may consist with Procreation and the bringing up of Children till they could shift for themselves; nothing being necessary to any Society, that is not necessary to the ends for which it is made.

J. Locke, *Two Treatises*, II, 83, p. 365.

49 ibid., II, 81, p. 364.

50 Locke briefly mentions that women maintain possession of the fruits of their own labor in discussing, and denying, the right of conquest. "For as to the Wife's share, whether her own Labour or Compact gave her a Title to it, 'tis plain, Her Husband could not forfeit what was hers." ibid., II, 183, p. 438.

51 ibid., II, 82, p. 364.

52

> In Beasts of Prey the *conjunction* lasts longer: because the Dam not being able well to subsist her self, and nourish her numerous Off-spring by her own Prey alone ... the Assistance of the Male is necessary to the Maintenance of their common Family, which cannot subsist till they are able to prey for themselves, but by the joynt Care of Male and Female.

ibid., II, 79, p. 363.

53 Locke does contend that in the state of nature everybody can use force:

> And that all Men may be restrained from invading others Rights, and from doing hurt to one another, and the Law of Nature be observed, which willeth the Peace and *Preservation of all Mankind*, the *Execution* of the Law of Nature is in that State, put into every Mans hands, whereby every one has a right to punish the transgressors of that Law to such a Degree, as may hinder its Violation.

ibid., II, 7, p. 312. However, Locke does not offer examples drawn from domestic life, as Tyrrell in particular did.

54 ibid., I, 48, p. 210.

55 To attribute power to one of the parties does not necessarily eliminate conflict, as much as the reasons for complaint by the person who is in the subordinate position. Conflict is less visible, not necessarily less frequent and harsh.

56 ibid., II, 83, p. 365.

57 M. Seliger, *The Liberal Politics of John Locke*, London, George Allen & Unwin, 1968, p. 174, emphasizes that consent is the basis of interpersonal morality. J. Locke, *Two Treatises*, II, 14, pp. 317–18.

58 "It gives the Master but a Temporary Power over him, and no greater, than what is contained in the *Contract* between 'em." ibid., II, 85, p. 365.

59 To modern readers this conception obviously appears untenable, as does

the contention that consenting to a position of subordination inscribed in nature is a voluntary and free act. When Locke discusses the master/servant relationship, he argues against those, like Filmer, who made power over people descend directly from property in land.

60 J. Locke, ibid., II, 87, p. 367.
61 ibid., II, 74, pp. 358–60.
62 ibid., II, 77, p. 362.
63 ibid., II, 88, p. 368.
64 ibid., II, 87, p. 367.
65 This is one of the unclear points in Locke's theory, on which much ink (now computer scribbling) has been poured. P. Russell offers an analysis of the issues at stake, in "Locke on Express and Tacit Consent: Misinterpretations and Inconsistencies," *Political Theory*, 1986, vol. 14, pp. 291–306.
66 There is a gap between Locke's quasi-historical narrative about a family getting transformed into a political association, and Locke's description of how a *civil* society can be set up. Not all political societies are *civil*. To have a political society, consent to the monopolization of the use of force by an individual or a group may well be sufficient. But only where individuals follow the procedure indicated by Locke – all give up the right to use force to the community, and rulers accountable to the community are then chosen – do we have a political association that fulfills the aim for which individuals set it up – the protection of each one's life, liberty, and estate. Locke therefore offers us a normatively charged portrait of civil society, as he offers us a normatively charged picture of the domestic association. On the fact that not all political societies are "civil," see R. Ashcraft, "Locke's Law of Nature: Historical Fact or Moral Fiction?" *American Political Science Review*, 1968, vol. 62, pp. 898–915.
67 M. Seliger, *Liberal Politics*, pp. 213–14.
68 N. Bobbio, "Pubblico e privato. Introduzione a un dibattito," *Fenomenologia e società*, 1982, vol. 5, pp. 167–77.
69 There is the exception of captives taken in a just war. J. Locke, *Two Treatises*, II, 23–4, pp. 325–6. They have forfeited their own lives, by engaging in an action (an unjust war) that deserves death. Their rulers can thus decide to spare them and use their services, which is an indirect way of trading slavery for one's survival.
70 ibid., II, 6, p. 311.
71 ibid., II, 105, pp. 380–1, supposedly at least two.
72 ibid., II, 19, p. 321.
73

> Here, 'tis like, the common Question will be made, *Who shall be Judge* whether the Prince or Legislative act contrary to their Trust? ... To this I reply, *The People shall be Judge*; for who shall be Judge whether his Trustee or Deputy acts well, and according to the Trust reposed in him, but he who deputes him, and must, by having deputed him have still a Power to discard him, when he fails in his Trust? ... But farther, this Question ... cannot mean, that there is no Judge at all. For where there is no Judicature on Earth, to decide Controversies, amongst Men, *God* in Heaven is *Judge*: He alone, 'tis true, is Judge of the Right.

ibid., II, 240–1, p. 476.

74 J. Locke, *A Letter concerning Toleration*, J. Tully (ed.), Indianapolis, IN, Hackett Publishing Company, 1983, p. 49.
75 What about a group of servants who negotiate together with one master? Is not this a case in which a plurality of individuals will negotiate over the same resources? Leaving aside that, even in this case, one can imagine that each servant will discuss specific terms, it is apparent that Locke's model is counterfactual. The *divide et impera* device which Locke tacitly adopts well serves the head of household's desire to control a group of human beings who outnumber him.
76 M. Bovero, "Società di contratto, contratto sociale, democrazia reale. Sul significato del neocontrattualismo," *Teoria politica*, 1985, vol. I, pp. 3–20.
77 J. Locke, *Two Treatises*, II, 96, p. 375.
78 J. Locke, *An Essay concerning Human Understanding*, P.H. Nidditch (ed.), Oxford, Clarendon Press, 1979, XXI, v, p. 236; for the definition of power, XXI, i-ii, pp. 233–4.
79

> For that which acts any Community, being only the consent of the individuals of it, and it being necessary to that which is one body to move one way; it is necessary the Body should move that way whither the greater force carries it, which is the *consent of the majority*: or else it is impossible it should act or continue one Body, *one Community*, which the consent of every individual that united into it, agreed that it should; and so everyone is bound by that consent to be concluded by the *majority*.

J. Locke, *Two Treatises*, II, 96, pp. 375–6. On this point, J.W. Yolton remarks that if unanimity were always necessary to "move" a community, we should still be in the state of nature. The consent of the members "acts" the community, that is, it enables it to function as one body. *Locke and the Compass of Human Understanding*, Cambridge, Cambridge University Press, 1970, p. 182. The consequence is that a majority has to be found for the family, where there are only two members.
80 Or to assign to a third party, such as the magistrate, the task to arbitrate between the two parties, when conflict arises. But if the intervention of a third party is necessary every time husband and wife are not unanimous, how could marriage exist in the state of nature, where individuals are supposed to be able to regulate their relationship autonomously? Locke repeatedly contends that conjugal society is brought into existence and maintained by husband and wife, without the intervention of public authority. To make of the magistrate the condition without which marriage cannot work would undermine Locke's basic assumption that human beings do not depend on public power to institute and regulate inter-personal exchange. The arbitrator is therefore called in only in extreme situations – as happens with all social relations – when one of the parties trespasses the proper limits, and threatens to turn the relationship into a "state of war."
81 J. Locke, *Two Treatises*, II, 82, p. 364. M.L. Shanley emphasizes that there is no majority in a conjugal society, but does not explore the implications

of this factor. "Marriage Contract and Social Contract in Seventeenth-Century English Political Thought," *Western Political Quarterly*, 1979, vol. 32, pp. 79–91.

82   J. Locke, *Two Treatises*, I, 48, p. 210.

83   Except those savage families in America that are held together by "lust." Thomas Hobbes, *Leviathan*, C.B. Macpherson (ed.), Harmondsworth, Penguin Books, 1980, I, 13, p. 187.

84   J. Locke, *Two Treatises*, II, 2, p. 308.

85   And what Locke, in the *Essay*, XXVIII, 10, p. 353, calls the "Law of Opinion":

> Vertue and Vice are Names pretended, and supposed every where to stand for actions in their own nature right and wrong: And as far as they really are so applied, they so far are co-incident with the *divine Law* above-mentioned. But yet, whatever is pretended, this is visible, that these Names, *Vertue* and *Vice,* in the particular instances of their application, through the several Nations and Societies of Men in the World, are constantly attributed only to such actions, as in each Country and Society are in reputation or discredit. Nor is it to be thought strange, that Men every where should give the Name of *Vertue* to those actions, which amongst them are judged praise worthy; and call that *Vice,* which they account blamable: Since otherwise they would condemn themselves, if they should think any thing *Right,* to which they allow'd not Commendation; any thing *Wrong,* which they let pass without Blame. Thus the measure of what is every where called and esteemed *Vertue* and *Vice* is this approbation or dislike, praise or blame, which by a secret and tacit consent establishes it self in the several Societies, Tribes, and Clubs of Men in the World: whereby several actions come to find Credit or Disgrace amongst them, according to the Judgment, Maxims, or Fashions of that place.

86   Locke's restrictive interpretation of the subjective theory of rights is the pillar upon which he constructs his theory of limited political power. Grotius, Pufendorf, and Hobbes established a parallel between what each individual can do in his personal transactions, and what a people can do in instituting civil society. It was apparent that a permissive interpretation justified absolute authority. Locke shows that a restrictive one can do the trick, and introduce limits on the rulers. After all, the relationship between ruled (as "one body") and ruler is a dual one, as is the relationship between husband and wife, master and servant.

87   On the historical and structural relationship between state of nature and civil society, see R.A. Goldwin, "Locke's State of Nature in Political Society," *Western Political Quarterly*, 1976, vol. 29, pp. 126–35.

88   J. Locke, *Two Treatises*, II, 27, p. 328.

89

> These Men having, as I say, forfeited their Lives, and with it their Liberties, and lost their Estates; and being in the *State of Slavery*, not capable of any Property, cannot in that state be considered as any part of *Civil Society*; the chief end whereof is the preservation of Property.

ibid., II, 85, p. 366.

90

Man being born, as has been proved, with a Title to perfect Freedom, and an uncontrouled enjoyment of all the Rights and Privileges of the Law of Nature, equally with any other Man, or Number of Men in the World, hath by Nature a Power, not only to preserve his Property, that is, his Life, Liberty and Estate, against the Injuries and Attempts of other Men; but to judge of, and punish the breaches of that Law in others.

ibid., II, 87, pp. 366–7.

91 P. Laslett, "Introduction" to J. Locke, *Two Treatises*, p. 116, contends that property, in the narrow sense of the possession of external resources, gives the political quality to personality. In other words, full political agency appears to require possession of external resources, as well as of personal ones.

92 ibid., pp. 122–4.

93 ibid., II, 123, p. 395.

94 ibid., II, 129, pp. 397–8; 130, p. 398.

95 The most recent, and extreme version of this interpretation is offered by Robert Nozick in his *Anarchy, State, and Utopia*, New York, Basic Books, 1974.

96 Supposedly partial, for citizens at least retain the right to pass final judgement on how the government takes care of the common good.

97 The tension between the private and public aspects of the right to interpret the law of nature is well illustrated by the potential conflict between the rights of proprietors and the rights of the propertyless. Civil society is supposed to defend every individual's property, for only by doing so do we comply with the duty to preserve the lives of human beings, which do not belong to us, but to God. Commentators, such as James Tully, have recently debated whether the right not to be starved to death is a perfect or an imperfect right for Locke. If it is a perfect right, redistribution may be the only means to ensure that it is respected, especially in a society, such as the seventeenth-century one, in which unequal accumulation of property has occurred, and private distribution of surplus may well leave many in danger of starvation. Can the state confiscate property to feed the hungry? Can the state impose taxation on proprietors, or does it have to obtain their consensus? Locke is silent on the former, but clearly says that consensus is indispensable to taxation.

98 With the exclusion of the right of rebellion. This was, of course, a very radical statement at the time. If we set Locke's writings in the politics of his time, his theory can be interpreted as empowering the "people" to a remarkable degree. This is the view emphasized by R. Ashcraft in *Revolutionary Politics and Locke's Two Treatises of Government*, Princeton, NJ, Princeton University Press, 1986.

4 A NEW PUBLIC

1 I wish to thank Stephen Darwall for attracting my attention to this point. On this theme see John Colman, *John Locke's Moral Philosophy*, Edinburgh, Edinburgh University Press, 1983, pp. 5–7.

2 By Shaftesbury, among others.

> The civil union, or confederacy, would never make right or wrong, if they subsisted not before. He who was free to any villainy before his contract, will and ought to make as free with his contract when he thinks fit. The natural knave has the same reason to be a civil one, and may dispense with his politic capacity as oft as he sees occasion. 'Tis only his word that stands in his way.... A man is obliged to keep his word. Why? Because he has given his word to keep it.... Is not this a notable account of the original of moral justice, and the rise of civil government and allegiance?

Shaftesbury, *Characteristics of Men, Manners, Opinions, Times, etc.*, Hildesheim, NY, Georg Olms Verlag, 1978, vol. I, pp. 109–10.

3 *The Fable of the Bees*, London, 1714, and 1723, with the commentary, was received with harsh criticism and dismissing sarcasm. But Mandeville's work presented an even greater threat to accepted views of human nature than Hobbes's theory. It seemed fairly easy to dismiss the latter. It was enough to look around to see the absurdity of Hobbes's psychology and politics. On the contrary, Mandeville offered a plausible, although disturbing, interpretation of the dynamics that hold together civilized Europe. They are the dynamics of manipulation, deception, and hypocrisy. Politicians socialize human beings to behave in a way which will make society flourish. Instincts are selfish, antisocial, and debasing. Their destructive potential can be blocked, and their energy turned toward socially acceptable aims. However, approvable behavior is the product of successful socialization, rather than of authentic morality. M.M. Goldsmith, *Private Vices, Public Benefits*, Cambridge, Cambridge University Press, 1985, offers an accurate portrait of Mandeville's impact on Augustan England. Hutcheson himself openly polemicizes with Mandeville. The title-page of *An Inquiry into the Original of our Ideas of Beauty and Virtue*, in *Two Treatises* (from now on, *Inquiry*), London, 1725, reads: "In which the Principles of the late Earl of Shaftesbury are Explain'd and Defended, against the Author of the *Fable of the Bees*." All the works by Hutcheson are quoted from the editions reprinted in *Collected Works of Francis Hutcheson*, Hildesheim, NY, Georg Olms Verlag, 1969 and 1971, facsimile editions.

4 As T.D. Campbell remarks:

> Hutcheson's political theory requires to be set in the context of his meta-ethics; the moral sense doctrine permeates his entire political philosophy and some analysis of it is a necessary prelude to a proper evaluation of his legal and political ideals.

"Francis Hutcheson: 'Father' of the Scottish Enlightenment," in R.H. Campbell, and A.S. Skinner (eds), *The Origins and Nature of the Scottish Enlightenment*, Edinburgh, John Donald Publishers 1982, p. 168.

5 I use this term to indicate the translation of moral perceptions of good and evil into binding rights and duties.

6 F. Hutcheson, *A System of Moral Philosophy* (from now on, *SMP*), London, 1755, vol. II, bk II, ch. IV, iii, p. 218.

7 For example, in I. Hont and M. Ignatieff (eds), *Wealth and Virtue*,

Cambridge, Cambridge University Press, 1985: J. Moore and M. Silver-thorne, "Gershom Carmichael and the Natural Jurisprudence Tradition in Eighteenth-Century Scotland," pp. 73–87; I. Hont, "The 'Rich Country–Poor Country Debate' in Scottish Classical Political Economy," pp. 271–315; and M. Ignatieff, "John Millar and Individualism," pp. 317–43. I tend to see the two terms as identifying the same political theory, centered around the notions that communal values are axiologically superior to individual values, that the good of the community has primacy over individual interest, and that participation by male citizens is intended to curb those very private interests. If we take classical republicanism as merely meaning that public participation is essential to maintain liberty, then Hutcheson is a classical republican. But I would contend that quite a lot of thinkers, even in modern times, should then be considered classical republicans.

8 As for Natural Law theory, Stoicism is the fundamental reference of this line of thought. But early eighteenth-century British moralists emphasize Stoic moral philosophy, rather than its juridical implications. Hutcheson adopts the Stoic definition that virtue is *vita secundum naturam*, in *An Essay on the Nature and Conduct of the Passions and Affections* (from now on, *Essay*), London, 1728, Preface, p. XVII.

9 F. Hutcheson, *SMP*, II, III, I, ii, p. 150.

10 ibid., II, III, I, ii, pp. 152–3.

11 ibid., II, III, I, ii, pp. 151–2.

12 As will be clarified below, reason is not responsible for moving us to act in a way rather than another. In other words, it is not a source of obligation in itself. However, it can make us understand what our obligations are, and order them hierarchically. Whether reason can, as in Locke, suspend our desires, so that we are then free to choose what is morally better, is a question debated by Hutcheson, to which he does not give a clear-cut answer. He takes a Lockean position in *Essay*, sec. I, I, ii, pp. 32–3.

13 Shaftesbury, *Characteristics*, I, p. 108.

14 "There is therefore, as each one by close attention and reflection may convince himself, a natural and immediate determination to approve certain affections, and actions consequent upon them; or a natural sense of immediate excellence in them." F. Hutcheson, *SMP*, I, I, IV, iv, p. 58. D. Daiches Raphael, *The Moral Sense*, London, Oxford University Press, 1947, p. 34, contends that Hutcheson never considers that reason may be a faculty of immediate apprehension. To an empiricist, this might undermine the assumption that reason only manipulates material received through the senses – immediate apprehension may lead back to innate ideas. According to W. Frankena, "Hutcheson's Moral Sense Theory," *Journal of the History of Ideas*, 1955, vol. 16, pp. 356–75, Hutcheson attacks reason as the organ of moral judgement because he takes that judgement to be analogous to the aesthetic one. The problem with sensation is that it is a private experience. D. Daiches Raphael, *Moral Sense*, p. 9. "There is a further characteristic of sensation, which is not known to be possessed by it, but for which there is good evidence, namely the characteristic of being private to the person sensing." J. W. Smith, "The British Moralists and the Fallacy of Psychologism," *Journal of the History of Ideas*, 1961, vol. 22, pp. 185–204, wonders whether Hutcheson's

insistence on the objectivity of moral values makes sense given his insistence on the moral sense. But Hutcheson may indirectly be addressing the problem of the private nature of sensation. *Inquiry,* I, VI, 10, p. 75:

> Both are *natural* Powers of *Perception,* or *Determinations* of *the Mind* to receive necessarily certain Ideas from the presence of Objects. The *internal Sense* is, *a passive Power of receiving Ideas of Beauty, from all Objects in which there is Uniformity amidst Variety.*

15 F. Hutcheson, *SMP,* I, I, III, i, p. 38.

16 ibid., I, I, II, v, pp. 24–5.

17 F. Hutcheson is credited with being the first philosopher who distinguishes between exciting and justifying reasons. W.T. Blackstone, *Francis Hutcheson and Contemporary Ethical Theory,* Athens, GA, University of Georgia Press, 1965, p. 7.

18 F. Hutcheson, *SMP,* I, I, III, iv, pp. 44–5.

19 And we derive happiness from contemplating ourselves being benevolent. This second order pleasure occupies a central position in Hutcheson's early writings, where he is concerned with understanding the dynamics of the moral sense in detail. But in the *System* the pleasure derived from *being* benevolent becomes more prominent. I shall venture to say that this may be due to the fact that the *System* is Hutcheson's most "political" work. From the point of view of the political implications of morality, benevolence is what matters, rather than the pleasure which we derive from contemplating ourselves being morally approvable.

20

> The acts of the will may be again divided into two classes, according as one is pursuing good for himself, and repelling the contrary, or pursuing good for others and repelling evils which threaten them. The former we may call *selfish,* the latter *benevolent.*

ibid., I, I, I, v, p. 8.

21 In *Inquiry,* II, II, vi, p. 135, Hutcheson contends that the fact that benevolent actions benefit the doer only constitutes an additional motive for performing them.

22 F. Hutcheson, *Essay,* Preface, p. VIII. The pleasure of virtue is the highest of which we are capable, and it is therefore in our interest to be virtuous.

23 F. Hutcheson, *SMP,* I, I, IV, vi, p. 61.

24 ibid., I, I, II, xii, p. 36.

25 ibid., I, I, IV, xii, p. 77.

26 A theme which will be central to Hume's thought.

27 ibid., II, III, I, ii, p. 152.

28 ibid., I, I, II, vi, p. 25.

29 ibid., I, II, III, i, pp. 252–3.

30 K. Haakonssen, "Natural Law and the Scottish Enlightenment," *Man and Nature,* 1985, vol. 4, pp. 47–80, emphasizes that Hutcheson appears to distinguish morality and legality, and consequently, morality and politics, on the ground that politics should only enforce perfect rights, while morality regards imperfect rights. But he does not mention the distinction between morality and legality as two inquiries concerned with two aspects of actions.

31 F. Hutcheson, *SMP,* I, I, II, vi, pp. 25; I, I, III, i, p. 41; I, II, III, i, 238.

32 ibid., I, I, III, iv, p. 45.
33 ibid., I, I, III, iii, p. 42.
34 ibid., I, I, II, vi, p. 26.
35 ibid., I, I, II, v, p. 25.
36 ibid., I, I, V, iii, p. 84.
37 In the specific sense that rights and duties are reciprocally defined: for every right there exists a corresponding duty. See R. Tuck, *Natural Rights Theories*, Cambridge, Cambridge University Press, 1981, p. 1.
38 F. Hutcheson, *SMP*, I, II, IV, i, p. 282:

> These powers [the moral sense and reason] suggest the rules or laws of this state of liberty, and all states are denominated from what the laws and obligations of them enjoin or require, and not from such conduct as the passions of men may hurry them into contrary to the laws of those states.

39 ibid., I, II, III, i, p. 252. And *jus*, as Hutcheson remarks in a note to this passage, is distinct from *right*: "the *jus* ensues upon the *rectum*."
40 ibid., I, II, III, i, p. 253. The passage continues:

> Or we may say more briefly, a man hath a *right* to do, possess, or demand any thing "when his acting, possessing, or obtaining from another in these circumstances tends to the good of society, or to the interest of the individual consistently with the rights of others and the general good of society, and obstructing him would have the contrary tendency."

41

> To each right there corresponds an *obligation,* perfect or imperfect, as the right is. The term obligation is both complex and ambiguous. We primarily say one is obliged to an action "when he must find from the constitution of human nature that he and every attentive observer must disapprove the omission of it as morally evil."

ibid., I, II, III, vi, p. 264.
42 ibid., I, II, III, i, p. 253.
43 And because we have no ground for forbidding him to do so.
44 In other words, can we have a good society in which individuals are not other-regarding, provided that they do not harm others?
45 ibid., I, I, VII, xii, p. 139.
46 ibid., I, I, VI, i, p. 100.
47 ibid., I, I, I, vi, p. 10.
48 F. Hutcheson, *Inquiry*, II, III, viii, pp. 163–4.
49 F. Hutcheson, *SMP*, I, I, VIII, i, pp. 148–9.
50 ibid., I, II, V, i, p. 293.
51 ibid., I, II, IV, ii, p. 281; iii, p. 283.
52 ibid., I, II, V, ii, p. 299.
53 ibid., I, II, V, ii, pp. 300–1.
54

> All *adventitious real rights* arise from a transaction of some of the original rights of *property* from one to another. And all *personal adventitious rights* are constituted by transferring to others some parts of our natural liberty, or of our right of acting as we please, and of

obliging ourselves to certain performances in behalf of others.

ibid., I, II, VII, i, p. 340.
55   ibid., II, III, I, v, p. 161.
56   ibid., II, III, I, v, p. 159.
57   Through which, Hutcheson emphasizes, "men profess to give mutually equal values." ibid., II, II, XIII, i, p. 64.
58

Such a servant, whether for life or a term of years, is to retain all the rights of mankind, valid against his master, as well as all others, excepting only *that* to his labours, which he has transferred to his master.

ibid., II, III, III, i, p. 200.
59

The tender sentiments and affections which engage the parties into this relation of marriage, plainly declare it to be a state of equal partnership or friendship, and not such wherein the one party stipulates to himself a right of governing in all domestick affairs, and the other promises subjection.

ibid., II, III, I, vii, p. 163.
60   A hedonistic moral theory moreover lowers the standard required to be a member of the universe entitled to consideration. Hutcheson obviously includes animals, at least as objects, if not subjects of morality. "'Tis true brutes have no notion of right or of moral qualities: but infants are in the same case, and yet they have their rights, which the adult are obliged to maintain." ibid., I, II, VI, iii, p. 314.
61   As already recollected, adultery on either part must be punished equally. And, in condemning rape, Hutcheson says: "'Tis a strange corruption of manners and sentiments in any nation which boasts of maintaining liberty and equality in rights to all their people, that such cruel injustices to any, even of the lowest condition, should escape without severe punishment." ibid., II, III, I, iv, p. 157.
62   ibid., II, III, IV, iii, p. 219.
63   ibid., II, III, IV, I, p. 212.
64   ibid., I, I, I, vi, pp. 10–11; also I, I, VIII, iv, pp. 158–9, on the negative consequences of partiality.

As the notion of one's own highest happiness, or the greatest aggregate or sum of valuable enjoyments, is not generally formed by men, it is not expressly desired or intended. And therefore we cannot say that every particular calm desire of private good is aiming correctly at that sum, and pursuing its object under the notions of a necessary part of that sum.... In like manner we have calm benevolent affections toward individuals, or smaller societies of our fellows, where there has not preceded any consideration of the most extensive system, and where they are not considered formally as parts of this largest system, nor their happiness pursued as conducing to the greatest sum of universal happiness.

65   ibid., II, III, IV, vi, pp. 224.
66   ibid., II, III, V, iii, p. 229.

67 I. Kant, *The Metaphysical Elements of Justice*, J. Ladd (ed.), New York, Macmillan Publishing Company, 1985, p. 79.

68 I wish to emphasize that the example is not entirely accurate, for in complying with our obligation to respect the perfect rights of others we are not particularly virtuous.

> In general, the fulfilling the *perfect Rights* of others has little *Virtue* in it; for thereby no *Moment* or *Good* is produc'd more than there was before; and the *Interest* engaging to the Action is very great, even the avoiding all the Evils of *War* in a *State of Nature*. But the *violating perfect Rights*, or even *external ones*, is always *exceedingly evil*, either in the immediate, or more remote Consequences of the Action.

F. Hutcheson, *Inquiry*, II, VII, vii, pp. 268–9.

69 It is noteworthy that Hutcheson, like Pufendorf, and probably following him, does not have a proprietary model of the relationship between the person and her natural endowments. Rights are perceptions of the moral sense, and reciprocals of duties. But, as in Pufendorf, the consequences of granting individuals the right to transfer part of their natural liberty by "alienating" it to others reintroduces the consequences if not the premises of the proprietary model.

70 F. Hutcheson *A Short Introduction to Moral Philosophy*, Glasgow, 1757, p. [i].

71 ibid., II, IV, ii, p. 141.

72 F. Hutcheson, *SMP,* I, II, IV, iii, p. 284.

73 ibid., I, II, IV, iv, p. 286.

74 ibid., I, II, V, ii, p. 299; II, II, XV, i, p. 89.

75 The perfect rights of "mankind as a system" are various and somewhat unexpected. They include: to prohibit suicide; to require the reproduction of the species; to force parents to discharge their duties toward children; to prevent homosexual intercourse, intercourse with animals, and abortion; to prevent waste of resources; to help the innocent in danger; to punish the aggressor; to publicize inventions; to compel each person to work; and to prevent or punish the profanation of tombs. ibid., II, II, XVI, i-vii, pp. 105–10.

76

> Mankind, as a system, seems to have rights upon each individual, to demand of him such conduct as is necessary for the general good, and to abstain from what may have a contrary tendency, tho' the wrong conduct no more affects one individual than another. Of these rights and obligations some are of the perfect kind, where compulsion may be just; others are of a more delicate obligation, not admitting compulsion, where our duty must be left to our own prudence and sense of virtue.

ibid., II, II, XVI, i, p. 105.

77 "There are others of the imperfect kind, to be left generally to the prudence and virtue of persons concerned, to which correspond the general duties or offices incumbent on each individual towards mankind in general, previous to any special tye." ibid., II, II, XVI, viii, p. 111.

78 ibid., II, II, XVI, iv, p. 108.

79 F. Hutcheson, *Essay*, I, I, i, p. v.

80

> The Ideas raised in different Persons by the same Object, are probably different, when they disagree in their Approbation or Dislike; and in the same Person, when his Fancy at one time differs from what it was at another. This will appear from reflection on those Objects, to which we have now an Aversion, tho they were formerly agreeable: And we shall generally find that there is some accidental Conjunction of a disagreeable Idea, which always recurs with the Object.

But then Hutcheson contends:

> But there does not seem to be any Ground to believe such a Diversity in human Minds, as that the same Idea or Perception should give pleasure to one and pain to another, or to the same Person at different Times; not to say that it seems a Contradiction, that the same Idea should do so.

Inquiry, I, I, pp. 4, 5–6.

81   F. Hutcheson, *SMP*, II, II, XVII, i, pp. 119–20.
82   "It is true indeed, that the Actions we approve in others, are generally imagin'd to tend to the *natural Good* of *Mankind*, or that of some *Parts* of it." F. Hutcheson, *Inquiry,* II, I, ii, p. 111.
83   F. Hutcheson, *SMP,* II, II, XVI, viii, p. 111.

CONCLUSION

1   J. Locke, *Two Treatises of Government*, P. Laslett (ed.), New York, Mentor Books, 1965, II, 3, p. 308.
2   This problem arises even if we elect representatives who are supposedly accountable to their electors. The argument runs parallel to Rousseau's argument about the impossibility of having someone else represent our will. According to Rousseau, individuals are free only at elections, and at no other time. The same can be said here of transferring, although conditionally, our interpretative capacity. This does not mean that we should not do it. (It would be unrealistic for me to suggest that.) But the problems raised by transferring our interpretative capacity reopen the question of the relationship between direct and representative democracy.
3   A critical reader can object: Why should equality necessarily imply a growing presence of a public regulator? Cannot we leave individuals alone in managing their set of perfect rights, and really limit the intervention of the state to marginal cases? We surely can, as radical libertarians do. But it is noteworthy that libertarians accept the possibility of self-enslavement – and therefore the reintroduction of asymmetrical power relations, and the creation of private domains of different sizes – as a consequence of transactions between persons who have a nearly absolute control over their personal resources, and are left completely alone in managing them.
4   Among feminist writers, for example, S. Tenenbaum, "Woman through the Prism of Political Thought," *Polity,* 1982, vol. 15, pp. 90–102.
5   For Locke they are inviolable because essential to the person as God's property.
6   Locke moves religious experience from the public to the private domain. This will indeed modify that experience, but it shows that its allocation in

one or the other realm is a matter of historical contingency, not natural necessity. And it is well known that basic physiological activities can be practiced in public as well as in private, depending on contingent factors such as culture, historical time, and personal preference.

7   Although other practices developing in the same area, such as artificial insemination, surrogate motherhood, etc. may well require intense and pervasive public regulation.

8   The best example of this procedure which I can find in Locke is the institution of money, which is attained via tacit consent, and profoundly modifies the dictate of the law of nature prohibiting the accumulation of perishable resources. *Two Treatises*, II, 46–8, pp. 342–3.

9   The theoretical alternative to the hypothesis that individuals consciously assess the collective implications of their actions is presented by thinkers who rely on heterogeneity of ends to explain how social equilibrium can be the outcome of uncoordinated, discrete social relations. This line of thought, which starts with Smith and Hume, assumes that the modern *social* structure – be it the market, or the distribution of power roles to different agents, or evolutionary tendencies shaped by principles of adaptation and survival of the fittest – accounts for social stability. Politics can thus be reduced to a minimum. I find that this view is counterfactual, and considers politics merely as instrumental to maintaining social stability. Whereas I think of politics as a fundamental modality of the human condition.

10 But what about natural rights? Do they not provide a set of stable personal endowments, which can be considered a "prerequisite"? The problem with "natural rights" is that they are very formal indeed, and if we give them any specific content, we shall have to assume that society does not change at all over time, so that we shall know once and for all what we can legitimately claim as our personal domain. Thus, given that society does change over time, even if we maintain those rights as unviolable boundaries, their specific content will have to be redefined, and this is a matter for interpretation.

11 Locke already hints at this possibility, in commenting on the "law of opinion" in *An Essay Concerning Human Understanding*, P.H. Nidditch (ed.), Oxford, Clarendon Press, 1979, XXVIII, 10, p. 353:

> For though Men uniting into politick Societies, have resigned up to the publick the disposing of all their Force, so that they cannot employ it against any Fellow-Citizen, any farther than the Law of the Country directs: yet they retain still the power of Thinking well or ill; approving or disapproving of the actions of those whom they live amongst, and converse with: And by this approbation and dislike they establish amongst themselves, what they call *Vertue* and *Vice*.

R. Koselleck, *Critique and Crisis*, New York, Berg, 1988, pp. 59–60, interprets this activity as the elaboration of unwritten norms which are parallel to, and not always identical with, the laws of the state, although falling short of legal enforceability.

12 Which will be, in the context of a different moral theory, Smith's solution. Hutcheson himself refers every now and then to the impartial spectator, but he does not develop this theme. On the relationship between the

impartial spectator and the politician in Smith, see K. Haakonssen, *The Science of a Legislator: The Natural Jurisprudence of David Hume and Adam Smith*, Cambridge, Cambridge University Press, 1981.

13 F. Hutcheson, *A System of Moral Philosophy*, London, 1755, vol.I, bk.II, ch.III, iv, pp. 261–2.

14 Which is, ultimately, the reason why a political association becomes necessary at all.

15 It is noteworthy that Hobbes does point to an alternative, for the social contract is the moment when universal participation enables individuals to recognize that there are universally valid laws of nature, and that these can lead human beings out of the state of war.

16 One could say, following, J. Rawls, *A Theory of Justice*, Cambridge, MA, The Belknap Press, 1981, that the right has primacy over the good. But I wish to emphasize that I think of politics as an activity which is informed by both morality and legality, rather than assigning primacy to one or the other.

17 From this point of view, I do not think that we can say that the only task of politics is to coordinate rather than integrate individual activities. Insofar as we consciously reflect about how coordination can be attained, we think of the individuals attempting to coordinate as united in one institution, and concerned with what can ensure that coordination.

18 The self-reflective character of political activity, and of the association which is created through it, shows in the circularity of the definitions of politics available to us. The most widely used is Weber's:

> What do we understand by politics? The concept is extremely broad and comprises any kind of *independent* leadership in action.... Tonight, our reflections are, of course, not based upon such a broad concept. We wish to understand by politics only the leadership, or the influencing of the leadership, of a *political* association, hence today, of a *state* .... A state is a human community that (succesfully) claims the *monopoly of the legitimate use of physical force* within a given territory.

"Politics as a Vocation," in *From Max Weber*, H.H. Gerth and C. Wright Mills (eds), New York, Oxford University Press, 1958, pp. 77–8. C. Schmitt criticizes Weber for the circularity of this definition in *The Concept of the Political*, 1976, New Brunswick, NJ, Rutgers University Press, 1976, p. 20: "In one way or another 'political' is generally juxtaposed to 'state' or at least is brought into relation with it. The state thus appears as something political, the political as something pertaining to the state – obviously an unsatisfactory circle." In the footnote to this passage, Schmitt openly refers to Weber's "Politics as a Vocation" as an example of this supposedly vicious circle.

Bibliography

PRIMARY SOURCES

Aquinas, Th. (1949) *On Kingship*, Toronto, The Pontificial Institute of Medieval Studies.

Aristotle (1958) *Politics*, E. Barker (tr.), Oxford, Oxford University Press.

Aristotle (1976) *Nicomachean Ethics*, J.A.K. Thomson (tr.), Harmondsworth, Penguin Books.

Ascham, A. (1975) *Of the Confusions and Revolutions of Governments*, Delmar, NY, Scholars' Facsimiles & Reprints.

Bodin, J. (1979) *The Six Bookes of a Commonweale*, R. Knolles (tr.), New York, Arno Press Reprints.

The Digest of Justinian (1985) Th. Mommsen, P. Krueger, and A. Watson (eds), Philadelphia, PA, University of Pennsylvania Press.

Filmer, R. (1949) *Patriarcha and Other Political Works*, P. Laslett (ed.), Oxford, Basil Blackwell.

Gee, E. (1658) *The Divine Right and Originall of the Civill Magistrate from God*, London.

Grotius, H. (1901) *Of the Law of War and Peace*, A.C. Campbell (tr.), New York, M.W. Dunne.

Hobbes, Th. (1980) *Leviathan*, C.B. Macpherson (ed.), Harmondsworth, Penguin Books.

Hume, D. (1980) *A Treatise of Human Nature*, P.H. Nidditch (ed.), Oxford, Clarendon Press.

Hutcheson, F. (1969 and 1971) *Collected Works of Francis Hutcheson*, Hildesheim, NY, Georg Olms Verlag, facsimiles editions, 7 vols.

Kant, I. (1985) *The Metaphysical Elements of Justice*, J. Ladd (ed.), New York, Macmillan Publishing Company.

Locke, J. (1961) *Scritti editi e inediti sulla tolleranza*, C.A. Viano (ed.), Torino, Taylor.

Locke, J. (1963) *Works*, Darmstadt, Scientia Verlag Aalen, Reprints, 10 vols.

Locke, J. (1964) *Essays on the Law of Nature*, W. von Leyden (ed.), Oxford, Clarendon Press.

Locke, J. (1965) *Two Treatises of Government*, P. Laslett (ed.), New York, Mentor Books.

Locke, J. (1968) *The Educational Writings of John Locke*, J.L. Axtell (ed.), Cambridge, Cambridge University Press.

Locke, J. (1979) *An Essay Concerning Human Understanding*, P.H. Nidditch (ed.), Oxford, Clarendon Press.

Locke, J. (1983) *A Letter Concerning Toleration*, J. Tully (ed.), Indianapolis, IN, Hackett Publishing Company.

Mandeville, B. (1924) *The Fable of the Bees*, F.B. Kaye (ed.), Oxford, Clarendon Press.

Plato (1985) *Collected Dialogues*, E. Hamilton and H. Cairns (eds), Princeton, NJ, Princeton University Press.

Pufendorf, S. (1717) *Of the Law of Nature and Nations*, London.

Pufendorf, S. (1735) *The Whole Duty of Man, According to the Law of Nature*, London.

Shaftesbury (1978) *Characteristics of Men, Manners, Opinions, Times, etc.*, Hildesheim, NY, Georg Olms Verlag.

Suàrez, F. (1971) *De Legibus*, Madrid, Consejo Superior de Investigaciones Cientificas.

Tyrrell, J. (1681) *Patriarcha, non Monarcha*, London.

Tyrrell, J.(1692) *A Brief Disquisition of the Law of Nature*, London.

Tyrrell, J. (1718) *Bibliotheca Politica*, London.

SECONDARY SOURCES

Articles

Aldridge, A.O. (1951) "The Meaning of Incest from Hutcheson to Gibbon," *Ethics*, vol. 61, pp. 308–13.

Aldridge, A.O. (1972) "The State of Nature: An Undiscovered Country in the History of Ideas," *Studies on Voltaire and the Eighteenth Century*, vol. 98, pp. 7-26.

Ashcraft, R. (1968) "Locke's Law of Nature: Historical Fact or Moral Fiction?" *American Political Science Review*, vol. 62, pp. 898–915.

Ashcraft, R. (1980) "Revolutionary Politics and Locke's *Two Treatises of Government*," *Political Theory*, vol. 8, pp. 429–85.

Benhabib, S. (1988) "Judgement and the Moral Foundations of Politics in Arendt's Thought," *Political Theory*, vol. 16, pp. 29–51.

Blythe, J.M. (1989) "Family Government, and the Medieval Aristotelians," *History of Political Thought*, vol. 10, pp. 1–16.

Bobbio, N. (1980) "Pubblico, privato," in *Enciclopedia XI: Prodotti—Ricchezza*, Torino, Einaudi, pp. 401–15.

Bobbio, N. (1982) "Pubblico e privato. Introduzione a un dibattito" *Fenomenologia e società*, vol. 5, pp. 166–77.

Booth, W.J. (1981) "Politics and the Household. A commentary on Aristotle's *Politics* Book One," *History of Political Thought*, vol. 2, pp. 203–26.

Bovero, M. (1985) "Società di contratti, contratto sociale, democrazia reale. Sul significato del necontrattualismo," *Teoria politica*, vol. 1, pp. 3–20.

Brennan, T. and Pateman, C. (1972) "Mere Auxiliaries to the Commonwealth: Women and the Origins of Liberalism," *Political Studies*, vol. 27, pp. 183–200.

Butler, M.A. (1978) "Early Liberal Roots of Feminism: John Locke and the Attack on Patriarchy," *American Political Science Review*, vol. 72, pp. 135–50.

Chapman, R.A. (1975) "*Leviathan* Writ Small: Thomas Hobbes on the Family," *American Political Science Review*, vol. 69, pp. 76–90.

Colie, R.L. (1966) "John Locke and the Publication of the Private," *Philological Quarterly*, 1966, vol. 45, pp. 24–45.

Darwall, S.L. (1989) "Motive and Obligation in the British Moralists," *Social Philosophy and Policy*, vol. 7, pp. 133–50.

David, L. (1970) "The Correlativity of Rights and Duties," *Nous,* vol. 4, pp. 45–55.

Dunn, J. (1967) "Consent in the Political Theory of John Locke," *The Historical Journal*, vol. 10, pp. 153–82.

Feinberg, J. (1978) "Voluntary Euthanasia and the Inalienable Right to Life," *Philosophy and Public Affairs*, vol. 7, pp. 93–123.

Frankena, W. (1955) "Hutcheson's Moral Sense Theory," *Journal of the History of Ideas*, vol. 16, pp. 356–75.

Gauthier, D. (1977) "The Social Contract as Ideology," *Philosophy and Public Affairs*, vol. 6, pp. 130–64.

Gay, P. (1967) "The Spectator as Actor," *Encounter,* vol. 39, pp. 27–32.

Goldschmidt, M.L. (1954) "Publicity, Privacy, and Secrecy," *The Western Political Quarterly*, vol. 7, pp. 401–16.

Goldsmith, M.M. (1976) "Public Virtue and Private Vices," *Eighteenth-Century Studies*, vol. 9, pp. 477–510.

Goldwin, R.A. (1976) "Locke's State of Nature in Political Society," *Western Political Quarterly*, vol. 29, pp. 126–35.

Gouldner, A.W. (1960) "The Norm of Reciprocity: A Preliminary Statement," *American Sociological Review*, vol. 25, pp. 161–78.

Grady, R.C. II (1977) "Property and 'Natural Political Virtue': The Implications of Locke as a Liberal," *Polity,* vol. 10, pp. 86–103.

Greenleaf, W.H. (1966) "Filmer's Patriarchal History," *Historical Journal*, vol. 9, pp. 235–72.

van Gunsteren, H. (1979) "Public and Private," *Social Research,* vol. 46, pp. 255–71.

Haakonssen, K. (1985) "Hugo Grotius and the History of Political Thought," *Political Theory*, vol. 13, pp. 239–65.

Haakonssen, K. (1985) "Natural Law and the Scottish Enlightenment," *Man and Nature*, vol. 4, pp. 47–80.

Haydon, G. (1979) "Political Theory and the Child: Problems of the Individualist Tradition," *Political Studies*, vol. 27, pp. 405–20.

Hinton, R.W.K. (1967) "Husbands, Fathers, and Conquerors, I," *Political Studies*, vol. 15, pp. 291–300.

Hinton, R.W.K. (1968) "Husbands, Fathers, and Conquerors, II," *Political Studies*, vol. 16, pp. 55–67.

Hundert, E.J. (1977) "Market Society and Meaning in Locke's Political Philosophy," *Journal of the History of Philosophy*, vol. 15, pp. 33–44.

Jenkins, J.J. (1967) "Locke and Natural Rights," *Philosophy,* vol. 42, pp. 149–54.

Johnson, J.T. (1971) "The Covenant Idea and the Puritan View of Marriage," *Journal of the History of Ideas*, vol. 32, pp. 107–18.

Kelly, G.A. (1979) "Who Needs a Theory of Citizenship?," *Daedalus,* vol. 108, pp. 212–36.

Kirchkheimer, O. (1966) "Private Man and Society," *Political Science Quarterly,* vol. 81, pp. 1–24.

Krieger, L. (1964) "The Distortions of Political Theory: The XVIIth Century Case," *Journal of the History of Ideas,* vol. 25, pp. 323–32.

Lasch, C. (1974) "The Suppression of Clandestine Marriage in England: The Marriage Act of 1753," *Salmagundi,* vol. 26, pp. 90–109

Lasch, C. (1985) "Historical Sociology and the Myth of Maturity," *Theory and Society,* vol. 14, pp. 705–20.

Laslett, P. (1948) "Sir Robert Filmer: The Man Versus the Whig Myth," *William and Mary Quarterly,* vol. 5, pp. 523–46.

von Leyden, W. (1956) "John Locke and Natural Law," *Philosophy,* vol. 31, pp. 23–35.

McCloskey, H.J. (1971) "The Political Ideal of Privacy," *Philosophical Quarterly,* vol. 21, pp. 301–14.

Mattern, R. (1980) "Moral Science and the Concept of Persons in Locke," *Philosophical Review,* vol. 89, pp. 24–45.

Maxwell, J.C. (1951) "Ethics and Politics in Mandeville," *Philosophy,* vol. 26, pp. 242–51.

Michel, R.H. (1978) "English Attitudes toward Women," *Canadian Journal of History,* vol. 13, pp. 35–60.

Nadelhaft, J. (1982) "The English Woman's Sexual Civil War: Feminist Attitudes towards Men, Women, and Marriage, 1650–1740," *Journal of the History of Ideas,* vol. 43, pp. 555–79.

Okin, S.M. (1981) "Women and the Making of the Sentimental Family," *Philosophy and Public Affairs,* vol. 11, pp. 65–88.

Oppenheim, F.E. (1968) "Eguaglianza come concetto descrittivo," *Rivista di filosofia,* vol. 59, pp. 255–75.

Parry, G. (1964) "Individuality, Politics and the Critique of Paternalism in John Locke," *Political Studies,* vol. 12, pp. 163–77.

Pinkus, P. (1976) "Mandeville's Paradox," *Studies on Voltaire and the Eighteenth Century,* vol. 154, pp. 1629–35.

Pitkin, H. (1965) "Obligation and Consent, I," *American Political Science Review,* vol. 59, pp. 990–99.

Pitkin, H. (1966) "Obligation and Consent, II," *American Political Science Review,* vol. 60, pp. 39–52.

Pitkin, H.F. (1981) "Justice – On Relating Private and Public," *Political Theory,* vol. 9, pp. 327–52.

Reiman, J.H. (1976) "Privacy, Intimacy, and Personhood," *Philosophy and Public Affairs,* vol. 6, pp. 26–44.

Richards, B.A. (1968–9) "Inalienable Rights: Recent Criticism and Old Doctrine," *Philosophy and Phenomenological Research,* vol. 29, pp. 391–404.

Riley, P. (1965) "Locke and the Dictatorship of the Bourgeoisie," *Political Studies,* vol. 13, pp. 219–30.

Riley, P. (1976) "Locke on 'Voluntary Agreement' and Political Power," *Western Political Quarterly,* vol. 29, pp. 136–45.

Rorty, A.O. (1982) "From Passions to Emotions and Sentiments," *Philosophy,* vol. 57, pp. 159–72.

Russell, P. (1986) "Locke on Express and Tacit Consent: Misinterpretations and Inconsistencies," *Political Theory*, vol. 14, pp. 291–306.

Saraceno, C. (1983) "Interdipendenze e spostamenti di confine tra 'pubblico' e 'privato'," *Il Mulino*, vol. 82, pp. 784–97.

Schochet, G.J. (1967) "Thomas Hobbes on the Family and the State of Nature," *Political Science Quarterly*, vol. 83, pp. 427–45.

Schochet, G.J. (1969) "Patriarchalism, Politics and Mass Attitudes in Stuart England," *Historical Journal*, vol. 12, pp. 413–41.

Shanley, M.L. (1979) "Marriage Contract and Social Contract in Seventeenth-Century English Political Thought ," *Western Political Quarterly*, vol. 32, pp. 79–91.

Simmons, A.J. (1983) "Inalienable Rights and Locke's *Treatises*," *Philosophy and Public Affairs*, vol. 12, pp. 175–204.

Skarsten, A.K. (1954) "Nature in Mandeville," *Journal of English and Germanic Philology*, vol. 53, pp. 561–8.

Skinner, Q. (1966) "The Ideological Context of Hobbes's Political Thought," *Historical Journal*, vol. 9, pp. 286–317.

Skinner, Q. (1966) "The Limits of Historical Explanation," *Philosophy,* July vol. 41, pp. 199–215.

Skinner, Q. (1969) "Meaning and Understanding in the History of Ideas," *History and Theory*, vol. 8, pp. 3–53.

Smith, J.W. (1961) "The British Moralists and the Fallacy of Psychologism," *Journal of the History of Ideas*, vol. 22, pp. 185–204.

Tenenbaum, S. (1982) "Woman through the Prism of Political Thought," *Polity,* vol. 15, pp. 90–102.

Thomas, K. (1958) "Women in the Civil War Sects," *Past and Present*, vol. 13, pp. 42–62.

Thomas, K. (1959) "The Double Standard," *Journal of the History of Ideas*, vol. 20, pp. 195–216.

Tuck, R. (1986) "A New Date for Filmer's *Patriarcha*," *Historical Journal*, vol. 29, pp. 183–6.

Waldron, J.J. (1981) "Locke's Account of Inheritance and Bequest," *Journal of the History of Philosophy*, vol. 19, pp. 39–51.

Walzer, M. (1984) "Liberalism and the Art of Separation," *Political Theory*, vol. 12, pp. 315–30.

Warrender, H. (1979) "Political Theory and Historiography: A Reply to Professor Skinner on Hobbes," *Historical Journal*, vol. 22, pp. 931–40.

Weintraub, J. (1990) "The Theory and Politics of the Public/Private Distinction," presented at the meeting of American Political Science Association, San Francisco, CA.

Yolton, J.W. (1958) "Locke on the Law of Nature," *Philosophical Review*, vol. 67, pp. 477–98.

Books

Arendt, H. (1958) *The Human Condition*, Chicago, The University of Chicago Press.

Arendt, H. (1961) *Between Past and Future*, New York, The Viking Press.

Arendt, H. (1982) *Critique of Judgement: Lectures on Kant's Political Philosophy*, Chicago, The University of Chicago Press.

Ashcraft, R. (1986) *Revolutionary Politics and Locke's Two Treatises of Government*, Princeton, NJ, Princeton University Press.

Benn, S.I. and Gaus G.F. (eds), (1983) *Public and Private in Social Life*, London, Croom Helm.

Berelson, B. and Janowitz, M. (eds), (1953) *Public Opinion and Communication*, Glencoe, IL, The Free Press.

Blackstone, W.T. (1965) *Francis Hutcheson and Contemporary Ethical Theory*, Athens, GA, University of Georgia Press.

Bobbio, N. (1989) *Thomas Hobbes*, Torino, Einaudi.

Brandt, R. (ed.), (1981) *John Locke, Symposium Wolfenbuttel 1979*, Berlin, Walter de Gruyter.

Campbell, R.H. and Skinner, A.S. (eds), (1982) *The Origins and Nature of the Scottish Enlightenment*, Edinburgh, John Donald Publishers.

Colman, J. (1983) *John Locke's Moral Philosophy*, Edinburgh, Edinburgh University Press.

Cox, R.H. (1963) "Justice as the Base of Political Order in Locke," in C.J. Friedrich and J.W. Chapman (eds), *Nomos, VI. Justice*, New York, Atherton Press.

Daiches Raphael, D. (1947) *The Moral Sense*, London, Oxford University Press.

Daly, J. (1979) *Sir Robert Filmer and English Political Thought*, Toronto, University of Toronto Press.

De Franchis, F. (1984) *Dizionario giuridico, Inglese-Italiano*, Milano, Giuffré.

Donzelot, J. (1979) *The Policing of Families*, New York, Pantheon Books.

Dumont, J. (1977) *Homo aequalis*, Paris, Editions Gallimard.

Dunn, J. (1969) *The Political Thought of John Locke*, Cambridge, Cambridge University Press.

Dunn, J. (1975) *Rethinking Modern Political Theory*, Cambridge, Cambridge University Press.

Dunn, J. (1984) *John Locke*, Oxford, Oxford University Press.

Elshtain, J.B. (1981) *Public Man, Private Woman*, Princeton, NJ, Princeton University Press.

Foucault, M. (1978) *The History of Sexuality*, New York, Pantheon Books.

Franklin, J.H. (1973) *Jean Bodin and the Rise of Absolutism*, Cambridge, Cambridge University Press.

Franklin, J.H. (1979) *John Locke and the Theory of Sovereignty*, Cambridge, Cambridge University Press.

Gadamer, H.G. (1989) *Truth and Method*, New York, Crossroad.

Gierke, O. (1934) *Natural Law and the Theory of Society, 1500 to 1800*, Cambridge, Cambridge University Press.

Gilmore, M.P. (1941) *Arguments from Roman Law in Political Thought, 1220–1600*, Cambridge, MA, Harvard University Press.

Goldsmith, M.M. (1985) *Private Vices, Public Benefits*, Cambridge, Cambridge University Press.

Gough, J.W. (1956) *John Locke's Political Philosophy*, Oxford, Clarendon Press.

Gough, J.W. (1957) *The Social Contract*, Oxford, Clarendon Press.

Greenleaf, W.H. (1968) *Order, Empiricism and Politics*, London, Oxford University Press.

Haakonssen, K. (1981) *The Science of a Legislator: The Natural Jurispudence of David Hume and Adam Smith*, Cambridge, Cambridge University Press.

205

Habermas, J. (1975) *Legitimation Crisis*, Boston, MA, Beacon Press.
Habermas, J. (1989) *The Structural Transformation of the Public Sphere*, Th. Burger (tr.), Cambridge, MA, The MIT Press.
Hammick, J.T. (1887) *The Marriage Law of England*, London, Shaw & Sons.
Haw, R. (1952) *The State of Matrimony*, London, SPCK.
Hearnshaw, F.J.C. (ed.), (1967) *The Social and Political Ideas of Some English Thinkers of the Augustan Age*, New York, Barnes & Noble.
Hill, C. (1949) *The English Revolution, 1640: Three Essays*, London, Lawrence & Wishart.
Hill, C. (1980) *The World Turned Upside Down*, Harmondsworth, Penguin Books.
Hill, C. (1980) *Some Intellectual Consequences of the English Revolution*, Madison, WI, The University of Wisconsin Press.
Hirschman, A.O. (1977) *The Passions and the Interests*, Princeton, NJ, Princeton University Press.
Hont, I., and Ignatieff, M. (eds) (1985) *Wealth and Virtue*, Cambridge, Cambridge University Press.
Horkheimer, M. (1972) "Authority in the Family," in *Critical Theory; Selected Essays*, New York, Herder & Herder.
Horne, Th.A. (1978) *The Social Thought of Bernard Mandeville*, London, The Macmillan Press.
Howard, G.E. (1964) *History of Matrimonial Institutions*, New York, Humanities Press.
Jaggar, A.M. (1983) *Feminist Politics and Human Nature*, Totoma, NJ, Rowman & Allanheld.
Jensen, H. (1971) *Motivation and the Moral Sense in Francis Hutcheson's Ethical Theory*, The Hague, Martin Nijhoff.
de Jouvenel, B. (1963) *The Pure Theory of Politics*, Cambridge, Cambridge University Press.
Kanowitz, L. (1969) *Women and the Law: The Unfinished Revolution*, Albuquerque, NM, University of New Mexico Press.
Kendall, W. (1965) *John Locke and the Doctrine of Majority-Rule*, Urbana, II, University of Illinois Press.
Kenny, A. (1963) *Action, Emotion and Will*, London, Routledge & Kegan Paul.
Koselleck, R. (1988) *Critique and Crisis*, New York, Berg.
Krieger, L. (1965) *The Politics of Discretion*, Chicago, The University of Chicago Press.
Lamprecht, S.P. (1962) *The Moral and Political Philosophy of John Locke*, New York, Russell & Russell.
Lasch, C. (1977) *Haven in a Heartless World*, New York, Basic Books.
Laslett, P. (1966) *The World We Have Lost*, New York, Charles Scribner's Sons.
Lemos, R.M. (1978) *Hobbes and Locke: Power and Consent*, Athens, GA, University of Georgia Press.
MacIntyre, A. (1984) "The Relationship of Philosophy to its Past," in R. Rorty, J.B. Schneewind, and Q. Skinner (eds), *Philosophy in History: Essays on the Historiography of Philosophy*, Cambridge, Cambridge University Press.
Macpherson, C.B. (1962) *The Political Theory of Possessive Individualism*,

Oxford, Oxford University Press.

Marcuse, H. (1972) "Authority," in *Studies in Critical Philosophy*, London, NLB.

Moore, B. Jr (1984) *Privacy*, Armonk NY, M.E. Sharpe.

Nozick, R. (1974) *Anarchy, State, and Utopia*, New York, Basic Books.

Okin, S.M. (1979) *Women in Western Political Thought*, Princeton, NJ, Princeton University Press.

Padgen, A. (ed.) (1985) *The Language of Political Theory in Early Modern Europe*, Oxford, Oxford University Press.

Parry, G. (1978) *John Locke*, London, George Allen & Unwin.

Passmore, J.A. (1965) "The Malleability of Man in 18th-Century Thought," in E.R. Wasserman (ed.), *Aspects of the 18th Century*, Baltimore, MD, The Johns Hopkins University Press.

Pateman, C. (1988) *The Sexual Contract*, Oxford, Polity Press.

Plamenatz, J. (1963) *Man and Society*, New York, McGraw-Hill.

Pocock, J.G.A. (1975) *The Machiavellian Moment*, Princeton, NJ, Princeton University Press.

Pocock, J.G.A. (1975) "The History of Political Thought: A Methodological Inquiry," in P. Laslett and W.G. Runciman (eds), *Philosophy, Politics and Society*, Oxford, Basil Blackwell.

Pocock, J.G.A. (1985) *Virtue, Commerce, and History*, Cambridge, Cambridge University Press.

Pocock, J.G.A. and Ashcraft, R. (1980) *John Locke*, Los Angeles, CA, University of California, William Andrew Clark Memorial Library.

Polin, R. (1960) *La politique morale de John Locke*, Paris, Presses Universitaires de France.

Polin, R. (1963) "Justice in Locke's Philosophy," in C.J. Friedrich and J.W. Chapman (eds), *Nomos. VI. Justice*, New York, Atherton Press.

Pollock, F. and Maitland, F.W. (1923) *The History of the English Law*, Cambridge, Cambridge University Press.

Poster, M. (1978) *Critical Theory of the Family*, New York, Seabury Press.

Powell, C.L. (1917) *English Domestic Relations, 1487–1563*, New York, Columbia University Press.

Preston King and Parekh, C.B. (eds) (1968) *Politics and Experience*, Cambridge, Cambridge University Press.

Randall, J. (1978) *The Origins of the Scottish Enlightenment*, London, The Macmillan Press.

Rawls, J. (1981) *A Theory of Justice*, Cambridge, MA, The Belknap Press.

Riley, P. (1982) *Will and Political Legitimacy*, Cambridge, MA, Harvard University Press.

Robbins, C. (1959) *The Eighteenth-Century Commonwealthman*, Cambridge, MA, Harvard University Press.

Rorty, R., Schneewind, J.B., and Skinner, Q. (eds) (1984) *Philosophy in History*, Cambridge, Cambridge University Press.

Rosaldo, M.Z. and Lamphere, I. (eds) (1974) *Woman, Culture and Society*, Stanford, CA, Stanford University Press.

Salmon, J.H.M. (1959) *The French Religious Wars in English Political Thought*, Oxford, Clarendon Press.

Schmitt, C. (1976) *The Concept of the Political*, New Brunswick, NJ, Rutgers University Press.

Schneider, L. (1967) *The Scottish Moralists on Human Nature and Society*, Chicago, The University of Chicago Press.

Schochet, G.J. (ed.) (1971) *Life, Liberty, and Property; Essays on Locke's Political Ideas*, Belmont, CA, Wadsworth.

Schochet, G.J. (1975) *Patriarchalism in Political Thought*, New York, Basic Books.

Scott, W.R. (1900) *Francis Hutcheson, His Life, Teaching, and Position in the History of Philosophy*, Cambridge, Cambridge University Press.

Seliger, M. (1968) *The Liberal Politics of John Locke*, London, George Allen & Unwin.

Shorter, E. (1975) *The Making of the Modern Family*, New York, Basic Books.

Siltanen, J. and Stanworth, M. (1984) *Women and the Public Sphere: A Critique of Sociology and Politics*, New York, Saint Martin's Press.

Skinner, Q. (1978) *The Foundations of Modern Political Thought*, Cambridge, Cambridge University Press, 2 vols.

Skinner, Q. (1988) *Meaning and Context*, Cambridge, Polity Press.

Stein, P. (1988) *The Character and Influence of the Roman Civil Law*, London, The Hambledon Press.

Steinberg, J. (1978) *Locke, Rousseau and the Idea of Consent*, Westport, CT, Greenwood Press.

Stone, L. (1977) *The Family, Sex and Marriage in England, 1500–1800*, New York, Harper & Row.

Strauss, L. (1963) *Natural Right and History*, Chicago, The University of Chicago Press.

Tarcov, N. (1984) *Locke's Education for Liberty*, Chicago, The University of Chicago Press.

Trumbach, R. (1978) *The Rise of the Egalitarian Family*, New York, Academic Press.

Tuck, R. (1981) *Natural Rights Theories: Their Origin and Development*, Cambridge, Cambridge University Press.

Tully, J. (1988) *A Discourse on Property: John Locke and his Adversaries*, Cambridge, Cambridge University Press.

Vaughan, K.I. (1980) *John Locke, Economist and Social Scientist*, Chicago, The University of Chicago Press.

Weber, M. (1958) *From Max Weber*, H.H. Gerth and C. Wright Mills (eds), New York, Oxford University Press.

Weber, M. (1978) *Economy and Society*, G. Roth and C. Wittich (eds), Berkeley, CA, University of California Press, 2 vols.

Willey, B. (1953) *The Eighteenth-Century Background*, New York, Columbia University Press.

Williams, B. (1972) "The Idea of Equality," in P. Laslett and W.G. Runciman (eds), *Philosophy, Politics, and Society*, Oxford, Basil Blackwell.

Wood, N. (1983) *The Politics of Locke's Philosophy*, Berkeley, CA, University of California Press.

Yolton, J.W. (1970) *Locke and the Compass of Human Understanding*, Cambridge, Cambridge University Press.

Zaretski, W. (1976) *Capitalism, the Family, and Personal Life*, New York, Harper & Row.

Index